RECOLONIZATION AND RESISTANCE:
SOUTHERN AFRICA IN THE 1990s

Other books by John S. Saul

Socialism in Tanzania: Politics and Policies,
co-edited with Lionel Cliffe (in two volumes, 1972 and 1973)

Essays on the Political Economy of Africa,
co-authored with Giovanni Arrighi (1973)

Canada and Mozambique (1974)

Rural Co-operation in Tanzania,
co-edited with Lionel Cliffe and others (1975)

The State and Revolution in Eastern Africa (1979)

The Crisis in South Africa,
co-authored with Stephen Gelb (1981 and 1986, revised edition)

A Difficult Road: The Transition to Socialism
in Mozambique (1985)

Socialist Ideology and the Struggle for Southern Africa (1990)

The Two-Edged Sword: Namibia's independence struggle and its Legacy, co-edited with Colin Leys (1993)

RECOLONIZATION AND RESISTANCE:

SOUTHERN AFRICA IN THE 1990s

JOHN S. SAUL

P.O. Box 1892
Trenton, New Jersey 08607

Africa World Press, Inc.
P.O. Box 1892
Trenton, N. J. 08607

Copyright © John S. Saul 1993
First Printing 1993

All rights reserved. No part of this publication may be reproduced, stored in a retrieval system or transmitted in any form or by any means electronic, mechanical, photocopying, recording or otherwise without the prior written permission of the publisher.

Book Design: Jonathan Gullery
Cover Design: Carles J. Juzang

Library of Congress Cataloging-in-Publication Data

Saul, John S.
    Recolonization and resistance : southern Africa in the 1990s / John S. Saul.
    p.   cm.
    Includes bibliographical references and index.
    ISBN 0-86543-389-5. --ISBN 0-86543-390-9 (pbk.)
    1. Africa, Southern--Politics and government--1975–
2. Mozambique--Politics and government--1975– 3. National liberation movements--Africa, Southern. 4. Nationalism--Africa, Southern. I. Title.
DT1165.S28   1993
320.968--dc20   93-4675
                                                                            CIP

to the memory of H. H. Wilson

teacher, friend, conscience

Contents

Introduction
The Recolonization of Southern Africa?
ix

Chapter 1
The Southern African Revolution
1

Chapter 2
The End of the Cold War in Southern Africa
35

Chapter 3
The Frelimo State: From Revolution to Recolonization
57

Chapter 4
South Africa:
Between "Barbarism" and "Structural Reform"
89

Chapter 5
Structural Reform: A Model for the Revolutionary Transformation of South Africa?
143

Afterword
Strategies for Resistance in the 1990s
170

Introduction: The Recolonization of Southern Africa?

▼▼▼▼▼▼▼▼▼▼▼▼▼

The present book is, in effect, a sequel to my *Socialist Ideology and the Struggle for Southern Africa* (published by Africa World Press in 1990). That volume, drawing together a number of essays I had written during the 1980s, was by no means flush with optimism. "Despite all the recent advances in southern Africa," I wrote (citing the overthrow of the Portuguese empire, the fall of the UDI regime in Rhodesia and the dramatic revival of the resistance movement inside South Africa itself), "difficult times continue" — and I took the virtual collapse of Frelimo's development project in Mozambique as one particularly somber index of such "difficulties." Yet the essays in *Socialist Ideology,* for all their bleaker shadings, were still borne along on a wave of relative optimism. They reflected, certainly, a strong sense of how much had been accomplished in the region since the early 1960s. Thus, as the first chapter in this current collection (an overview of the "thirty years' war" of liberation in the region) also makes clear, it was important that "the Southern African Revolution" had despatched into the history books the cruel defenders of unalloyed and unapologetic white rule (Caetano, Smith, Botha). It was important, too, that some of the successor regimes (the "Frelimo state" in Mozambique, for example) had begun to experiment with socio-economic alternatives to the neo-colonial molds in which so much of post-colonial Africa had been cast.

As my first chapter also demonstrates, however, the 1980s found counter-revolution to be at least as prominent a feature as revolutionary change within the region as a whole. Perhaps the full implications of that counter-revolution were underestimated in the *Socialist Ideology* volume. It is impossible to do so now, South Africa's aggressive policy of destabilization having complemented so effectively Western capitalism's reinforcement of its hegemony in southern Africa (with the "structural adjustment" offensive of the IMF and World Bank a particularly crucial vector of this latter process). Sketched in chapter one, the theme of imperial consolidation is reinforced in chapter two by an analysis of the way in which a "post-Cold War"/"New World Order" context now frames the region. Such is the present writ of Western power, in fact, that one is even tempted to view the fate of a country like Mozambique as evidencing an effective "recolonization" of that country.

Is "recolonization" too powerful a metaphor? The third chapter of this book, which focuses on "the Frelimo state,"[1] concludes by looking at some of the ways in which such a description might be depressingly accurate. This is not that chapter's only order of business, however; for it seeks, as well, to contribute to the contemporary reassessment — so essential if lessons are to be learned for future rounds of progressive endeavor in southern Africa — of how the southern African revolution (at least in its specifically Mozambican manifestation) went astray. Has previous commentary — my own included — placed too much emphasis on "external variables" (destabilization by South Africa principal among them)? Has the time come for a "paradigm shift" (Gervase Clarence-Smith's phrase[2]) in our analysis of "the causality of the Mozambican crisis" that privileges the central importance of Frelimo's own errors of omission and commission? My answer, as outlined in the chapter, is a firm yes — and no.

True, the presumed imperatives of solidarity (including the fear of giving aid and comfort to the enemy!) may too often have blunted the writings of a first generation of observers of the southern African revolution. It is crucially important in current work to redress any such imbalance if an accurate history of that revolution is to be written.[3] Still, there is also a certain all-too-fashionable negativism to much of the "paradigm-shifting" that is currently taking place, a shifting of South African destabilization to the status of a "residual variable," for example, that is not honest to the true weight of that factor in the Mozambican equation. And there is also, currently, an overstatement of the misguided nature of the Frelimo project itself that fails to capture the full complexity of developments inside Mozambique. Such, at any rate, is the argument advanced in chapter three.

Note, however, that any shifting of paradigms that may now be taking place amongst Africanists is not confined simply to the case of Mozambique; as we will see, it reflects a profound sea change, in scientific circles, in the discussion both of Africa as a whole and of the development challenge more broadly conceived. Although some of the criticism of Frelimo might be called "leftist" (even "ultra-leftist" — and misleading to the extent it is the latter), more of it implies an abandonment of much that is progressive in left discourse about Africa. The Marxist flag under which I earlier asserted the southern African revolution to be advancing is, in the context of recent global events, a far more tattered standard than when many of the essays in *Socialist Ideology* were first written. Nonetheless, the Marxist tradition remains a principal point of reference for what follows — and, it seems to me, the single best vantage-point for the kind of honest critique of Frelimo's failed practices that undoubtedly is necessary (and which chapter three seeks to facilitate).

And what, in any case, of South Africa, surely still a site of potent advance for the southern African revolution and a major — and crucially important — exception to any portrait of regional recolonization? Alongside its account of the ebb and flow of developments elsewhere in southern Africa, the first chapter of this volume underscores the dramatic re-emergence and rapid growth of resistance inside South Africa itself, from the 1970s onwards. And if that chapter does break off its account of the South African situation at a point of apparent stalemate (1988), there is chapter four to carry the story forward, through the revival of resistance in 1989, the unbanning of the ANC, the release of Nelson Mandela, and into the current negotiations' round. Dramatic advances indeed, advances full of potentially positive implications not only for the people of South Africa but also for the beleaguered populations of the Frontline states.[4]

Yet, as that chapter also demonstrates, "negotiations" in South Africa are still framed by a stalemate between contending parties that does not augur well for any smooth transition to a genuinely democratic constitution, a stalemate that actually evokes the chilling possibility of a precipitous descent into chaos and "barbarism." Moreover, even if constitutional questions are resolved peacefully and equitably, the difficulties of mounting a radical/socialist challenge to the established structure of socio-economic power will be formidable. Here again the terminology of "recolonization" — or perhaps, more accurately, that of "neo-colonialism" — may be thought to reveal something important about the fate that stalks black South Africans as the full and overbearing logic of the capitalist economy, world-wide and local, is brought to bear upon them.

Mere fatalism is not an adequate response to this set of circumstances, however. Nor is it likely to be the response of the very large number of South Africans who are loath to withdraw from class struggle over socio-economic outcomes (a case in point: the involvement, in late 1991, of *three-and-a-half million* South African workers in a massive strike-cum-stay away directed against the government's imposition of a new value-added-tax). At the same time, any lapse into rhetorical "leftism" as guide to theory and practice will not be of much assistance either. Here again we can take our cue from the South Africans themselves: much of chapter four as well as chapter five in its entirety are given over to examining the on-going attempt by many South Africans to discover new means — means I find to be illuminated by use of the concept of "structural reform" to encompass them — of both conceiving and advancing their demands for a more profound transformation of their circumstances.

In South Africa, then, we find not only on-going efforts to keep alive the project of "transformation," but also efforts to revitalize the Marxist tradition itself in order to lend additional clarity and theoretical resonance to that project. In the rest of the badly-battered region, only slowly recovering from the dashing of previous hopes, such innovative efforts may be less advanced — but there, too, fresh voices have begun to be heard. Needless to say, any elaboration of the Marxist tradition along novel lines more relevant to the present needs of southern Africa must be further enriched by feminist and anti-racist insights and must be more profoundly aware than ever of the necessary centrality of genuinely democratic practices to the success of radical undertakings. There is also the distinct possibility that even a more sophisticated radicalism may not prove adequate to the task at hand; such is the bleakness of much of the terrain in present-day southern Africa (including South Africa itself) that it is easy to be pessimistic about prospects there. Nonetheless — a brief "Afterword" to the present volume reinforces the point — there is sufficient evidence of resistance to the wave of "recolonization" now threatening to engulf the region to affirm that in southern Africa the struggle, at the very least, does continue.

INTRODUCTION   XIII

1   Frelimo first emerged in the early 1960s as the liberation movement, FRELIMO - the *Frente de Libertaçao de Moçambique* - and later, in power, became the Frelimo party (the Partido Frelimo). Since most of my numerous references to Frelimo in this book are to the party in power I have adopted the lower case form of this acronym throughout.
2   Gervase Clarence-Smith, "The Roots of the Mozambican Counter-Revolution," *Southern African Review of Books*, 2, #4 (April-May, 1989), p. 10; as we will see in chapter three the notion of a possible "paradigm shift" in the study of Mozambique is also broached by Alex Vines in his *RENAMO: Terrorism in Mozambique* (London: James Currey, 1991), p. 74, and, at least implicitly, by a number of others.
3   For a related analysis of the Namibian case that attempts to contribute to the writing of just such an "accurate history" see Colin Leys and John S. Saul (eds.), *The Two-Edged Sword: Namibia's independence struggle and its legacy* (London: James Currey, 1993).
4   See, on this subject, Robert Davies, "Post-Apartheid Scenarios for the Southern African Region," *Transformation*, #11 (1990).

Chapter 1
The Southern African Revolution[1]

▼▼▼▼▼▼▼▼▼▼▼▼▼

Writing in The Socialist Register *1969[2] Giovanni Arrighi and I painted a bleak picture of independent Africa's prospects, suggesting the likely "stability of existing neo-colonial structures" for the foreseeable future and arguing that "the 'Latin Americanization' of independent Africa is well underway." Twenty years later, when the present essay was written (once again, for* The Socialist Register*), this had proven to be an accurate prophesy, although, to be honest, we could not have predicted, even in our wildest imaginings, just how catastrophic for Africa this denouement to the continent's march towards independence would prove to be. However, surveying the scene at the beginning of 1989 — as the present essay attempted to do — I was also drawn back to another aspect of our original article.*

Was there a bright side to the picture in 1969? "Hope," we argued, "must instead be focused upon the liberation struggle in southern Africa, the implications of which are bound to have truly continental dimensions."

> In the "centers" of southern Africa the peasantry has been effectively proletarianized and the social structure produced by the pattern of development in which the white settlers play the hegemonic role leaves little, if any, room for a neo-colonial solution. Moreover, in the periphery of this region (the Portuguese territories) the neo-colonial

solution has been blocked by the "ultra-colonialism" of Portugal and the peasant revolution which has ensued is creating subjective conditions for socialist transformation which are generally absent elsewhere in independent black Africa.

We did counsel against "any illusions concerning the nature and short-term prospects of the struggle in southern Africa," but concluded that, "at the present historical moment, this [struggle] provides the main, if not the only, leverage for revolutionary change in Sub-Saharan Africa."

The point stands. Of course, the conventional wisdom of imperial planners of the time was very different. 1969 was also the year of the notorious *National Security Study Memorandum 39*,[3] a National Security Council report which apparently induced Henry Kissinger to conclude, in the words of one of the memorandum's scenarios, that "the whites are here to stay [in southern Africa] and the only way that constructive change can come about is through them. There is no hope for the blacks to gain the political rights they seek through violence...." Unfortunately for the likes of Kissinger, history in southern Africa was already moving forward with seven-league boots. Contrary to *NSSM 39*, "the outlook for the rebellions" in the "Portuguese territories" of Mozambique and Angola was *not* "one of continued stalemate." Nor could the "white regime" of Rhodesia "hold out indefinitely," its internal security system able to "meet foreseeable threats." Indeed, not even South Africa could, "for the foreseeable future...maintain internal security," even if it has been able, on balance, to "effectively counter insurgent activity."

A mere five years later the comfortable assumptions of *NSSM 39* lay in tatters, the military victories of liberation movements in Africa having been the major precipitant of 1974's Portuguese coup; it was this coup, in turn, that paved the way for the installation of radical governments in Angola and Mozambique and for the escalation of armed struggle in Rhodesia. Nor was the mood of challenge borne by such changes to stop at the South African border. Victories elsewhere in the region were a source of inspiration there, but, in any case, stirrings in South Africa had their own dynamic. The dramatic signs of renewed working-class militancy visible in 1973's wave of strikes, and the youth-centered militancy in the townships soon to come to a head: the Soweto events of 1976, announced that the long, dark night of the 1960s — when "internal stability," imposed at bayonet point by Emergency Regulation, had indeed been the order of the day — was over.

In short, a revolutionary process was now afoot in the region, bearing (or so, at times, it seemed) the promise of a socialist future for southern Africa. This essay will attempt to evaluate that promise, perhaps on firmer ground than was available in 1969, at the very outset of the revolutionary revival Arrighi and I sought to divine. However, it will be necessary, first, to trace in more detail the ebbs and flows of the process in question. Unfortunately, this essay will also have to specify the nature of the counter-revolution to which revolution in southern Africa has given rise. For the counter-revolutionary project mounted by Pretoria and its allies has been savage, setting new precedents of cruelty and cynicism. And it has determined that, whatever the achievements of the past two decades, the struggle for southern Africa is still very far from being resolved.

I. Liberation Struggle and the Radicalization of Nationalism

The launching of liberation struggles in the Portuguese colonies (Mozambique, Angola and, outside the southern Africa region but important to outcomes there, Guinea-Bissau) and in white minority-dominated Rhodesia transpired in a continental context of "successful" nationalisms. The skilled machinations of such departing colonial powers as Britain and France meant that, in general, the decolonization effected with the granting of independence in the 1950s and 1960s would only be a "false" one, a prelude to neo-colonialism and class collaboration with the rising elites of tropical Africa. For various good reasons of their own, Portugal and the Smith regime that seized power in Rhodesia by means of 1965's "unilateral declaration of independence" (UDI) refused to risk this ploy of attempting to coopt the emergent nationalist leadership into formal positions of authority. Nationalists in southern Africa would have to stand and fight, a requirement that was to make some difference to the terms of the decolonization bargain ultimately struck.

Not that all such nationalists could be considered immune to temptation, if and when a "neo-colonialism" were to be placed on offer. Struggles would continue within the movements in Lusophone Africa and Rhodesia/ Zimbabwe until very late in the day as to what the class content of liberation should actually be, once the relevant minority regime was forced to the bargaining table. Nonetheless, there was a radicalizing logic to guerilla warfare that began to imprint itself on movements like Frelimo in Mozambique, the MPLA in Angola and even ZANU in Zimbabwe in discernible ways. Mozambique provided, perhaps, the classic case. It became apparent to many within the Frelimo leadership that a guerilla struggle like the one launched in northern Mozambique in 1964 required a level of genuine popular participation in and identification with the emancipatory process very different from that evidenced in prior nationalist mobilizations. After all, the potential risks of throwing in their lot with the guerillas were great for the peasantry. And the liberation movement needed not merely the peasantry's passive acceptance of its presence, but its active support — in scouting, in provisioning, in the carriage of materiel. Rejecting the *foco* approach — once in heated direct exchange with Che Guevara himself during the latter's African excursion — Frelimo opted instead for its own version of "people's war."[4]

This meant beginning to construct rudimentary democratic structures in the expanding liberated areas, beginning to exemplify popularly based programmes in the health and education spheres, beginning to raise promising questions about such issues as the emancipation of women and even beginning to experiment with certain forms of collective production. This was a radicalization of practice on the ground that also fed back into the movement's theorization of its undertakings, giving rise to a remarkably indigenous process of discovery of the strengths of Marxism as a framework for revolutionary endeavor. This was not, of course, a level of insight that was automatically won. A fierce struggle broke out within the movement in the late 1960s, between those who were willing to accompany this kind of radicalization process and those, hankering for a "false decolonization" of their own, who resisted it. At best, these latter pined for quick military victories in order to bring the Portuguese "to their senses," even as they sought to advance their own interests within the movement by politicking along tribal and racial lines or by conceiving self-aggrandizing economic schemes.

In the event, the latter wing of the movement lost out and the proponents of an increasingly radicalized nationalism carried the day. Perhaps, as some observers have argued, there is a danger of romanticizing this achievement (a point that is further discussed in chapter three). The Frelimo-inspired political structures were still cast in a discernibly military mould, with, critics would argue, a degree of centralization of authority that could translate all too readily into a dangerous kind of "vanguardism" in the post-liberation phase — especially when the model had to be generalized to that considerable proportion of the country which had not been directly touched by the experience of the liberated areas.[5] Nonetheless, principles of democratic empowerment were being established as well as the beginnings of a left perspective very different from the obscurantist banalities of the "African Socialism" school that had been so prominent heretofore on the continent. Even though still primarily the possession of the revolutionary vanguard itself, this new perspective manifested a much clearer and more forthright understanding both of the workings of capitalist imperialism and of the dynamics of class formation *within* African societies. Most importantly, it was to provide the springboard for the attempt to implement socialist development strategies in such countries as Mozambique and Angola after the military defeat of Portugal — and the fall of that country's fascist government — paved the way for independence.

From Mozambique to Zimbabwe

The growing success of the armed struggle in Mozambique also gave a firm leg up to the Zimbabwean liberation movement. Although there were some signs, in the early 1960s, that Britain might be prepared to countenance a "false decolonization" in Rhodesia, the seizure of power by the Smith regime soon put paid to that idea while (at best) neutralizing Britain's notional responsibility for the fate of its quasi-colony. Military confrontation would prove necessary there as well in order to force the pace of change. It took some time for the popular movement in Zimbabwe to bring this necessity into focus, however. For it was riven with divisions of the most wasting kind, framed not in terms of genuine ideological differences but by the kind of jockeying for position between petty bourgeois politicians that so often in Africa has activated debilitating organizational rivalries (ZANU vs. ZAPU, in the Zimbabwe case) and even ethnic rivalries (Ndebele vs Shona, for starters). Yet ZANU was ultimately — in the early 1970s — to avail itself of Frelimo's offer to open up a more effective military front in Zimbabwe via the newly liberated areas of Mozambique's Tete Province and thereby work (especially after Mozambique's own independence provided an even more secure base) to undermine, slowly but surely, the viability of the settlers' UDI project.

Yet the escalation of armed struggle did not serve to radicalize the movement there as profoundly as had been true of Mozambique, this despite the fact that in Zimbabwe, too, the ideological discourses of the movement were increasingly cast in

Marxist terms. Internecine politicking remained very much the order of the day, both between ZANU and ZAPU as rival claimants to nationalist primacy and within the two movements themselves. Various attempts to transcend these limitations on a new, more ideologically progressive basis (the ZIPA initiative of the mid-70s, designed to displace the old guard leadership and initially viewed with some favour by the host Frelimo government in Mozambique, provides a case in point) collapsed. Guerilla advances, arguably not as deeply rooted in popular assertions on the ground as had been Frelimo's, also seemed, in their impact, to be less integrated into the circuits of the exile leadership's politics. This, plus the fact that end-game in Zimbabwe saw the reassertion of the imperial factor (via Britain's orchestrating of the Lancaster House decolonization talks), narrowed considerably the further revolutionary potential of the popular movement's victory — though many felt, nonetheless, that the saliency of the land question in Zimbabwe and the existence of a relatively large African working class might serve to keep pressure on the leadership to deliver on the radical promise implicit in much of its rhetoric.[5]

If, however, the promise of radicalization ultimately appeared in somewhat muted form in Zimbabwe, the nationalists' victory there became an important piece in the regional pattern of advance against the redoubts of white minority rule, bringing the front-line of struggle ever closer to the region's core, South Africa. Moreover, South Africa was itself stirring during this period, the 1970s witnessing the dramatic revival of the popular movement there. As we shall see, the presence of a vast and remarkably creative working class in the latter country promises, perhaps more firmly than elsewhere in the region, that liberation there will take on an increasingly socialist edge. Yet the intricate interpenetration of racial oppression and class exploitation — and of both nationalist and socialist responses to such domination — have lent a note of unpredictability to this process. Look, for example, at the very terms of the revival we have mentioned.

Bear in mind that the 1960s represented a trough in the history of popular resistance in South Africa. That resistance had peaked in the 1950s with various dramatic campaigns of mass action, but the apartheid state all too soon had managed to regain the upper hand, using the post-Sharpeville Emergency Regulations to ban popular organizations like the African National Congress (ANC) and the Pan-Africanist Congress (PAC); to jail, ban or drive into exile large numbers of activists; to crush, in short, all open opposition. In fact the state had dealt the popular movement not merely a crushing physical blow but also a psychological one of deeply demobilizing proportions. As the banned organizations (most importantly, the ANC) struggled to reestablish a political — and now, of necessity, military — presence relevant to the new terrain, a vacuum was created that would only slowly be filled.

South Africa: the struggle revives

But filled it was, in the first instance by the emergence of the Black Consciousness movement. An ideological project that paralleled other cultural nationalist expressions of the time (like "Black Power" in North America), it was largely the creation of petty-bourgeois intellectuals (albeit many of them of impressive stature, like Steve Biko), with separatist overtones, limited strategic sense and a minimal grasp of the possible role of the popular classes in effecting social change. However, as a reaffirmation of racial pride and of the sentiment of resistance to the apartheid dispensation, Black Consciousness was significant. Perhaps, as its themes began to permeate the ambience within which new generations were growing up, its immediate importance was more psychological than political. But not for long. For it was a fresh generation of youth who, as students, would soon rock the apartheid system to its foundations. Thus, in 1976, in Soweto and elsewhere, they squared off not merely against "Bantu education" and the imposition of Afrikaans as a medium of instruction, but against the entire system of oppression that they despised and now chose not to fear.

Of at least equal centrality to the rebirth of resistance was the stirring of the black working class, prefigured in various ways in the late 1960s and early 1970s and finding its most dramatic early expression in the strikes of Durban (in particular) in 1972-73. But perhaps dramatic confrontation was less crucial, at this point, than the more mundane process that also marked the 1970s, that of laying the organizational foundations of what was to become a wide range of vigorously independent trade unions. True, in the Soweto events, the fit between students and workers was often less than smooth, even producing some conflict and tension. Moreover, the most solidly grounded of the new unions (those that would soon come together under the banner of FOSATU, for example) were often loath to move quickly and assertively onto the terrain of politics *per se*. In part this reflected a particular reading by some union activists of the history of the 1950s when, they felt, SACTU, the trade union wing of the Congress Alliance, had all too uncritically subordinated the consolidation of its presence on the shop-floor to the demands of nationalist mobilization. There was also some suspicion that the vanguardist pretensions of the ANC (and, perhaps even more to the point, those of the ANC's close ally, the South African Communist Party) might ultimately be pursued at the expense of the working classes' own interests.

Despite such tensions it bears emphasizing that what was being created in the 1970s was the context for creative interaction between a revived popular democratic politics and an increasingly radical working-class project. In the next section we will examine in more detail how these two strands have come together to create a particularly promising and South Africa-specific version of radicalized nationalism. First, however, something further must be said about the peculiarly regional nature of the radicalization process we have begun to trace. Self-evidently, the region's political economy is tied together by the omnipresence of the long arm of South Africa, the latter's hegemony forged by long years of southern African history. Small wonder, then, that the process of liberation should itself spring across national frontiers.

Thus, the 1975 victory over Portugal of nationalist forces in Mozambique and Angola, as well as the Angolan repelling of a South African invasion force in 1975, had great and visible resonance — being, without doubt, one of the inspirations that produced Soweto. Nor is it entirely accidental that the next dramatic popular outburst in South Africa — the school boycotts in Cape Town and beyond in 1980 — came hard on the heels of ZANU's victory and the realization of Zimbabwean independence. Of course, the unfortunate fact is that these kinds of linkage also fueled the fires of counter-revolution in South Africa, making the Frontline states prime targets for South African "destabilization" tactics in the next round. If victories on the "front-line" had helped the South African movement to rebuild its self-confidence, it soon became apparent that the fate of such states was even more dependent on the pace with which the South African movement could build its own revolution in the region's heartland — and thus remove, from within, the chief source of their destabilization. Phrased in such terms the regional nature of the revolutionary process we are discussing was to become ever clearer with each passing year.

II. The Socialist Promise

In the first flush of independence, however, and in the former Portuguese colony of Mozambique in particular, the prospect of consolidating the revolutionary promise of the liberation struggle seemed strong. True, the colonial inheritance from the Portuguese was a grim one, Portugal's status as the most backward country in Europe having left its grotesque mark on its colonies. Thus Mozambique was relatively undeveloped even by African standards, while much of such development as the Portuguese had facilitated was designed to service the South African economy — via the movement of migrant labour, the provision of transport outlets to the sea, the planned marketing of power from the Cabora Bassa dam project. The precipitant flight of the Portuguese settler community at independence merely brought further into crisis an already distorted system, now undermining the network of commercialization and key agricultural and industrial sectors in ways that the new Frelimo government would have had trouble adjusting to even under the most favorable of circumstances.

But the circumstances were to prove far from favorable. Mozambique set itself to support the struggles of its Zimbabwean allies for freedom, providing a crucial rear base for the ZANU guerillas and immediately implementing sanctions against the Smith regime at very great cost (the Mozambican town of Beira, one of Rhodesia's chief outlets to the sea, becoming almost immediately a ghost port, for example). There were other costs to this act of solidarity, the most expensive, in retrospect, being Rhodesia's invention of the National Resistance Movement (the MNR or Renamo), conjured up from the dregs of Portugal's former colonial security apparatus to raise the costs of Frelimo support for ZANU by creating havoc inside Mozambique. A pin-prick at first, the Renamo tactic was to become a major instrument of destabilization once taken over by the South Africans in the wake of Zimbabwean independence. Economic dependence on South Africa also gave Frelimo's enemies leverage. Yet despite problems inside the country and without, the new government did seek to concretize its socialist aspirations.

It attempted, for example, to generalize the politically empowering experience of the liberated areas to all other parts of the country via the mechanism of the "dynamizing groups," structures of democratic participation established in rural settings, neighbourhoods and workplaces. Truly stirring developments began to occur in the social services sphere, in education, health and the like, and significant changes were also projected in the area of women's emancipation. The economy, too, began to be brought under state control and planning — if at a pace, dictated by the vacuum created in many sectors by Portuguese abandonment of various economic enterprises, that sometimes ran ahead of Frelimo's own better judgement. Within two years of achieving independence Frelimo had become a "vanguard party" of "Marxist-Leninist" provenance and was conceiving large, even grandiose, plans of national economic development centered on state ownership and planning and peasant-based cooperativization.

Destabilization works

The catastrophic forestalling of such plans is a long and painful story, one dealt with more fully in chapter three of the present volume.[7] Certainly weaknesses in Frelimo's own project provide part of the explanation. Was its vanguardism too closed and self-righteous, its "Marxism-Leninism" too frozen and inflexible, its economic planning too preoccupied with high-tech, large-scale solutions and too little preoccupied with peasant needs and incentives? Probably; but even as Frelimo moved at its 1983 Fourth Congress to profit from the lessons of its mistakes, its space for further manoeuvre had already narrowed disastrously by dint of the regional war waged by South Africa that was fast enveloping the country. Soon Frelimo found itself suing for peace with South Africa (at Nkomati in early 1984), backing away from even that minimal level of concrete assistance it had felt able to give the ANC.

Frelimo also found itself forced to treat much more solicitously than would have been its preference the minions of international capitalism (the global aid network and the IMF, for example) and forced, concomitantly, to allow a much wider space for "the logic of the market" to determine its choices both domestically and internationally. It seems fair to say that Frelimo's earlier errors had been primarily those of a genuinely left leadership become too triumphalist and too self-confident of its ability to force the pace of advance. Yet many observers now feared that new strata were emerging around the state apparatus and in the private sector that might begin to have a vested interest in moving the country ever more definitively away from the vestiges of its socialist project. As with somewhat parallel developments in Angola — developments produced in the context of an even more direct and aggressive intervention by South Africa and the United States — the results in Mozambique had come, by 1990, to provide a sobering reminder of the limits to what could be achieved on the periphery of an untransformed region.[8]

Developments in Zimbabwe are also sobering, as earlier comments in this essay have already anticipated. South Africa has sought to create trouble for an independent Zimbabwe certainly, even if in much more modest ways than has been the case in either Mozambique or Angola. But the main barrier to a Zimbabwean revolution has been largely self-generated, in ways anticipated during the process of liberation itself (when, as noted, the victorious movement remained less transformed by the practice of armed struggle than might have been hoped). True, in choosing to approach the existing settler/capitalist economic structure very gingerly, the ZANU leadership argued that they were merely profiting from the negative lessons of Mozambique's experience while also taking necessary cognizance of the hostile regional terrain. Yet it soon appeared that the leadership had come to make such a virtue of this apparent necessity that their revolutionary credentials were rendered increasingly suspect. Ibbo Mandaza has summarized the process in the following terms: "As the African petty bourgeoisie began gradually to find access to the same economic and social status as their white counterparts, so, too, did it become increasingly unable to respond to the aspirations of the workers and peasants....It became imperative, as an act of survival for the new state, to put a rein on its mass base....Political principles and ideological commitments appeared mortgaged on the altar of private property!"[9]

To be sure, advances were made via this route in terms of "substantial levels of food production, the growth of a layer of medium to small peasant producers, a maintenance of infrastructure, improved educational and agricultural services for much of the population and an absence of racial polarization." Yet even the commentator who makes these points confesses himself uneasy with Mugabe's "commandist style of leadership" and his "demobilizing [of] democratic forms of organization after independence."[10] And other observers emphasize Zimbabwe's extensive, often quite supine, accommodations with international capitalism, the state's self-interested muzzling of the working class and its stalling of any very meaningful programme of rural transformation (cooperativization, the beginnings of land reform and the like). And they note the fact that the Zimbabwean polity — despite the running start towards a more fundamental transformation ostensibly provided it by the experience of armed struggle — has nonetheless come to be marked by additional negative features all too familiar from developments in African states elsewhere on the continent. Thus, what has transpired is less the mobilization of the mass of population along class lines (as "workers and peasants") and more the instrumentalization of that population as ethnic constituencies (whether as "Shona" vs. "Ndebele" or in terms of intra-Shona distinctions) for regional political barons jockeying for power and privilege at the center of the system. Nor has quasi-capitalist accommodation been altogether successful even in strictly economic terms, as Zimbabwe, too, finds itself increasingly in a mendicant posture towards the IMF and its attendants.[11]

We must be cautious here. Sobering facts about the presently visible denouements to liberation from white-minority rule in the countries we have been discussing should not blind us to the importance of what has been achieved. This is especially clear once we have grasped the fact that — given the centrality of South Africa — revolution in the countries in southern Africa cannot be fully realized until that revolution encompasses the entire region. How much more clearly exposed was South Africa by the late-1980s than had been the case a decade and half earlier, and how much further south had the front line of struggle in the sub-continent been pushed? Wasn't Zimbabwe, in spite of its contradictions still on that front-line and still rock solid, for example, in its military support for a besieged Mozambique? And wasn't that front-line itself to be pushed further south when, as a direct result of a substantial military set-back suffered at the hands of the Angolans and their Cuban allies, South Africa was forced to accept the reality of a democratic political future for its own colony of South-West Africa/Namibia?

Independence in Namibia

Once again, the answer to this latter question must be "yes" — and "no." The 1989 re-entry of the United Nations onto the scene in Namibia to supervise the transition to majority rule was indeed something to celebrate, even if the terms of that re-entry were, finally, decided over the heads of SWAPO (Namibia's liberation movement) through negotiations between a range of other players — the Americans and the Soviets, the Cubans and the Angolans, and, not least, the South Africans themselves. Some have argued that, as a result, South Africa was able to undermine, in significant ways, the UN's ability to counterbalance structures of social control that Pretoria has spent decades implanting on the ground in Namibia,[12] and that the run-up to the April (1990) election of a Namibian constituent assembly saw both South Africa and various vested interests based inside Namibia itself warp the country's transition to independence too much in their own favour. In fact, SWAPO, despite its victory, did fail in that election to obtain the 67% of the poll that would have given it a free hand in constitution-making.

But this result also reflected growing public awareness of SWAPO's own checkered record in exile (the word of its treatment of detainees in its Angolan camps being particularly important in this regard). Moreover, the result probably had the additional beneficial effect of forcing SWAPO constitution-makers to be more responsive to the demand to seed the new constitution with democratic guarantees than might otherwise have been the case. Less savoury was the fact that, as the realities of the new counter-revolutionary dynamics of the region (to be further discussed in the following section but marked, not least, by South Africa's continuing economic hegemony) sank in, the new SWAPO government found itself much less inclined than its most fervent supporters had hoped to challenge the terms of its inherited structure of economic dependence. Very quickly, it became clear that apparent liberatory advance in Namibia would prove to be at least as flawed and as contradictory as it has been elsewhere in the region.[13] By 1990, then, only some profound change in South Africa itself — one that radiated, in turn, back through the Frontline states — seemed to hold any real transformatory promise for the region. We thus return to the heart of the matter, to the prospect for revolution within South Africa.

There, the key revolutionary "moment" (prior, at least, to the release of Nelson Mandela in early 1990 and the entry into the new South African politics of "negotiations" discussed in chapter four) proved to be the insurrection of 1984-1986, an insurrection that displayed graphically both the strengths and weaknesses of the South African movement, broadly defined. Towards that moment the seeds of resistance planted in the 1970s continued to grow.[14] Now, however, the two broad strands of above-ground resistance earlier identified began to interpenetrate even more markedly than had hitherto been the case. Certainly working-class activism as focussed around trade union initiatives became increasingly important. So much so that the dominant classes, caught off balance, sought (following the terms of the Wiehann Commission) to coopt this fledgling movement through recognition of black trade union rights within the framework of existing and quite restrictive labour relations structures. Although a heated debate ensued within trade union circles as to whether to run the risks of registration under these terms, ultimately the process of legalization was turned back against the regime, seized upon from below to carve out further space for working class assertion. The organizational drive continued, notably in the mines (where the National Union of Mineworkers gained increasing prominence), with the formation of the Congress of South African Trade Unions (COSATU) in

November 1985 ultimately defining a high water mark in this union sphere. Thus, by 1987, it was estimated that this union central had as many as one million signed-up members.

Community-based activism also grew apace. Students/youth continued to be important; the 1980 boycott movement which fanned out from the Cape demonstrated this, as did the prominence of school boycotts and youth militancy in the insurrectionary moments of 1984-86. But community activism was now much more broadly based, the general ambience of defiance giving rise to a range of community-centred resistances running well beyond the classroom. These surfaced in every area where the impact of the regime's deepening economic crisis and its authoritarian practices could be felt (in rent strikes and consumer and transportation boycotts, for example) and gave rise to a rich array of community organizations throughout South Africa. These organizations activated workers where they lived and reinforced their growing radicalization, while also providing a particularly important nexus for the entry of women into the struggle. It was this kind of ferment, too, that was to press (some) churches more firmly into the ranks of militancy. As a result, when the initiative was taken in 1983 to organize nationally to resist the government's imposition of a new tri-cameral parliamentary system (involving token chambers for Indians and "Colcoreds" and continued exclusion of Africans), the building blocks for the resultant umbrella organization, the United Democratic Front, were already in place. In the UDF, it has been estimated, were two million people represented by some six hundred constituent bodies. They were successful, in the first instance, in undermining the legitimacy of the tri-cameral elections but were now also girded for further confrontation with the apartheid system.

We alluded earlier to the interpenetration of the two strands of resistance. This feature now became very marked, full of promise for the increasing efficacy and increasing radicalization of the resistance movement — although also problematic in certain particulars. As suggested above, the trade unions harbored some (notably within the FOSATU camp) who approached the broader political arena gingerly, concerned to root the workers' struggle as firmly as possible on the shop-floor and suspicious of the merely "populist" intentions of certain political leaders. As a result, it was often the best-organized of trade unions that chose to keep at arm's distance from the UDF. At the same time, the community activism of their own membership was a force drawing such unions into a more overt role in the political arena, making them, before long, active partners in many of the boycotts and stay-aways that became such a prominent part of the struggle that fanned out from the Vaal Triangle after September 1984. Moreover, there were also unions emerging (SAAWU and GAWU, for example) that actually placed primary emphasis upon community organization and nationalist politics. As pressure for greater trade union unity developed, these two wings of the workers' movement (increasingly distinguished as "workerist" and "populist") found themselves linked together in a relationship, sometimes debilitating and sometimes creative, that produced the aforementioned COSATU.

The re-emergence of the ANC

Particularly germane to the way in which these different emphases now began to play themselves out was the reemergence of the African National Congress to a position of centrality within the broad resistance movement. As I have argued elsewhere,[15] the ANC's resurgence sprang from a combination of its historical legitimacy, its ability (unlike the rival Pan-Africanist Congress) to retain unity and coherence in exile, and its unique promise, exemplified by an escalating level of sabotage actions ("armed propaganda" in the ANC's lexicon), to lend military muscle to any confrontation with the state. Moreover, as the struggle escalated, the ANC showed itself particularly skilled politically in bringing the broad array of popular resistance into focus around its own slogans and programmatic demands, even in periods when popular actions seemed to have been running, spontaneously, well ahead of any direct ANC mobilization. Examples to be mentioned include the anti-SAIC and anti-Republic Day campaigns; the Free Mandela initiative; the widely-publicized emphases upon such slogans as, first, "ungovernability" and then "from ungovernability to people's power;" and the successful attempt to bring the Freedom Charter back into prominence as a crucial touchstone of the democratic movement's demands. In addition, in organizational terms, the ANC proved successful in linking itself to the most important new initiatives being mounted above ground inside the country — with the UDF, for example, and, more indirectly but equally importantly, with a rapidly crystallizing COSATU.

This trend was not uncontested, of course. There were rivals to this ANC-UDF-COSATU alliance that was slowly but surely emerging center-stage in resistance circles in South Africa, notably those who continued to define their politics quite self-consciously with reference to a relatively unalloyed version of the Black Consciousness tradition (Azapo, the National Forum, the National

Council of Trade Unions/NACTU). Such resistance to ANC-UDF-COSATU hegemony sometimes presented itself in leftist terms, attempting to rationalize its racially exclusivist preoccupations as radicalism by highlighting the centrality of the "*black* working class" to its project. Not particularly convincing in many of its protestations, this tendency has remained, in any case, a comparatively minor one within resistance circles. In practice, the real debate over the probable definition of the revolutionary content of the South African movement has tended to take place *within* the major alliance identified above.[16]

Not that analyzing the struggle over the probable socio-economic "content" of some future liberation of South Africa is a straightforward exercise. To begin with, there is the question of the precise degree of radicalism represented by the ANC's own nationalist project. Certainly the most prominent ANC ideological formulae have tended to emphasize, over the years, the advisability of a two-stage process of liberation (national liberation-cum-democratization first, and socialism later) — even if, more often than not, the working class is presented as being the single most crucial element to the liberatory alliance (and therefore, the ANC line hints, some kind of guarantor of socialism in the next round). No doubt there have been tactical considerations at play here. Racial oppression is a particularly prominent reality in South Africa, and it has been tempting to develop a politics that centres on mass sensitivity to that fact. Not only might this be expected to broaden the class alliance of blacks pushing for change, it could even speak, it has been argued, to workers in a genuinely radicalizing manner. For with the state's repressive role etched in color, workers might be more inclined to broaden the "trade union consciousness" generated at the workplace into a potentially hegemonic project that implies the actual overthrow of that state. In addition, presenting the struggle as being, first and foremost, a struggle for "de-racialization" and "democratization" could be expected both to add to the coalition of international supporters committed to the overthrow of apartheid and to help to split the white community inside South Africa itself in ways not likely to be available if the emancipatory project were defined, immediately, in more clearly radical terms.

Yet there are also obvious dangers to such a "judicious" approach. If working-class power and socialist priorities are not established absolutely firmly from the outset, how is the pull towards mere petty-bourgeois nationalism to be countered? For, as the period of insurrection was to demonstrate, the nearer the movement comes to power, the more active will be liberal forces within the white business community and amongst members of the black petty-bourgeoisie (including those within the ANC itself) in seeking to narrow the nationalist agenda; moreover, the complexities of dealing with South Africa's sophisticated economy can be expected, in and of themselves, to exert a formidably de-radicalizing pressure upon any post-liberation government, helping to pull it towards what, at best, might prove to be merely some all too "reasonable" form of deeply-compromised "social democracy."

Set against this, however, is the ANC's own discernibly radical tradition (this in part associated with the South African Communist Party, and therefore, admittedly, something of a mixed blessing — given the difficulties that party has had in freeing itself from its long-term Stalinist incubus). Important, too, is the continuing pattern of radicalization of the township youth, ever more inclined (accurately enough) to underscore the links between capitalist exploitation and racial oppression in South Africa. And, finally, there are the trade unions, some of the most important of which (the Metalworkers are a good example) are very far from manifesting mere "trade union consciousness" in their increasingly socialist claims upon the future. In part the ANC has had to go to school to such unions in re-establishing its preeminent position within the South African movement, and this is yet another promising portent. Moreover, as noted above, "Charterist" elements have had to jockey with the so-called "workerists" within COSATU in ways that have not split the union or the broader movement and may even have strengthened them — by foreshadowing the manner in which the issues of the future can be openly debated. In short, the imperatives thrown up by South Africa's class structure seem one potential inoculation against the tailing off of successful struggle there into the mere Africanization of capitalism.

Needless to say, rendering permanent the South African revolution will be a source of on-going struggle even in a post-apartheid South Africa. Yet it is one thing to speculate about the post-apartheid future, another to reach that future by, in the first instance, actually overthrowing the apartheid state. In the 1984-86 period, when the pace of change in South Africa seemed to be accelerating geometrically, "futurology" was the vogue. True, questions of class alliance germane to determining the likely long-term socialist content of liberation in South Africa are also relevant to defining the most appropriate line-up of class agents for change in any more immediate phase of struggle. Yet, as the failure of insurrection was to demonstrate, there are also quite specific questions that arise regarding the modalities of insurrectionary practice itself. In fact, these are questions that the popular movement inside South Africa only really began to wrestle with *after* South Africa's repressive Emergency Regulations had dealt that movement a severe setback. This essay will return to the consequent debate in its next section. Here, however, a brief look at some of the strengths and weaknesses of the revolutionary challenge presented by the 1984-86 near-insurrection is in order.

The insurrectionary moment

The range of incident that comprised the insurrection was significant, certainly — and so, cumulatively, was the number of South Africans involved. And it did shake the dominant classes, especially when domestic unrest also began to trigger off more dramatic sanctions activity from abroad (including, not least importantly, those "market-induced sanctions" that saw the international banking community reconsidering the viability of South Africa's investment climate). Nonetheless, questions could be asked as to how effectively the insurrection was actually organized. Certainly there were those who felt, even at the time, that the UDF as a national body was top-heavy and in too much of a hurry, and that, by not comprehending the need to further consolidate local organization, it became more merely parasitic of popular energies boiling away at that level than it should have been.

Of course, it is also true that, as events wore on, more emphasis was given to the genesis of streets committees, peoples' courts and the like, institutions that promised to provide greater resilience and an even greater sense of purpose and accomplishment at the base. And in some spheres remarkable examples of novel kinds of creativity did appear. Thus in education, in part at ANC urging, the tactic of mere boycott of the schools was scrutinized critically. Then, with the linking of parents groups to those of students in such organizations as the National Education Crisis Committee, exciting programmes began to be devised that sought to reclaim the schools as, in effect, quasi-liberated territory upon which to build new social relations and devise new syllabi. It was in this context, for example, that the slogan "People's Education for People's Power" replaced that of "No Education Before Liberation!" Perhaps, in the end, the problems characteristic of South Africa's insurrectionary moment were primarily ones of timing: the insurrection was nipped too quickly in the bud by state repression to permit the movement to profit promptly from its mistakes and to deepen its project dramatically.

All the more disappointing, then, that the movement could not defend itself better from the state when the crunch came. This was especially so in light of the fact that a promise had been made by the ANC, both in the year or two immediately proceeding the insurrection and also in 1985, in the heat of battle, at the movement's Kabwe Consultative Conference. The promise was that the ANC would be able to shift its military presence from mere "armed propaganda" (however important that might be) to actively arming and defending the resistance on the ground in the townships. What actually transpired along these lines was very much less than that. And what of the goals of insurrection? Certainly the strategic focus of the dramatic events of the time was less than clear, in part because, almost inevitably, no one center had real control over such events and in part because there often seemed operative the implicit premise that mere revolt, as widespread as possible, would produce relevant "negotiations." The ANC, at the center of events in many important ways, did position itself deftly for such negotiations, as a string of visitors, including a weighty group of senior business people, trooped dutifully to Lusaka. Yet this was not, immediately, to prove adequate as a road to power.

III. Counter-revolution and Future Prospects

The nature of the South African state's response to the growth of revolutionary challenge, both domestically and in the region at large, has already been anticipated at several points in this essay. We have noted, in particular, the key role played by South African destabilization in undermining much of the promise of socialism in such countries as Mozambique and Angola. In Angola this involved direct military intervention from the very dawn of Angolan independence (November 11, 1975) when, with American encouragement, South African troops drove for Luanda. Only the eleventh hour military assistance of Cuba saved the MPLA government. But this was merely the first phase of the long and wasting war South Africa (and its American ally) was to inflict upon Angola, both directly and by essential support provided to its local cat's-paw in the fray, the UNITA movement of Jonas Savimbi. As noted, South Africa was defeated in southern Angola in 1988, but at great cost to Angola: left behind was a country in tatters, seeking economic succor from the IMF and forced to request the departure of the ANC, with its military bases, from its soil as part of 1988's peace accords.

This latter seemed, at the time, to be no insignificant concession, especially given the fact that one of the key goals of South African destabilization was, all along, a quarantining of ANC presence in the Frontline states. A second goal was to undermine the possibility of the front-line establishing an alternative grid of regional economic activity (under the auspices of the Southern African Development Coordination Conference, for example) outside the historically established economic overlordship of South Africa — this being an even more pressing aim in Mozambique, where Zimbabwe's possible alternative links of transportation to the sea have been a chief target of Renamo activities, than in Angola. But there was also a third, quite self-conscious goal behind South African aggression: to turn the promise of nationalist victory and, in particular, of socialist assertion in the region to mud, the better to undermine the resonance of such advances inside South Africa itself and to facilitate the broader counter-revolutionary goals of South Africa's Western allies.

True, opinions have differed from time to time within the imperial camp as to when the process of military destabilization and consequent concessions made by the target regime could be said to have gone far enough. With the Nkomati Accord, for example, most Western actors, including, somewhat surprisingly, the Reagan White House, chose to remove Mozambique from the top of their international hit-list, looking, increasingly, to the IMF and tied aid to finish the job of reabsorbing that weakened country into the global circuits of capital. Yet South Africa itself preferred to drive on with its cruel project of destruction in Mozambique, seeking further to neutralize that country by, in effect, destroying the very fabric of its social life — targeting, through Renamo, essential economic linkages, murdering trained personnel and, literally, terrorizing the population. (In Angola, in contrast, as South Africa prepared to retire from the fray, the United States, at least momentarily, actually promised to pick up the slack in support for UNITA and to block Angola's entry into the IMF!) Elsewhere in the region — albeit somewhat less dramatically — South Africa has also been prepared to use economic leverage (the sanctions that helped topple an awkward Lesotho government in 1986 or the economic whip that is constantly being cracked over the head of Zimbabwe) and destabilization in a lower key (lightening raids into Botswana and Zimbabwe or the stirring of the pot of disunity in the latter country by sponsorship of the so-called "super-ZAPU") to gain tactical advantage.

State repression and the Emergency

No less crucial has been the use of the iron fist where the threat to Pretoria's interests is even more acute — inside South Africa itself. True, some measure of preemptive accommodation to be struck with black forces pressing for change has been, from time to time, part of the apartheid regime's domestic strategy, the attempted cooptation of the new trade union movement mentioned earlier being a case in point — this in turn being merely one component of a broader "reform" package of the late 1970s that was designed to peel away a significant stratum of urbanized, relatively better-off blacks into acceptance of the legitimacy of an only marginally altered system. As we have seen, mass mobilization around an emerging programme of far more meaningful liberation quickly put paid to such a tactic. But voices could still be heard, (from some sections of the business community for example) — and particularly in the context of the subsequent insurrection — suggesting that more substance be given to the reform initiative.

Yet only the most bold were prepared to suggest that anything even approximating a complete deracialization (and color-blind bourgeois democratization) of South Africa might be the best means to insulate South African capitalism from going down with the country's structure of racial oppression (cf. Zac De Beer's well known comment that "we dare not allow the baby of free enterprise to be thrown out with the bath-water of apartheid"). For most in the white community any such changes seemed, for a very long time, either absolutely unthinkable on first principles or (at best) far too risky. On the other hand, half measures of "reform" did not work either. In consequence, the state's initial response to insurrection was to be, almost exclusively, a repressive one. When, in turn, this repression seemed to "work" — producing, at least momentarily, a measure of social stability — most nay-sayers in the business community and elsewhere lapsed into relatively comfortable passivity once again.

The modalities of repression utilized inside South Africa in the immediate post-insurrection years were no less ruthless than those developed by Pretoria in its regional counter-revolutionary activities. Indeed, lessons learned in Mozambique and Angola were actually being carried back into South Africa for application in the black townships. As noted, in the late 1970s the apartheid regime seemed momentarily to convince itself that it could find black intermediaries who might actually help sell "reform" and cooptation to the broader mass of urbanized blacks and thus legitimize the neo-apartheid system. By the mid-1980s, however, any black allies were much more obviously cast for the role of fellow policemen, junior partners in the repressive apparatus.

True, the cutting edge of repression was still the police force *per se* and, increasingly, the army, the latter now also involved, within the framework of an innovative and remarkably comprehensive "National Security Management System," in what was, for it, the relatively unconventional task of scourging the townships. The toll of death, arbitrary arrest and torture, crackdown on the media and banning of individuals and organizations that followed with the imposition of the partial Emergency of 1985 and the nation-wide, far more draconian Emergency of 1986, is well known. But enter, in addition, the vigilantes, black gangs with foot-soldiers drawn from *lumpen* elements but focussed around the initiatives of urban councillors and businessmen, of Bantustan politicians and warlords, who chose to profit from the existing system. These were killers to whom the police either turned a blind eye or else actively trained, and they were encouraged to stalk the democratic movement with lethal intent, as seen in the debacle of Crossroads in 1985-86 or in the depredations carried out by Buthelezi and his Inkatha minions in Pietermaritzburg in 1987-88. Here was a "scorched earth" approach to the project of neutralizing dissent fully worthy of Renamo.

More could be written about the barbarities of repression. Though less visible to the outside world because of severe restrictions on media coverage of developments in South Africa, 1988 actually witnessed an intensification of the crackdown. That this should still be necessary after several years of the Emergency was indicative of just how deep resistance ran. Nonetheless, the costs to the movement of this state action should not be underestimated. As *The Weekly Mail* put the point at the time:

> Dealing with opponents on the left [is] one of the few areas where the government showed no hesitation and a clear-cut, imaginative policy. They produced a constant supply of new methods of repression, the best example of which was the Emergency restriction order.... Individuals, organizations, even funerals, were subjected to the most extraordinary list of incomprehensible restrictions, dished out so fast that nobody could keep track....The government started the process by restricting 17 organizations in February, including the United Democratic Front and Azapo, with a partial restriction on COSATU. This dealt with the major and best known orga-

nizations. Gradually, as new bodies began to reveal themselves or old bodies took up the cudgels, they were dealt similar blows....It was a new form of prison without bars.[17]

Of course, there were plenty of bars as well, and other equally merciless tactics. Thus "some of the major resistance leaders of the 1980s, the people who pioneered the UDF-style of non-violent opposition, were dubbed violent terrorists and sentenced to long terms of imprisonment in the 'Delmas' treason trial." (No reference cited.) Or take those churches that tried to step into the partial vacuum left by the February restrictions. "Government response: the clergy were water-cannoned by police in Cape Town, the headquarters of the SACC (South African Council of Churches) and the Southern African Catholic Bishops Conference were mysteriously bombed, and the Reverend Frank Chikane's mother received a hand grenade in the post." (No reference cited.) When 143 (white) conscripts announced that they would not honor their call-up for military service it looked, momentarily, as if the state might discuss seriously the possibility of alternative service with the End Conscription Campaign (ECC). Colder heads prevailed, however, and the ECC merely joined the list of restricted organizations. Assassination continued to be a favorite tactic of the powers that be, both at home (where the list of victims grew) and abroad, where a pattern of physical removal of ANC activists (about fifty between 1981 and 1988) peaked with the murder of the ANC's Paris representative, Dulcie September. When, as 1988 progressed, more and more student and youth organizations became a particular target for state attack, the implications were sobering. If the apartheid government was not even marginally interested in finding real intermediaries for dialogue about a different kind of future, what alternatives were open? As youth representatives put the point: "Underground is not a healthy terrain for struggle for an organization that wants to reach the masses, make statements and operate above-board. But conditions of near-illegality have been forced on us."[18]

Debating tactics

Clearly, the Emergency narrowed the terrain for above-ground activity, but had that terrain disappeared altogether? What could be done, for example, to follow through on the insight, produced by failed insurrection, that a firmer base would have to be built at the grassroots level both to keep the struggle alive in the short-run and to prepare a base for any future dramatic confrontation? There were those who argued that, given the strength of the regime, a politics of bargaining and negotiation with the state was the only viable politics in any case. An analogy with the trade unions' entry into the industrial relations system (the better to find space for further manoeuvre and demand) was sometimes suggested — unflaggingly so by Steven Friedman of the South African Institute of Race Relations, for example.[19] Could not township organizations also group around concrete local demands, analogous to the workplace demands that had given such force and presence to trade unions, in order to make concrete advances, to build strength and gradually to transform the South African situation?

Of course, this was already being done on some fronts (with rent strikes in many townships) and plotted on others (the aforementioned NECC programme for the schools, for example). Nor did it seem inevitable that an extension of this approach need collapse, by definition, into mere reformism: it might instead imply a more determinedly revolutionary (but tactically adept) project of "structural reform."* It was by thinking along such lines, as I wrote after a clandestine visit to South Africa in 1988, that

---

* My suggestion is that what was being groped towards was something analogous to the practices codified by Andre Gorz in his conceptualization of "structural reform" — which, incidentally, he distinguished quite self-consciously from "reformism" (see his "Reform and Revolution," *The Socialist Register 1968*. (London: Merlin Press, 1968). As it happens, this approach can lead to a far more revolutionary understanding of the kind of activities being identified here than could Friedman's studied "pragmatism." For Gorz suggests that in periods when revolution is not immediately on the agenda, organization for reform can be a revolutionary act — provided the gains demanded and won are self-consciously understood by the political movement in question as implicating, systemically, a series of further demands; and provided, as well, that the mobilization of people around such demands leads to the crystallization of organizational forms that mark a process of cumulative empowerment and developing revolutionary potential. In a situation like that of South Africa in the late-1980s this approach might have meant certain visible advance on specific fronts (thereby giving people a necessarily *concrete* sense of the on-going struggle in the short-run) while also building the popularly-based organizational infrastructure crucial to another, more successful round of confrontation sometime in the future. Might more of this kind of strategic thinking have given a greater sense of focus to the 1984-86 insurrection? An even more important question, at the time of my originally writing this article, was whether possibilities for such a "structural reform" approach still existed in the South Africa of the Emergency. In the event, the revival of even more assertive kinds of resistance in 1989 — combined with the significant rethinking of its options by the state that culminated, later that same year, in its unbanning of the ANC and (in February 1990) its release of Mandela from prison — produced a distinctive new terrain for politics in South Africa. For a discussion of the even greater possible relevance of Gorz's formulations to this new terrain, however, see chapters four and five, below.

some UDF activists even briefly floated, for discussion, the idea of participating in the local blacks-only elections, and thereby seizing hold of state-structured township councils as one possible way of giving fresh focus to popular resistance to the state. Ultimately the idea was rejected, since the councils are, in fact, so tightly controlled by the apartheid administrative apparatus that they grant the democratic forces little real room for manoeuvre. In fact, only the most obvious of collaborators concluded otherwise, while Bishop Tutu and others, at some risk to themselves, called for a renewed boycott of such structures in the October elections. For its part, the state used its powers (and considerable manipulation of the electoral procedures) to neutralize the boycott and to attempt — with no great success, as things turned out — to manufacture the appearance of support for those few blacks prepared to help make its system work. Continued boycott of the councils made sense, I think, but some further discussion of the merits of the boycott made sense too. In any case, this was merely one example among the many I found on my trip of the readiness of South African democrats to scrutinize past practice in their effort to devise new and more relevant tactics.[20]

The unions had also to operate on this ambiguous terrain, and had, in fact, a little more space within which to do so — since a scorched earth tactic is scarcely viable for the state in the factories and the mines. Yet the unions also found themselves on the defensive under the Emergency, the state and capital both having seized on the opportunity to roll back gains that had been made. Most dramatic was the state's harsh new Labour Relations Amendment Bill, designed to reverse the gains unions have made for themselves in recent years. There was also a much more pugnacious attitude on the part of employers in their wage bargaining (typified in 1987 by the aggressive reaction of so rhetorically liberal an employer as Anglo-American to the mineworkers' strike). Nonetheless, the unions did take up much of the slack in the political arena, expanding their role despite the restrictions. The dramatic three-day stay-away in June 1988 (jointly coordinated with popular political structures) which saw as many as three million workers off the job demonstrated this, as did COSATU's attempt (aborted by the state) to have an all-inclusive anti-apartheid conference in September of the same year. Of course, such moves were still some distance from any attempt to mobilize the workingclass at the point of production to, say, occupy the factories as part of a coordinated general strike. But they were significant, nonetheless.

The fact that the state ultimately banned the September meeting and, momentarily, the on-going attempt to regroup the struggle above ground had additional implications. It evoked, once again, the importance of also having an effective underground, not least a *military* underground. This, in turn, implied its own share of dilemmas. How, for example, was it possible to seek to split the white community by entering into dialogue with certain "liberal forces" while simultaneously attempting to raise the costs of apartheid for its beneficiaries by means of armed action? Nor was this an academic question. In 1988 it surfaced, within the ANC itself, in a debate over the relative merits of "hard" vs. "soft" targets — although in the end the movement made it clear that, as far as possible, it would continue to eschew inflicting civilian casualties. What the ANC would not deny itself, however, was the right to sustain some kind of armed activity.

Thus, that same year (1988), it "carried out an unprecedented number of guerilla attacks, despite security force claims that the movement's momentum had been broken. According to South African Police statistics, a total of 238 guerilla attacks took place in the first ten months of 1988, compared with 234 during the whole of last year, 230 in 1986, 136 in 1985 and 44 in 1984."[20] In addition to the familiar brand of exemplary sabotage ("armed propaganda"), many of these actions directly targeted army and police personnel. Moreover, it seemed true that, more so than previously, back-up for these actions — the training and logistics — was grounded within structures internal to the country, no small matter since South African destabilization in the region probably had begun to have a negative impact on the ANC's military capacity (lengthening supply lines and raising costs, for example, and, presumably, negatively affecting the ANC's ability to make its armed presence felt during the l984-86 insurrection).

Breaking the stalemate?

Despite this, it cannot be said that there was any real prospect that some militarily-premised knockout blow from the ANC would deliver a quick resolution to the struggle in South Africa. Still, the apartheid regime could not be considered to be all-powerful either, even at the height of its "Emergency." Underlying its repressive bluster were very real economic weaknesses and vulnerabilities signalled by continuing problems of slow growth, chronic unemployment, on-going balance of payment difficulties and vulnerability to sanctions (whenever, in international response to the renewed visibility of dramatic popular resistance, these would become a serious threat once again).[22] Nor was the political ground on which the government walked altogether solid. Quite apart from — and more important than — the well-publicized "rise of the right" (the Conservative Party, the neo-Nazi AWB), there was a visible lack of direction within the National Party camp itself, with "hard-liners" and "soft-liners" jockeying for position while able to produce only a mishmash of contradictory state policies. Soon, indeed, such tensions were to prove beyond the talents of even P. W. Botha — until his dramatic political demise in 1989 very much "the leader" as the last surviving member of apartheid's parliamentary class of 1948 — to master. Nor, as we now know, was a mere intensification of repression to prove an adequate policy refuge for his immediate successor, F. W. de Klerk.

Most important, in the end, was a reality that defined the outer limit and chief weakness of the state strategy of repression: the fact that the South African regime could stalemate its adversaries but not successfully legitimize its rule in the eyes of the vast mass of the black population. Not that that "black population" has been itself an unproblematic category: the intransigence of South Africa's apartheid regime ensured that some of the energy surging up from below turned sour when balked of fulfillment (the pathology represented by some of Winnie Mandela's activities in Soweto in these years is one example). And the regime found other fissures with the black community as well, including some former militants amongst the township youth who turned vigilante or informer as the police rallied to rebuild their own brand of township network or who permitted themselves to be mobilized by ruthless warlords, along patron-client lines, against progressive trends in Natal or Crossroads. Here were gruesome trends that would extend into the politics of the 1990s.

As noted earlier, the state also continued, in the late-1980s, with attempts to shore up its own strata of black intermediaries — new urban partners for the Bantustan elites already in place. Similarly, some fresh financial resources were dispensed, particularly to townships that had proven to be revolutionary flashpoints in the past, in the hopes of complementing the harrassment of local militants with a modicum of economic betterment for other residents. (Housing was a particularly popular sphere for experimentation in such up-grading of the living conditions of the more stabilized of black urban dwellers.) Nor could one rule out other kinds of "formative action," designed by capital and the state to further divide, rule and coopt* — even if, realistically speaking, there remained a low ceiling on what the regime seemed likely to offer in this way.

Despite such efforts by the apartheid regime, however, the long-term initiative really did lie with the resistance movement in determining just how fatal would be the fact that neither state nor capital could easily legitimate themselves in neo-apartheid South Africa. Thus, even in the darkest days — of 1987, of 1988 — it was possible to say that the Emergency of the 1980s was not the Emergency of the 1960s. For the psychology of resistance now ran very deep. Because of this, most anticipated that, inevitably, there would continue to be dramatic flash-points in South Africa: imagine the regime's own nightmares, during this period, regarding the likely mass reaction if Nelson Mandela were to die on its hands in prison! And yet flash-points are not a revolution, even if they can prove to be privileged moments for focussing revolutionary potential. How were the radical energies, undoubtedly present in South Africa, to find more effective focus in forcing the pace of change?

Certainly, by the late-1980s, it was evident that the popular democratic movement had learned some lessons. In its year's end round-up of developments in 1988, the *Weekly Mail* provided the mundane but instructive example of recent actions by the Western Cape Students' Congress: "The burning barricades, demonstrations violently broken up by police recalled the turmoil of 1985. But a new discipline and maturity underlay student action. Instead of ad hoc reactions, protests formed part of a co-ordinated programme marked by thorough canvassing of student opinion for properly mandated change." Moreover, the action's "major significance ... lay beyond the [large] numbers involved: it resulted in police reversing a decision to enter schools and ensure teaching took place."[23]

---

* Indeed, even progressive trade union leaders worried aloud about a possible stratification of the working class itself that might prove counterproductive to revolution. What, they asked, were the implications of a gap that was emerging between workers in full-time, often skilled or semi-skilled, employment, organized and relatively better off, *vis-à-vis* the marginalized and the unemployed or underemployed, piling up in the sprawling peri-urban shanty towns? Specifically, the unions attempted to counter the perils of a split between such strata with programmes for organizing the unemployed and such innovations as the "Living Wage Campaign" (albeit, to date, with only modest success). Yet this was just one of the many challenges attendant upon uniting and mobilizing a black population whose profile was constantly being reshaped by the vagaries of an increasingly complex South African economy — challenges likely to cast a shadow over any subsequent processes of transition in South Africa as well.

"Discipline and maturity." "A coordinated programme." Too often the image of South African protest in the western media, even when that coverage has been reasonably well-intentioned, has been that of the rock-throwing black mob, angry with good reason perhaps, but a mob nonetheless. A more accurate image of the history of the preceding decade and a half of resistance would be that of profound political creativity and an ever higher level of organizational achievement on the part of the South African resister. This considerable revolutionary energy which has distinguished the South African scene found powerful expression in an impressive array of organizations like COSATU, like the UDF, like the ANC, like a hundred others — organizations that focussed the commitment of tens of thousands of individuals; organizations bent but not broken by repression.

This, and the renewal of a psychology of resistance, were by 1989 the key facts about contemporary South Africa to be noted by those who would wish to see it transformed. As the further events of that year — the continuing revival of mass resistance and the neutralizing of the effects of the state's Emergency regulations — were soon to demonstrate (see chapter four which discusses the transition in South Africa from the politics of mere repression to the current politics of "negotiations"), it was these organizations that would refuse to give the regime peace, thereby renewing the promise of, ultimately, finding the key to liberation. As I have hinted, within and between such organizations the potential for significant contradiction exists, not only over the question of how best to advance the current struggle for democratic enfranchisement but also over the socio-economic content of any such "democratization" as begins to emerge. Nonetheless, with the dawn of the 1990s, it was clear that these organizations had already served to empower the workers of South Africa, to empower the black population of South Africa, in significant ways; it was clear, too, that they would be central actors in the on-going fight to enlarge the terms of that empowerment.[24]

IV. Conclusion

In the end, it is the promise represented by the trajectory of such organizations that also gives resonance to Magdoff and Sweezy's characterization of South Africa, penned some years ago: "Its system of racial segregation and repression is a veritable paradigm of capitalist superexploitation. It has a white monopoly capitalist ruling class and an advanced black proletariat. It is so far the only country with a well developed, modern capitalist structure which is not only 'objectively' ripe for revolution but has actually entered a stage of overt and seemingly irreversible revolutionary struggle."[25] Irreversible? In fact, Magdoff and Sweezy themselves did contemplate other possibilities, warning that "a victory for counter-revolution — the stabilization of capitalist relations in South Africa, even if in somewhat altered form — would ... be [a] stunning defeat for the world revolution". (No reference cited.)

By the end of 1988, and despite the recent drama of the "insurrection," it appeared that some such "stabilization" had indeed occurred. And even if the van of history were to move forward again (as in the next few years it did) it was not certain how readily the established structure of racial privilege and capitalist power that lay behind constitutional forms could effectively be challenged. For many such reasons, it seemed wise not to be "triumphalist" regarding South Africa (and even less so, of course, regarding the increasingly battered Frontline states). Thus, no matter how often it might be said that fundamental change is — must be! — inevitable in South Africa, such change is something that remains *to be won*. In 1988, the apartheid state still remained to be overthrown, while, even more dauntingly, the logic of capitalism ("racial" or otherwise) that has been so integral to the repressive South African system still remained to be qualified and/or reversed.

But if triumphalism was no answer, it seemed equally unwise, as the 1980s drew to a close, to despair. Reflect back upon the *National Security Study Memorandum 39* with which this chapter began. As stated at the outset, the situation, twenty years on, suggested that things had come a long way since 1969 — in what is still, measured as "historical time", a relatively short span. *Pace* Kissinger and company, white power had not been "here to stay;" the southern African revolution had at least seen to that. In addition, and despite cruel setbacks, there was also a crystallization of advances — in organizational and ideological terms — that provided a legacy upon which the southern African movement, broadly defined, might hope to mount future rounds of challenge. Recall the story (perhaps apocryphal, although one hopes not) about Mao Zedong and the events of 1789. How did he evaluate the outcome of the French Revolution, he was asked. "It's too soon to tell," he replied.

True, as well, of the southern African revolution. In South Africa, at least, the prospect of continuing advance remained strong as the events of 1989 began to unfold.[26] Undoubtedly such advance would occur at much greater cost than could be wished, and it was likely to be a bit murkier in its outcome than might have been predicted a few short years previously, in the heat of insurrection. But advance there would surely be. And what of the broader claims made on behalf of the struggle in southern Africa? Was there also a possibility that Magdoff and Sweezy's hopes for the world-wide resonance of developments in South Africa would then be realized? "A victory for revolution, i.e., a genuine and lasting change in basic power relations in South Africa," they write, "could have an impact on the balance of global forces comparable to that of the revolutionary wave that followed World War II." In retrospect, this may well seem too grandiose a claim. Still, the basic premise remains a sound one: yes, the stakes in South Africa — in southern Africa — are high.

This essay (first written in early 1989 and only revised in modest ways for publication here) does provide a base-line for assessing southern Africa on the eve of the 1990s. Three years on, however, the situation had continued to evolve and in ways not altogether for the better. This is particularly true of the Frontline states, notably Mozambique and Angola: the first years of the new decade confirmed that they had both been so bloodied by the regional counter-revolution that almost none of their original promise could be said to have survived intact. The further unravelling of such countries (indeed, their virtual recolonization), and the context that facilitated such an outcome, are the focus of the next two chapters. In South Africa itself the promise remained more visible. As will be discussed in chapter four, the post-insurrectionary setback there did indeed prove to be temporary and, as the mass democratic movement regained some momentum, the South African state under President F. W. de Klerk began itself to revise its own approach. Thus, as the new decade dawned, the release of Nelson Mandela (on February 3, 1990) symbolized a new phase in the politics of South Africa. But this "new phase" — marked, in the first instance, by a process of "negotiations" over a new constitutional dispensation — was itself not to prove a straightforward one, either in producing quickly a political democratization of that country (De Klerk, for all the boldness of many of his moves, proving to be racked still by many of the contradictory impulses that had so scarred the project of his immediate predecessor, P. W. Botha), or in realizing the broader revolutionary possibilities invoked above by Sweezy and Magdoff.

1. This chapter was first published, under the same title, in *The Socialist Register 1989*. Useful, I hope, as an overview of how southern Africa stood on eve of the 1990s, it has been revised, although not extensively, for republication here; a further updating of this analysis is to be found in subsequent chapters of the present volume. In addition, I am currently preparing a more thorough, book-length manuscript, *The Thirty Years' War: The Struggle for Southern Africa, 1960-1990*, on many of the themes introduced in the present chapter.
2. Giovanni Arrighi and John S. Saul, "Nationalism and Revolution in Sub-Saharan Africa," *The Socialist Register 1969* (London: Merlin Press, 1969).
3. "National Security Study Memorandum 39" of 1969 was published, with a useful introduction by Barry Cohen and Mohamed A. El-Khawas, as *The Kissinger Study of Southern Africa* (Nottingham: Spokesman Books, 1975).
4. On Mozambique see, inter alia, John S. Saul (ed.), *A Difficult Road: The Transition to Socialism in Mozambique* (New York: Monthly Review Press, 1985).
5. For a further discussion of this and related issues see ch. 3, below.
6. On this subject see chapter 4 ("Zimbabwe: The Next Round") in my previous African World Press volume, *Socialist Ideology and the Struggle for Southern Africa* (Trenton: Africa World Press, 1990).
7. See, in addition, chapter 3 ("Development and Counterdevelopment Strategies in Mozambique") in my *Socialist Ideology... (ibid.)* as well as the on-going discussion of Mozambican developments to be found in the pages of *Southern Africa Report* (SAR), available from TCLSAC, 427 Bloor St. W., Toronto M5S 1X7, Ontario.
8. See my article, "Mozambique: The Failure of Socialism?" in SAR, 6, #2 (November, 1990), as well as chapters 2 and 3, below.
9. In Ibbo Mandaza (ed.), *Zimbabwe: The Political Economy of Transition, 1980-1986* (Dakar: CODESRIA, 1986), p. 51.
10. J. Hyslop, reviewing A. Astrow, *Zimbabwe: A revolution that lost its way?* in *South Africa Labour Bulletin* (Johannesburg) 12, 6/7 (August/September, 1987); see also, in this special issue of *SALB* on "Labour in Post-Independence Zimbabwe", the debate feature entitled "The Political Economy of Zimbabwe: Is Zimbabwe in Transition to Socialism?," as well as Ian Phimister, "Zimbabwe: The inheritance of the anti-colonial struggle" in *Transformation* (Durban), 5 (1987).
11. See, for example, Lionel Cliffe, "Where They Pushed or Did They Jump? Zimbabwe and the World Bank", *SAR*, 6, #4 (March, 1991), and Lee Cokorinos, "Zimbabwe Ten Years After: Prospects for a Popular Politics," *SAR*, 6, #1 (July, 1990).
12. Victoria Brittain, "Stacking the Deck in Namibia," *SAR*, 4, 4 (March, 1989).
13. On this subject see the special Namibian issue of *SAR*, 7, #2

(November, 1991), notably the article by Chris Tapscott entitled "Namibia: A Class Act?;" for a study of the deeply contradictory history of the development of the struggle for liberation in Namibia see Colin Leys and John S. Saul (eds.), *The Two-Edged Sword: The independence struggle in Namibia and its legacy* (London: James Currey, 1993).

14 John S. Saul and Stephen Gelb, *The Crisis in South Africa*, revised edition (New York: Monthly Review Press, 1986); see also, inter alia, Rob Davies, Dan O'Meara and Sipho Dlamini, *The Struggle for South Africa*, new edition (London: Zed Press, 1988). There is a wealth of sources on the various phases of the evolution of events in South Africa, most importantly such regularly published South African journals as *The Weekly Mail, Work in Progress, South African Labour Bulletin, Transformation* and *South African Review*.

15 See chapter 5 ("South Africa: the Question of Strategy") of my *Socialist Ideology and the Struggle for Southern Africa* (op. cit.).

16 Ibid.

17 Anton Harber, "On the Move. To Nowhere," *The Weekly Mail* (Johannesburg), 4, 46 (December 23, 1988 to January 12, 1989); this issue contains a number of articles usefully reviewing South African developments in 1988.

18 Quoted in Shaun Johnson and Vusi Gunene, "Under siege. Slogan-chanting students retreat underground," *The Weekly Mail* (ibid.).

19 See Friedman's regular column in *The Weekly Mail*, as well his suggestive pamphlet *Reform Revisited* (Braamfontein: South African Institute of Race Relations, 1988).

20 John S. Saul, "Without Proper Papers: Inside South Africa," *Monthly Review*, 40, 8 (January, 1989), pp. 9-10.

21 Gavin Evans, "The figures show ANC's alive and bombing," *The Weekly Mail*, (op. cit.).

22 See the special issue of *SAR* on "Apartheid Economics," 4, #4 (March, 1989) as well as various papers prepared in 1988 under the auspices of the Johannesburg-based Labour and Economic Research Centre; these papers, the product of a collective effort coordinated by Stephen Gelb, were subsequently published, in book form, as Stephen Gelb (ed.), *South Africa's Economic Crisis* (Johannesburg: David Philip, 1991).

23 Gaye Davis, "Tough DET clamps 'throw down gauntlet to students'," *The Weekly Mail* (op. cit.).

24 Not that such on-going efforts by popular forces to organize on the complex terrain that South Africa offers can ever be straightforward or easy of achievement, as we will see below in discussing the politics of the negotiations phase. I also reflect on the even more complicated challenge of mobilizing popular energies for radical/socialist change in the socio-economic structure in chapters four and five.

25 Harry Magdoff and Paul Sweezy, "The Stakes in South Africa," introducing a special issue of *Monthly Review*, 37, 11 (April, 1986), on "South Africa in Struggle."

26 For a valuable discussion of the likely future impact of changes in South Africa back into the region — the next round, in effect, of the dialectic between South Africa and southern Africa traced in this chapter — see Rob Davies, "Post-Apartheid Scenarios for the Southern African Region," *Transformation*, #11 (1990).

Chapter 2
The End of the Cold War in Southern Africa[1]

▼▼▼▼▼▼▼▼▼▼▼▼

Peace in southern Africa is still a long way from being realized, as the strife in Mozambique and Angola has dragged on and as the fitful character of the negotiations process in South Africa still leaves plenty of room there for violence, both state and privately sponsored. Moreover, as is obvious, the mere "breaking-out of peace" is not always an unqualified advance. In southern Africa, for example, such peace as has been achieved represents as much or more the success of a process of pacification by the imperial centers and of reabsorption of the region into the global capitalist system as it does any positive resolution of underlying development problems. For, as discussed in the previous chapter, conflict in southern Africa has turned to a considerable degree on warring definitions of the future nature of politico-economic structures there: non-racial vs. apartheid approaches in the political realm; socialist vs. capitalist options in the economic realm. Despite this fact, however, some commentators have tended to view developments in southern Africa from a very different perspective, one that has emphasized, almost exclusively, the centrality of East-West confrontation to an explanation of regional conflict. Not surprisingly, such commentators are also inclined to view "the end of the Cold War" as being the primary engine of "peace" in southern Africa. We begin our own analysis by examining carefully this premise.

The Disappearing Soviets

The disappearing Soviets. A cause for celebration? Who can feel any nostalgia for the palsied regimes of Eastern Europe — even though one may have legitimate fears for the future of such countries as they advance all too heedlessly into the maw of international capitalism? Striking a balance sheet on the implications for southern Africa of the "end of the Cold War" is a little more complicated, however. How is one to assess the costs and benefits of the virtual disappearance of both a Soviet presence and of a "Soviet model" from the lists in that region of the world?

Disappearance? A bit of an overstatement perhaps, although it is true, quite literally, of the German Democratic Republic, until recently so important a presence in various crucial sectors (education, police) of a country like Mozambique.[2] Yet even the Soviet Union seems well on the way to becoming a very minor player indeed — while apparently actively bent on rationalizing just such a minor role for itself. Thus, as the Soviets prepare to cut and run from southern Africa, their line of argument — one aspect of their "new political thinking" — is becoming depressingly familiar. Notions of international class struggle and the clash of global systems, once the stock in trade of Soviet ideologists, are now muted in the extreme; while, in the words of one Soviet historian of Africa, the new approach takes as its thrust

> that humanity and human values should take precedence over national and class interests in international relations. Ideological differences between East and West would thus play a secondary role to concerns such as the need to avoid nuclear war and famine and environmental issues. The Soviets want to reduce their military presence all over the world and seek political resolutions to the major theaters of conflict. In essence, foreign policy now seeks to achieve stability in areas in which the Soviet Union is involved, particularly those in which there are — or could be — regional conflicts.[3]

But do Soviet thinkers and policy-makers genuinely believe that "humanity and human interests" have taken precedence, in southern Africa or elsewhere, over the hard-edged pursuit of "business as usual" in Western policy-making? Surely the primary function of such a jejune formulation must be that of putting the best face possible on the bald fact of the Soviet Union's own global retreat. It represents one kind of ideological fallout from the

Eastern bloc's economic collapse and from the fact that, in Fred Halliday's formulation, the communist movement's attempt "to erect an alternative, more desirable and viable, that would replace the anarchy and viciousness of capitalism with a more humane and rationally directed form of economic activity . . . has foundered" — with the communist societies themselves having "succumbed to a mode of production and a political system far stronger than them."[4] Nor has the ideological rot come to a halt with formulations of the "humanity and human interests" variety. As any positive commitment to socialist solutions slips away in Eastern Europe, the case for such solutions in southern Africa is also actively downgraded by Soviet observers. As Soviet deputy foreign minister Anatoly Adamishin put the point, speaking to reporters after the 1989 signing of the Angola peace accord in Brazzaville: "I personally don't think they are going to build socialism in this part of the world."[5]

True, the Soviets have never been entirely enthusiastic about socialist endeavors in southern Africa, all along consigning them to their second eleven as being, at best, mere "states of socialist orientation:" the class prerequisites for genuine socialism not quite right, the commitment to Marxism-Leninism not quite sound, and so on. The extended debate around this issue (Mozambican leaders launched vigorous protests against such formulations, for example) appears particularly surreal in retrospect, of course, with the Eastern European countries which chose thus to judge their Third World counterparts now admitted to have been so shallow of socialist purpose themselves. But the studied scepticism exemplified by an Adamishin operates on new premises, in any case. Partly what is in play is the rankest sort of opportunism: balked of global purpose, an economically-straitened Soviet Union now seeks, first and foremost, to escape from costly overseas entanglements. And it seeks as well — through its pragmatic acceptance of Western hegemony on the periphery of the world system — to curry favour with the capitalist centres of finance and technology to which it increasingly looks for its own economic salvation.

But such opportunism/pragmatism appears, increasingly, to be accompanied by an ever-deeper recasting of basic ideological guidelines. If, in the Soviet Union (although not in the rest of Eastern Europe) there remains some creative tension between Marxist/socialist premises (however deformed) and capitalist/liberal premises, it is the latter that, increasingly, seem to be carrying the day — especially in approaching the global scene. Thus, following Adamishin's lead, Soviet analyst Vladimir Kokorev has curtly dismissed the Frontline states as merely indulging in "a complex intellectual game" and not taking care of domestic problems: "They have real problems of economic development and rebuilding. Mozambique has the problem of hunger. They [Frontline governments] try to use socialist slogans for their own gains." As for South Africa, Kokorev again seems to summarize an increasingly commonly-held Soviet position: "We don't want to see it as an East-West problem or a capitalist-socialist problem, but only in terms of a racism problem."[6]

In short, in the words of Kokorev's colleague at the Soviet Institute for African Studies, Leonid Fituni:

> the positions of both the USSR and the USA concerning the principal question, the question of apartheid, are basically very close....The principles of the new political thinking, the proclamation of the priority of human values over class values, necessitate the rejection of a dogmatic, sectarian approach in the problem of allies and fellow-travellers in the struggle for a democratic South Africa.[7]

More generally, Fituni affirms that "the Soviet Union has no special interests in southern Africa...nor does the Soviet Union foster any aspirations hostile to the interests of the West. Aware of Western economic involvement in southern Africa and of its reliance on the region's raw materials, the USSR has no intention of undermining industrialized countries' historic trade links with this part of the world."[8]

Benefits — and costs

Of course, one should not romanticize the motives behind the Soviet Union's previous ties with southern Africa, compounded as they were of significant dollops of Great Power aggrandizement and patronizing self-interest. But there was also a positive side. Eastern European military assistance was critical to the success of armed struggle in Mozambique and Angola, and also helped sustain at least some credible guerilla presence in South Africa over an extended period. ("It is to Brezhnev, as much as anyone else outside South Africa itself, that credit for cracking the racist bloc should go," writes Halliday.[9]) Most dramatically — alongside the even more dramatic involvement of Cuba — the Soviets in Angola have helped turn back South African aggression on more than one occasion.

And there has also been the fact of Eastern economic assistance, never without strings to be sure and, in the end, never likely to be enough, but far from negligible. True, when Vilas mourns that "because of the economic and political crises in the USSR and Eastern Europe, abundant and cheap socialist support for progressive governments overseas no longer exists," he mourns a day that never did exist — not in southern Africa (and least of all, over the years, in a beleagured Mozambique). The Soviet Union always acted to keep the southern African socialisms at arms' length from COMECON, for example. And the fact remains, more clearly revealed now than ever, that the "socialist bloc" was always too weak and too compromised to have readily provided a viable alternative economic orbit for countries seeking to realize genuine development in Third World settings. In such a context Vilas' further argument that "since the Russian Revolution the chances of socialist transformation in the periphery of capitalism have always been linked to the availability of resources, cooperation, and assistance from more developed socialist countries" — if true — may seem to be even more a counsel of despair than he imagines.[10]

Moreover, the question of the quality of communist aid to southern Africa is at least as important as the question of its quantity. Let us focus for a moment on the price paid for Soviet prominence (and Brezhnevian largesse) by the movement for liberation, broadly defined, in southern Africa. Of course, some will argue that there has been, in fact, little attempt to construct socialism in the region; others that any such attempts have been thus far (in the words of South African Communist Party Secretary Joe Slovo) "both premature and wrong."[10] These are misleading perspectives, although socialism in southern Africa has indeed been blighted by the cruel drag of "objective conditions" and dogged by inadequacies of conceptualization and implementation. It is all too tempting, as well, to push forward to a rather abstract evaluation of socialist endeavor in countries like Mozambique and Angola without giving real (rather than merely notional) weight to the most important brake on their creativity: externally-imposed, imperially-crafted wars of destabilization.

But, "the price paid for Soviet prominence?" It bears emphasizing, in the present context, how much the participation of southern African socialist leaderships in the universe of discourse of "actually-existing socialisms" blighted their initiatives. True, up to a point one could argue that "official Marxism-Leninism" merely reinforced weaknesses already inherent in the Mozambican and Angolan projects. Thus, the ideological premise of "vanguardism" can be seen as feeding the familiar arrogances of militarism and triumphant African nationalism; and the fetishizing of the "forces of production" and "proletarianization" can be seen as comfortably intersecting with classic syndromes of "big-projectitis" and suspicion of the peasantry. Yet the fact remains that other socialist paths were possible, and might have been followed — and that the Eastern European factor weighed very negatively in the balance that produced far too little democracy and far too much inflexibility in socio-economic policies in southern African socialist circles.

In part this sprang from the allure of the then still apparently successful "Soviet model," and in part from the international economics and geo-politics of the situation. When I talked recently to a friend (and senior Frelimo leader) in Maputo,[12] he referred to a long series of discussions he and I had had over the years (including a period when I had taught at the Frelimo party school); he recalled that I had often emphasized the costs of Frelimo's embracing the particularly lifeless brand of Marxism on offer from the Soviets as the ideological instrument for codifying its radical intentions. "We should probably have listened more to you," he said lightly, then added in a wry voice: "Of course you didn't have in your briefcase the military hardware that we felt we needed!"

We shall return to assess some possible implications of now removing the incubus of "the Soviet model" from within the socialist camp in southern Africa. First another, more broadly geo-political question suggests itself: is one possible benefit of the downgrading of the Cold War factor in southern Africa (or, differently put, of the Soviet Union's conversion to cooperation with the West in seeking "humane" outcomes there!) the lifting of the weight of Western hostility to progressive socio-economic experimentation? Not likely; for the Western countries have proven to be far from gracious winners in this respect. After all, though the Cold War may have taken on a certain life of its own in explaining Great Power behavior, it was the meeting of challenges (mounted under whatever rubric, national capitalist or socialist, as Gabriel Kolko has recently demonstrated so convincingly)[13] to the dictate of global capitalism that has underlain U.S. interventionism since the Second World War.

Now, as Craig Murphy has argued, the new positioning of "the dependent Third World" will probably render it "even more subordinate" to "the North" than previously. "By contributing to the demise of the Third World challenge to postwar North-South relations and by privileging institutions of international civil society that encourage market discipline on Third World development policies, the Reagan administration began to confront the challenge of reconstructing the North-South historical bloc(k)"; relieved of "the threat that Third World states will join the Soviet camp," this process can continue in an even more unchecked manner.[14] The collapse, in the face of the rawest kind of liberal economics (read "global neo-conservatism"), of such modest bows in the direction of global Keynesianism as the "New International Economic Order" can be seen as a case in point, perhaps.[15] Moreover, "the coercive institutions of the old North-South bloc(k) have, if anything, been strengthened by the thaw in East-West relations" (not least in those cases where Northern intervention against Third World "anarchy" is being most ostentatiously "multilateralized" via the United Nations).[16] In tandem, the U. S. military also "faces South. There is no question that both the President's public statements and the Pentagon's formal planning envision a more active U.S. military role in the Third World."[17]

The Mozambican case

This, then, is the kind of world that confronts southern Africa, whether (*pace* "the new thinking") the Soviet Union were to remain a protagonist of "socialism" in the region or not. The unashamed and ever-increasing aggressiveness of the IMF/World Bank vis-a-vis the states of the region is merely the most graphic case in point here — something I witnessed at close hand on a recent return visit to Mozambique. My own association with the Mozambican revolution began in the 1960s when I moonlighted, occasionally, from my job at Tanzania's university and helped out with English-language translations at Frelimo's headquarters in Dar es Salaam. My commitment to the Mozambican struggle was deepened by a trip to the liberated areas of Mozambique in l972; first-hand participation in 1975's dramatic independence celebrations in the newly-renamed capital of Maputo; numerous subsequent visits to the country, including attendance at several key Congresses and meetings; and even a spell of full-time employment, teaching at the Eduardo Mondlane University and in Frelimo's party school.

Through these years I passed close enough to the flame of Mozambique's revolutionary process to see how real was the sense of humane purpose that came to motivate so many Frelimo cadres, how sincere, too, their grasping for a Marxist methodology that would help codify the radical thrust of their undertakings. I had seen enough, in any case, to insulate me from both the ultra-left abstractions of a Michel Cahen[17] and the crass cynicism of a

Heribert Adam with his suggestion that recent developments have "reduced Frelimo's...versions of freedom ideology to rhetorical socialism...In a crunch, the elite therefore adjusts ideological interpretations as arbitrarily as they adopted them. No conversion is involved, as is frequently assumed, because a collective ideological commitment hardly existed in the first place."[19]

Still, my own visits of the mid-1980s had also revealed the progressive decay of Frelimo's high promise, a decay by now self-evident to all observers, and one that has been particularly well documented in articles by Judith Marshall, John Loxley and Otto Roesch, among others.[20] But I had not been back to Mozambique for several years when, in mid-1990, I returned there to attend a conference. It very quickly became apparent that even the instructive contributions of Marshall and the others had not quite prepared me for what I was about to witness.[21]

The conference itself was a revelation. Officially convened by the Frelimo party and the Ministry of International Relations, it was entitled "Rethinking Strategies for Mozambique and Southern Africa." The number of delegates invited from Western establishment circles was remarkable enough. Even more remarkable was the strong pitch in favour of adopting quite unalloyed "free market" policies to deal with Mozambique's development problems that was formally presented by each of the three senior governmental ministers (Pascoal Mocumbi, Jacinto Veloso and Armando Guebuza) who spoke. Guebuza was particularly hard-boiled in this respect, acknowledging the hardships that the structural adjustment programme had brought to many in Mozambique with the matter-of-fact assertion that the market economy solution does in fact make the rich richer and the poor poorer, bringing with it more social injustice as "the price of progress."

Indeed, it was the World Bank's own representative in Mozambique who sounded more of a warning note. He suggested that the Mozambique government had become rather too naive in its dealings with international capital, not being willing or able to drive the kinds of hard bargains with firms and Western agencies that might actually defend the country's interests. Not that this representative himself queried the premise that a wide range of benefits could flow from more or less total immersion in the international marketplace. But it was rather disconcerting, as I said in my own address to the conference, to find the World Bank standing marginally to the left of spokespersons from the Mozambican government. Equally disconcerting, I continued, was the small inclination on the part of any of the ministers to take seriously the fact that, even if a certain kind of socialism could be said to have "failed," there was still good reason for measured scepticism as to whether capitalism could succeed under the conditions in which Mozambique found itself.

Most remarkable of all, however, was a briefing given exclusively to conference delegates by Mozambique's President, Joaquim Chissano. Chissano seemed to be addressing himself most directly to the more establishment-style delegates from Germany and the United States (in particular, perhaps, the extremely right-wing former Reagan ambassador to South Africa, Herman Nickel). In doing so, however, he also starkly revealed to everyone just how supine Mozambique has become:

> The US said, "Open yourself to...the World Bank, and IMF." What happened? We are told now: "Marxism! You are devils. Change this policy." OK. Marxism is gone. "Open market economy." OK, Frelimo is trying to create capitalism. We have the task of building socialism and capitalism here.
>
> We went to Reagan and I said, "I want money for the private sector to boost people who want to develop a bourgeoisie." Answer: $10 million, then $15 million more, then another $15 million. You tell me to do away with Marxism, the Soviet Union and the GDR and give me [only] $40 million. OK, we have changed. Now they say, "If you don't go to a multi-party system, don't expect help from us."

Chissano did note that the structural adjustment programme being followed by the Frelimo government had deepened the hardships of the Mozambican people at least as much as it had produced economic advance. And he warned that "the readjustment programme must start showing results, or we must take other directions." But what "other directions?" As Chissano said rather forlornly in capping this threat, "We don't see which other way. We are totally dependent on inputs from outside. If they are not forthcoming in the correct manner it is no use."

The debate will continue about what has brought Mozambique to its current sorry pass; indeed, I will return to this question at much greater length in the following chapter. Already, however, we have mentioned the dead hand laid on the Mozambican experiment by Soviet-style socialism. And attention must also be paid to the hurtful combination of an unpromising historical starting-point inherited from Portuguese colonialism; a relentless siege imposed upon the country by outside forces (notably the architects of South Africa's destabilization strategy); and a Frelimo development project marred by significant failings of its own. Old Frelimo friends, people of genuinely left instinct and intent, were in a reflective mood, prepared to discuss more openly than had sometimes been the case the party's failings. Not that anything I heard or saw caused me to revise my earlier opinion: first and foremost amongst the causes of Mozambique's so-called "failure of socialism" has been the ruthlessness of the aggression launched against it (and the willed destruction of the basic fabric of Mozambican society attendant upon it).[22]

Indeed, I came to feel that I had, if anything, underestimated the broader imperialist underpinnings of the grim destabilization of Mozambique. At the seminar itself, as well as in other discussions, a pithy epigram attributed to the Caribbean social scientist Horace Campbell took on ever increasing resonance: "The IMF is the economic wing of the armed bandits!" There have been many indications, over the years, that South Africa's destabilization tactics dovetailed neatly with the Reagan doctrine of Third World "rollback." After all, these tactics had been applied in earnest only upon Reagan's entry into the White House. Now private discussions with Frelimo veterans underscored the extent to which Samora Machel had premised his own tactics in the early 1980s on his grasp of the fact of US/South African connivance in destabilization. The neutralization of American hostility was thus front and center in the calculations that underlay the signing of the Nkomati Accord.

As things turned out, Machel had underestimated the extent to which South Africa was an independent actor. South African and American policies as to the best methods of dealing with Mozambique diverged after the Nkomati Accord — the Americans apparently accepting it as rather more of a supine Mozambican surrender to the reality of *force majeure* and the logic of the international market-place than the South Africans were prepared to do. As a result, destabilization continued. Yet Chissano's words, quoted above, give some further measure of the ruthlessness with which the Americans (alongside other Western powers) have been prepared to follow up economically on the advantage bequeathed them by South Africa's direct physical weakening of an "enemy regime."

At the same time, some Frelimo veterans were also prepared to discuss, more frankly than ever, the weaknesses of their own project. Perhaps the mistake was in going for the vanguard party structure in the first place, one of them said. Certainly, he continued, we were wrong, all of us at the top, in fostering a cult of personality around Samora, whatever his undoubted virtues and the particular strength of his dedication to a popularly-based development strategy. This personality cult my informant saw as being the biggest change, politically, in the transition from the Mondlane period to the Machel period, and the most questionable one. Mention was also made of Samora's failure, in the breathing space provided by the end of the Zimbabwe war, to do something about the military. In particular, this might have involved removing the dead-wood amongst the army's commanders — both those who were not up to meeting the novel demands of the independence period (so different from the days of the liberation struggle), and those who had failed to resist the temptations to corruption. Did Samora feel too close, from guerilla days, to members of this leadership cadre to take the necessary steps? Yet a transformed army could have made a great difference in containing Renamo as South Africa first began to reactivate the latter group.

Then, as the war escalated, Samora seemed to lose his nerve and his self-possession, the period from 1983 to 1985 revealing graphically (Frelimo friends argued) some of the costs of excessively centralized and personalized rule. True, a vibrant and critically-focussed meeting of the Central Committee in 1986 did see the beginnings of a revitalization of Frelimo — and of Samora. Moreover, it seems quite plausible that it was precisely as Machel now began to move to transform the situation, giving promise, for example, of at last shaking-up the army, that the South Africans determined to kill him.

To be sure, despite the frankness displayed regarding such questions, one was still tempted to cavil at times about what was being left unsaid. Were even my most reflective Frelimo friends sufficiently self-critical, for example, about the extent to which party/state directives and controls had tended (with whatever good intentions) to straitjacket initiatives from below and failed, in consequence, to facilitate vitalization of unions, women's organizations, "civic associations" and the media? Was enough being learned not only from the shortfalls of Mozambique's own efforts at socialist construction but also from the now starkly revealed shabbiness of Eastern European practices? Still, it was refreshing to find that for some Mozambicans — though perhaps not yet enough of them — work has begun on a task that stands as essential to the Left the world over: that of studying, self-critically and with more effective tools than have been available in the past, socialism's setbacks.

The Real War in Angola

For the moment, however, we must return to the mournful words of President Chissano, cited above. They make bleak reading — unless, of course, you happen to be a Chester Crocker, found recently reflecting on the imperial taming of a battered and broken Mozambique during his term as Assistant Secretary of State for Africa in the State Department during the Reagan years. If Chissano epitomizes the confusions of defeat, Crocker perfectly defines the smug inhumanity of the victors — and the glib rewriting of the history of socialist Mozambique's destruction. "When Mozambique's imaginative leadership cast confrontation aside in 1983-84 to conclude its non-aggression pact with South Africa," Crocker writes, "it demonstrated the 'power of the weak,' reaching out to play a constructive region-wide role and seeking to engage Pretoria in a reciprocal framework of economic, security and political links. Ironically, South Africa's failure to respect fully its own obligations under the Nkomati Accords only added to Maputo's leverage, credibility and external backing!"[23]

Of course, the situation has not always been quite so one-sidedly amenable to Western command as these quotations from Chissano and Crocker might suggest. Witness the complicated politics that have played themselves out around the Angola/Namibia negotiations in the past few years. Thus, it was Eastern-backed military success — at Cuito Cuanavale — that paved the way, in the last round, for progress in those negotiations. At the same time, it has proven all too easy to misinterpret such developments. Take, for example, a significant article by Michael McFaul,[24] the one close analysis of recent diplomatic-cum-political developments in southeastern Africa we have. Careful, and eminently "liberal" in tone — yet the analysis manages to just miss the point, doing so in a way that is particularly germane to the argument of the present chapter (and, indeed, to the overall thrust of this book). McFaul's thesis: that the "Reagan Doctrine" failed in Angola and that "the settlement between Angola, Cuba and South Africa was achieved despite, not because of, the 'Reagan Doctrine.'"

McFaul emphasizes, instead, the importance of "the diplomatic efforts of Assistant Secretary of State Chester Crocker," and (correctly) of the "changes in the local military balance in southern Africa" mentioned above. He also notes — significant for our purposes — the contribution of Soviet "new thinking" which "generated a more sympathetic attitude toward both negotiations and improved relations between Angola and the West." But what of his fourth factor: "changes in Angolan foreign and domestic policy" — presented, blandly, as demonstrating that "the dismal state of the Angolan economy provided the primary impetus for Angola's attitude toward peace with South Africa and better relations with the United States. Angola's attempt to reconstruct its economy on the Soviet model had failed, not least because of a lack of aid from the Eastern bloc."

Well, yes — and no. Imagine consigning to a footnote, in the context of such argument, the fact that "Angola's defense budget devours half of the total government budget, and the war has taken over 500,000 lives, displaced another 1.5 million people, and caused an estimated $12 billion damage in physical destruction." As McFaul continues (in the same footnote), "It is thus somewhat artificial to separate Angola's security requirements from its economic dilemmas."

Precisely. Yet McFaul has managed to do just that — while blurring, as well, the broader imperial logic that has forced upon Angola such "security requirements." He argues, for example, that "most economic destabilization in Angola is a result of South African assistance to UNITA," thus managing more or less to ignore the importance both of direct South African military intervention — and of the United States' own considerable assistance to UNITA. Downplayed as well is the fact that South Africa has, in effect, acted as U.S. proxy in knocking the economic props out from under the Angolan government, thus rendering it more pliable. Not that South Africa can be interpreted as merely an American puppet in so acting; Botha and company also had quite pressing local motives for their Angolan (and Mozambican) adventures beyond merely servicing the U.S. goal of whipping these countries into line. Yet it is precisely the most obvious questions that constantly need posing in cases like this: why, for example, do the regional aggressions of P. W. Botha and Saddam Hussein earn such different responses from "the West?" The answer is all-too-obvious.

McFaul also notes, as if to clinch his argument, that "if the Reagan doctrine aimed to overthrow the Angolan government, it failed. Although the Angolans suffered tremendous losses during the last few years on the southern front, Luanda shows no sign of capitulating." And yet what is creeping back, cap in hand, to the World Bank and the IMF if not "capitulation?" True, the presence of the Cubans, and the network of linkages established deep within the American polity by Jonas Savimbi, have lent a supra-economic frenzy to American involvement in Angola that continues to the present day. Reagan/Bush have not, therefore, been as ready to accept the (effective) surrender of Angola as they were to accept — against the contrary policy of South Africa — the "surrender" of the Mozambicans after 1984's Nkomati Accord.

But the underlying logic *vis-à-vis* Angola is the same and is, in fact, beginning to take hold. The Chester Crocker seen above so comfortably rewriting the story of Mozambique's capitulation could as easily as McFaul have written the latter's conclusion to the Angolan story: "By seeking to engage these countries with economic assistance and commerce rather than Stinger missiles, to co-opt antagonists rather than confront them, American policy-makers could protect U.S. interests more effectively and without the loss of human life." But this is merely polite-speak. Surely the lesson of recent southern Africa history is quite other than Crocker confesses, or McFaul imagines: it is "not necessarily war but war if necessary." We underestimate, at our peril, just how successful the Reagan doctrine has been and just how far the West may still be prepared to go as, more self-consciously than ever, it "faces South."

As for the Soviet Union, McFaul at least can see that "the 'vanguard country' in the 'world revolutionary process,' Gorbachev's Soviet Union, is fast becoming a leading force for the status quo." Yet he fails to draw the obvious corollary: if Gorbachev did not, as McFaul stresses, walk away entirely from Angola, he was certainly quite comfortable to be walking away from the struggle for any kind of socialist Angola. That said, we may still conclude that the destruction of Angolan socialism (such as it was[25]) was a much more important determinant of American accommodation in southwestern Africa than the fading of the Soviet regional presence.[26]

The Future: South Africa and Beyond

The message is clear: peace (such as it is) in southern Africa has its price. Nor, we find, should we overestimate the importance of the single factor of the removal of the Soviet bogey from the southern African equation in making sense of developments there. Are there also dangers in *underestimating* it? Perhaps so; take South Africa, for example. The rapid thaw in the Cold War almost immediately made it far more difficult for hard-liners in South Africa itself to justify their intransigence, at home or abroad, as some kind of last-ditch defense against communism. Developments in Eastern Europe have thus simultaneously forced De Klerk's hand — democratization was now, dramatically, in the air world-wide — while weakening the case of those within his own camp who might oppose any more advanced reform agenda. In addition, the apparent weakening of the Soviet Union (a key ANC ally) on the one hand, and of the "idea of socialism" as a global option on the other, may also have moved the powers-that-be to conceive the ANC as freshly available for various "reasonable" and "pragmatic" compromises. In short, the "end of the Cold War" was one factor suggesting the existence of a new window of opportunity for a successful liberal reformism, one crafted, precisely, to preempt revolution.

Whether the increased cooptability of the ANC was indeed a correct lesson to draw is another question. In South Africa, certainly, the Soviet collapse has had important resonance within the mass movement, but in ways that remain quite difficult to assess in any definitive manner. True, as many South African and Western "liberals" now hope, the post-February terrain in South Africa may produce an ANC less dependent on the Soviet Union and/or the South African Communist Party (SACP), and one more shot through than ever with middle-class elements and middle-class (read: merely national-democratic) aspirations. But not inevitably. The ANC has a left autobiography of its own and a mass constituency (including, most importantly, an active and often quite self-consciously socialist working-class/trade union component) that will not readily countenance any backsliding from the attempt to democratize the economy.[27] Indeed, to the extent that the Soviet model fades into the background, the movement may prove capable of being even more open — less crudely vanguardist — towards that constituency as well as more subtle in creating the space for economic creativity.

This is still an open question, then, though there are many who feel these latter possibilities more accurately define the situation of the SACP than that of the ANC itself. Here, after all, is the only Communist party in the world that is still growing — and it is doing so by leaps and bounds. In part, it is the party's tough, militant, even militaristic image, pure and simple, that attracts young South Africans. But equally marked is the movement into the party of a body of working-class activists and intellectuals from the most democratic and anti-Stalinist centers of the trade union movement.[28] They are drawn by the evidence, in Joe Slovo's own writings for example, of a de-Stalinization of line and a democratization of practice that they feel shows promise of keeping a genuinely democratic socialist impulse on the South African agenda. In part, of course, any evolution the SACP is undergoing stems from the need to respond to the vibrancy of mass action inside South Africa; but Slovo himself has argued in private conversation that many past rigidities of line reflected imperatives derived from the party's dependence on Soviet backing. How thorough will the shedding of Stalinist residues (still frozen, some argue, in the party's own internal practices and beyond mere Soviet influence) prove to be? To what kind of policy thrusts will it give rise (especially in the economic sphere where the constraints, national and international, upon radical innovation are considerable)? How, on new terrain, will the party seek to realize the distinctiveness of its more autonomous "working-class" line and practice *vis-à-vis* its ANC ally? These remain tough questions for the post-apartheid, post-Cold War era.

I discuss these and related points at some length in chapters four and five, below, and will not further anticipate their argument here.[29] But make no mistake: an ever deepening thrust towards democratization of the struggle for political and economic transformation is a possibility in South Africa, as is the crystallization of a programme of "structural reform" in the socio-economic sphere that could cut between the twin programmatic extremes of romantic (and ultimately self-defeating) ultra-leftism on the one hand and "mere [readily cooptable] reformism" on the other. At the same time, the global context we have begun to sketch remains crucial to the way such possibilities might be expected to play themselves out. For this context threatens to choke off the full flowering of such possibilities at every turn. Thus, there can be little doubt that De Klerk has been further nudged towards reform by actors inside and outside the country who seek to de-racialize South African capitalism sufficiently to make it less vulnerable to radical attack. To this end, such actors manifest a profound interest in various constitutional "refinements" that might help blunt majority rule and in economic arrangements that might help encourage "reasonable" policies from any post-apartheid government. Already, denizens of the World Bank and the IMF hover about the scene in South Africa, as do other smooth purveyors of Western aid and of "sound advice."[30] It is just such actors who are charged with exacting the "price of peace" — in this case the price of a peaceful transition to "democracy" — from all those who would seek to build a more just and equitable (even socialist) post-apartheid South Africa.

As noted, other players (such as the militant trade unions or an ANC that continues to deepen the terms of its democratic vocation) are likely to be crucial to the struggle to resist this kind of narrowing of the South African revolutionary impulse. And so, too, might be a de-Stalinized SACP. Yet, whatever the prospects in a changing South Africa, it may well be that "de-Stalinization" has come too late for there to be any immediate possibility of renewed socialist advance in the Frontline states. True, not everyone on the left will be equally uncomfortable with the much freer run of global capitalist dictate in the Frontline states. As we will document in the following chapter, an embrace of the "revolutionary logic" of ascendant capitalism seems to be the underlying premise of the *Politique Africaine* school's apparent pleasure in the destruction of the "predatory" African state in all its manifestations;[31] it is certainly the bottom-line for all those post-Warrenite "Chicago Marxists" critiqued, not so long ago, by Manfred Bienefeld.[32] Yet Bienefeld, in reiterating the case for use of a revised "dependency framework" to identify the very low ceiling placed on African development aspirations by a capitulation to World Bank orthodoxy, seems much closer to an accurate fix on the immediate (gloomy) prospects for the frontline.

Still, if underdevelopment and endemic poverty for the vast mass of frontline populations will not be conjured away by "more and better capitalism," this means some of the impulses that have given rise to earlier socialist struggles in southern Africa are also likely to revive themselves. It may well be that the old leaderships (of Frelimo, of MPLA) can no longer be the most effective midwives of such impulses, of course. The burden of the past (and the ideological oversimplifications of the Cold War era) rests heavily on a leader like Joaquim Chissano, for example, who can now summarize the situation by suggesting that "Marxism was creating problems for us"[32] — proceeding to elide "Marxism" with official Soviet-style "Marxism-Leninism" in such a way as to leave himself almost no conceptual middle-ground for blunting the charge of the most unadulterated free-market nostrums.

Not that one need argue, from a progressive point of view, that all the recent changes in Mozambique are pure retreat. Indeed, in some instances they seem more a case of too little change, too late. Stronger steps towards effective democratization, if that is what is happening in Mozambique, are certainly welcome, capping a lesson socialists have had to take more firmly to heart everywhere in recent years. And there may be a general kind of wisdom, too, in seeking to let markets do some of the work that has broken the back of the planning apparatus in Mozambique. Regrettably, however, one senses that these changes are not being made in a measured manner, the better to deepen the effectiveness of a popularly-rooted project. Instead they seem more the grasping at straws of a leadership left reeling by the pounding it has taken, a leadership desperate to keep afloat on the turbulent seas of (continuing) destabilization, ever more assertive post-Cold War imperial demands and ever deeper reintegration into the global capitalist system.

In some cases, too, it seems that the weakest attributes of many Frelimo leaders have become magnified — benevolent authoritarianism now turned into something overtly non-benevolent. Take, for example, the hard version of Mozambique's present development strategy cited earlier from Minister Guebuza's remarks at the conference. As I pointed out in my own conference intervention, it may be no accident that the minister (Guebuza) who once offered up to the people of Maputo the hardship and high handedness of "Operation Production" (a programme of forced urban removal in 1983) in the name of socialism, is now prepared to offer the hardship of extreme polarization of incomes to that same people in the name of capitalist development.

Not all in Mozambique were on quite this wave-length, as I have noted above — even if it did seem, during my recent visit, that the most salient division one could discern within the Mozambican leadership lay between those who favoured a quite crude and aggressive project of entrepreneurial greed and corruption (a position exemplified most clearly by Guebuza himself and apparently packaged by those around him in crypto-racist terms as exemplifying the best kind of"African advancement"), and those who favoured a somewhat softer, more technocratic and "rational" version of "free market" strategy. Does there, in addition, linger within the Frelimo system something of Samora Machel's left-wing populist sense that Mozambique's development strategy should benefit, first and foremost, the poorest of the poor?

President Chissano himself may not have entirely lost sight of this bottom line of Frelimo's historical project — however impossible he finds it to give meaning to his best instincts in this regard. And even the senior leader who commented to me ruefully that "the Samoran project is over" did suggest that the Mozambican state remains a site of struggle where remnants of Frelimo's socialism might still be defended. For him, however, the main progressive "deposit" of the first fifteen years of Mozambican independence may lie elsewhere: as some kind of positive point of reference for future struggle, as an historical bench-mark lodged "in the minds of the people" and within the folds of a Mozambican culture still in the making.

In any case, he suggested, the clearest voice for a Mozambique that could eventually redeem some of the promise of Frelimo's original project may actually be that of those Maputo strikers who, early in 1990, sought to resist the inequities of Mozambique's structural adjustment package.[34] If this is so — if bottom-up regeneration is so crucial, in Mozambique and elsewhere — the chief contribution of the demise of "actually-existing socialism" may be simply to help undermine the continuing tendency for quasi-socialist discourses to mask authoritarian ones. Simply put, there is now less conceptual ground to hide on for the opportunist leaderships of a Zambia or a Zimbabwe who seek the solace of one-party solutions to political complexity in their countries. In settings where socialism has had some deeper meaning, in Mozambique and perhaps in Angola, the discourse of democracy is also in the air — and, as noted, carries some positive promise.[35] Not that this promise is to be measured exclusively in terms of elections or of the advance of "multi-partyism." Indeed, given the kinds of alternative parties (racist, regionalist) that are beginning to emerge in a "more pluralist" Mozambique, it is not hard to see Frelimo continuing to be the primary focus of support in any up-coming election for all those who wish Mozambique well.

To once again anticipate the argument of the following chapter, however: can we suggest that far more important than elections may be the opening up of space for the activity of newly autonomous popular organizations (the trade unions and women's organizations, for example) and other independent initiatives in the rural areas (cooperatives, for example)? Does this, in fact, promise an expression of the kind of voice from below — from an active "civil society" — that could begin to counterbalance all those other more negative pressures that have been pushing Mozambique to conform to global capitalist dictate? If so, the socio-economic terrain that confronts any such popular assertions seems sufficiently forbidding to suggest that they may well have to take on ever more radical (socialist?) overtones. Perhaps we can also predict that, if and when such radicalization occurs, something will have been learned from the past decade and a half of experience in the region. Isn't it likely that both the conceptualization and the practice of any post-Cold War socialism that begins to resurface in southern Africa will represent an advance on what has gone before?

Just what is to be learned? More must be said on this matter, certainly. But perhaps as good a way as any to contribute to this learning process will be to re-think the Mozambican experience in an even more fundamental way than has been possible in the present chapter. From revolution to recolonization in Mozambique: I turn in the next chapter to a discussion of what the task of further probing this dispiriting "transition from socialism to capitalism" might entail.

▼▼▼▼▼▼▼▼▼▼▼▼▼

1   This chapter is an expanded version of my article "From Thaw to Flood: The End of the Cold War in Southern Africa" that originally appeared in a special issue of Review of African Political Economy (ROAPE), 50 (March, 1991) on "Africa in a New World Order."
2   This text was written before the Soviet Union, in its turn, also disappeared; this fact renders outdated some of the specific ways in which arguments are made here, but does not, I think, undermine the general thrust of the argument.
3   Quoted in Steven Friedman and Monty Narsoo, *The New Mood in Moscow: Soviet Attitudes to South Africa* (Johannesburg: South African Institute of Race Relations, 1989), pp. 5-6.
4   Fred Halliday, "The Ends of the Cold War," *New Left Review*, #180 (March-April, 1990), pp. 22-3.
5   Quoted in Eddie Koch, "South Africa and the Soviets: from cold war to hot peace" in *The Weekly Mail* (Johannesburg), March 3, 1989.
6   Quoted in the article "South Africa is a racist problem — not a capitalist-socialist one say Soviets" in *Southscan*, 4, 14 (April 14, 1989), p. 106.
7   Leonid L. Fituni, "Looking from Moscow: The New Political Thinking and the South African Problem" (manuscript provided by a Soviet delegation to the Canadian Association of African Studies annual conference, Ottawa, 1989); this was subsequently published, in much the same form, as "A New Era: Soviet Policy in Southern Africa" in *Africa Report* (New York), 34, 4 (July-August, 1989), pp. 64-5. Fituni is identified as being head of the Department of International Crisis Management Studies of the Institute for African Studies, USSR Academy of Science, Moscow.
8   Fituni, *ibid.*. This formulation appears in both versions of his essay.
9   Halliday, *op. cit.*, p. 15.
10 Carlos Vilas, "Is Socialism Still an Alternative for the Third World?" *Monthly Review*, 42, 3 (July-August, 1990), pp. 105, 99.
11 I explore the issues raised in these paragraphs at greater length in ch. 3, below.

12 I draw this anecdote, and indeed much of the current section, from my article "Mozambique: The Failure of Socialism?" *Southern Africa Report* (SAR) (Toronto), 6, #2 (November, 1990).
13 Gabrial Kolko, *Confronting the Third World: United States Foreign Policy, 1945-1980* (Pantheon: New York, 1988).
14 Craig N. Murphy, "Freezing the North-South Bloc(k) after the East-West Thaw," *Socialist Review* (special issue on "North-South Relations in the New World Order"), 90/3
15 Winston Langley, "What Happened to the New International Economic Order," *Socialist Review,* (ibid.).
16 Murphy, *op. cit.*. Right-wing American pundit George Will recently has made central to his own rationale for an ever more aggressive American imperial role this notion of "anarchy," apparently intending it to substitute, as effective catch-all, for the now defunct "Communist menace;" no doubt we will hear much more along this and other related lines in the coming years.
17 Michael Klare, "Defense Policy in the 90s: The U.S. Military Faces South," *The Nation,* 18 June, 1990.
18 See Michel Cahen, letter in *Southern Africa Report,* 6, 1 (1990) (but see also his *Mozambique: La Revolution Implosée* (Paris: L'Harmattan, 1987)).
19 Heribert Adam and Stanley Uys, a paper entitled "From Destabilization to Neo-Colonial Control: South Africa's Post-Nkomati Regional Environment" presented to the South Africa Conference held at McGill University, Montreal, 17 May 1985.
20 See Judith Marshall, "On the Ropes: Socialism and FRELIMO's 5th Congress," *SAR,* 5, 2 (November, 1989), the feature "Economic Reform in Mozambique: Two Views" in *SAR,* 4, 2 (October, 1988) — which includes John Loxley, "Strategic Defeat or Tactical Retreat?" and Otto Roesch, "Classes in Formation?" — and Marshall's "Structural Adjustment and Social Policy in Mozambique" in *ROAPE,* #47 (Spring, 1990).
21 Here I draw again on my "Mozambique: The Failure of Socialism?" *(op. cit.).*
22 See chapter 3 ("Development and Counterdevelopment Strategies in Mozambique") of my *Socialist Ideology... (op. cit.)* and also chapter 3, below.
23 Chester Crocker, "Southern Africa: Eight Years Later," *Foreign Affairs* 68, #4 (Fall, 1989).
24 Michael McFaul, "Rethinking the 'Reagan Doctrine' in Angola," *International Security,* 14, #3 (Winter, 1989-90).
25 In fact, Angola's socialist endeavor was always much more sterile — and much more malformed by the dead hand of Stalinoid Marxism-Leninism — than was the Mozambican system. Change in this system would be welcome; however, "reform" and "democratization" along the lines dictated by the IMF and by Savimbi's backers are quite likely to prove to be worse than the disease. Moreover, so dis-

ruptive has been the impact of the war inflicted on Angola that a cycle of recurring violence and social chaos may be a more likely scenario than any smooth recolonization of this broken-backed society. On these and related themes see, for example, Frank Luce, "Angola's Quagmire: What Way Out?" SAR, 6, #5 (May, 1991).

26 My initial attempt to analyze the broader determinants of the outcome of the Angolan war along these lines was made at a joint Canadian/Cuban seminar on southern Africa held at York University in Toronto. It bears noting that this argument was received with marked hostility by some Cuban academics in attendance, who felt that such an emphasis on "the price of peace" (Angola's abandonment of anything remotely like a "socialist project") of the Angolan/Cuban victory qualified too much the (undoubtedly) positive role Cuban forces have played in helping preserve Angola's territorial integrity over the years.

27 For a discussion, along these lines, of the ANC see my essay "South Africa: The Question of Strategy" in *New Left Review*, #160 (November-December, 1986), which is also ch. 5 of my *Socialist Ideology... (op. cit.)*.

28 Mike Morris, "Why are Ex-Stalinists Joining the SACP?," *Southern Africa Report*, 6, #3 (December, 1990).

29 In the more detailed but closely related discussion of current prospects for a left project in South Africa to be found in those chapters, the possible nature of the kind of programme of "structural reform" referred to in the present paragraph is one of the main themes that is clarified and evaluated.

30 See, *inter alia*, Patrick Bond, "Closing In: The World Bank and the IMF in South Africa," *SAR*, 7, # 1 (July, 1991).

31 See, in particular, in the special tenth anniversary issue of *Politique Africaine* (#39, September, 1990) the articles by Dominique Darbon ("L'état predateur") and, notably, Jean-Francois Médard ("L'état patrimonialisé"), and, for a more detailed critique, chapter 3, below.

32 Manfred Bienefeld, "Dependency Theory and the Political Economy of Africa's Crisis," *ROAPE*, #43 (1988).

33 Interviewed in *Expresso* (Lisbon). May 12, 1990.

34 On this subject see also the valuable article by Judith Marshall entitled "Resisting Adjustment in Mozambique: the Grassroots Speaks Up," *SAR*, 7, #1 (July, 1991).

35 However, for a particularly sobering look at Angola in this regard see Victoria Brittain, "Angola: The Final Act," *SAR*, 7, #5 (May, 1992).

Chapter 3
The Frelimo State: From Revolution to Recolonization[1]

The sad trajectory of the Mozambican revolution has been devastating, almost beyond words, for Mozambicans. It has also been a sobering experience for those of us who have, over the years, supported and sought to interpret Frelimo's progressive development project in that country. "Frelimo's progressive development project?" It is a sign of the times that there seems to be something distinctly old-fashioned about even phrasing the issue in these terms. "Development project?" A misguided expression of modernist arrogance, surely. "Progressive?" Scepticism about the appropriateness of "socialist solutions" is so rife (even on much of the Left) that this term, too, seems highly suspect. And what about "Frelimo" itself? This is, apparently, the most suspect variable of all, to judge from much of the current writing about Mozambique.

Of course, it behooves all of us to understand better the sorry pass to which Mozambique has been brought under Frelimo leadership: from a country, admittedly backward, that nonetheless entered upon its independence in 1975 with high hopes to a country in tatters, possibly today the most desperately poverty-stricken in the world. Not so long ago, explanations of this disastrous trajectory began with the hard fact of South African destabilization. But increasingly — "a paradigm shift," we are told by British Africa-scholar Gervase Clarence-Smith[2] — the centre of gravity of accepted explanation seems to have moved, the blame for failure now falling more and more onto the the shoulders of Frelimo itself, and onto that movement's errors of omission and commission.

A useful corrective? Certainly those of us who have been closest to Frelimo over the years are, at least in part, guilty as charged. Can there be any doubt that we overestimated the scope of Frelimo's achievements and underestimated the seriousness of the weaknesses attendant upon its efforts? Yet I don't think it mere defensiveness to suggest the danger that the pendulum of explanation has begun to swing too far in the other direction; that the South African role in destroying Frelimo's undertakings now runs the risk of being underestimated rather than overestimated, and that the Frelimo project now runs the risk of being caricatured, negatively, beyond recognition. As we will see in this chapter, any such extreme rewriting of Mozambican history, if left unchallenged, could prove very costly indeed — not least in spawning a temptation, on the part of Mozambicans and others, to learn precisely the wrong lessons from the virtual collapse of the Mozambican state.

Something more general is also at stake. The alacrity with which the most negative interpretations of Frelimo's role in Mozambique have been seized upon in many quarters reflects not merely a "paradigm shift" in the study of Mozambique, but a virtual sea change in much of the discussion, even on the Left, of African development prospects. Some aspects of this change are healthy. Concerns about "democracy" — protean though the notion may be — will not so easily be ignored in future, for example. But some seem more to represent a failure of nerve, a loss of confidence, in the face of the grim fecundity of the "New World Order" and of trends towards the recolonization of southern Africa. Beware an African Studies in retreat — whether to the benevolent logic of the market or to the "moral economy" of the village — that casts more doubt than is necessary upon the possibility and/or wisdom of heroic purpose and revolutionary possibility. In discussing Mozambique, past, present and future, in the present chapter, I will also seek to comment on the "false solutions," both analytical and practical, that this broader trend places on offer.

I. A Paradigm Shift?

The range of criticisms of Frelimo practices is, in fact, quite broad, finding perhaps their most dramatic form in South African Communist Party veteran Joe Slovo's assertion, at a New York symposium on "The Future of Socialism", that Mozambique's attempted socialist project was "both premature and wrong!"[3] How are we to interpret this assertion? At one level it might be considered merely the application, by a long-time communist, of a rather conventional Third International Marxism to the Mozambican case. After all, even at the highest point of "fraternal relations" between Mozambique and the Soviet Union, the Soviets were never quite prepared to accord Mozambique any higher status than that of a "state of socialist orientation" because of its relatively "primitive" level of social relations.

Moreover, Slovo did not state clearly what he would have had the progressive leadership that found itself in power in Mozambique in the mid-1970s actually do with that power — thus rendering his own position, without any further elaboration, a rather too comfortable and passive one. Of course, he is also correct up to a point: the "backward conditions" Frelimo inherited ("the absolute level of undevelopment" as I have phrased it elsewhere), as well as the country's underdeveloped class structure and its extreme international vulnerability, would indeed have presented very real problems to any fledgling revolution in Mozambique. And yet the temptation to attach more importance to "necessary preconditions" than to concrete political and economic practices in explaining the strengths and weaknesses of an "actually-existing socialism" can also lapse into a singularly dismissive way of approaching the issue.

Slovo's position does not, in any case, represent the sort of "paradigm shift" other authors[4] have in mind when they use that phrase to summarize a recent redefinition of the terms of analysis of things Mozambican. At stake for them is less a preoccupation with such absolute limits as history had imposed upon Frelimo's ability to realize its aspirations than a debate over the relative importance of several more immediate factors in derailing the process of transformation in Mozambique. In Alex Vines' words, there is a move "in academic analysis ... away from the causality of the Mozambican crisis being South African destabilization, with the emphasis being shifted to a focus on Frelimo's agrarian policies as the roots of the problem." (No reference cited.) Or, in Clarence-Smith's more pungent phrasing: "In effect, Frelimo dug its own grave in the face of an apparently derisory enemy....Renamo exploits all the anger and resentment that Frelimo has created in the countryside through its policies."[5]

In fact, it is only the more extreme versions of this approach[6] that argue for a "paradigm shift" in anything like such stark terms. If we look at the most careful analyses of the war in Mozambique we find that a great deal of weight is still given — correctly — to the impact of Pretoria's sponsorship of Renamo and its ruthless destabilization tactics in Mozambique.[7] Thus, William Finnegan, while alert to the flaws in Frelimo's own project, emphasizes the importance of the fact that "few [new governments in Africa] have had the bad luck to live next door to a powerful foe ready to exploit their every misstep."[8] Even this formulation threatens to understate the case. For there is something remarkably cold-blooded about the current tendency to develop an approach to Mozambique that reduces South Africa's ruthless policy — "the destruction of an African country"[9] — to something like a residual variable. True, every historical situation is "over-determined," making it virtually impossible ever to hold enough other strands of determination "constant" to reach, confidently, some definitive account of any one of them. But we ignore at our peril (both moral and analytical) the conclusion of a U.S. State Department report that once described the war in Mozambique as "one of the most brutal holocausts against ordinary human beings since World War II."[10]

Not that fully grasping the centrality of this reality need blunt the edge of debate about the strengths and weaknesses of Frelimo's own broad project. It is here that we return to the hard fact that much of the texture of the debate about Mozambique is more fundamentally critical of Frelimo's undertakings than in the days when "scholar-activists" supportive of the movement (the Mozambican versions of Patrick Chabal's notorious "red-feet"[11]) were the chief contributors to the literature. A key point of reference in this respect is the work of Christian Geffray.[12] His case-study showed some of the ways in which, in one corner of the country, Renamo did use both the tensions that existed in and between local communities, and the negative reaction of some rural dwellers against Frelimo's economic mistakes and administrative highhandedness, to give some domestic political grounding to its activities.

Debate continues to swirl around the accuracy of Geffray's emphasis and the generalizability of his findings.[13] Moreover, Geffray himself would not use such data to blunt awareness of the extreme ruthlessness, even barbarity, with which Renamo has carried out what remains, essentially, a wrecker's role. Even so, such new material has served to sharpen the critical focus on Frelimo. It seems no accident that it is in a review of Geffray's book, prominently published in the *Times Literary Supplement* and provocatively titled "Between Two Terrors", that Peter Fry gives particularly vivid voice to a new orthodoxy-in-the-making on matters Mozambican, contrasting the misguided development efforts of the old Frelimo with those "who are supporting President Joaquim Chissano in his attempt to set Mozambique on a course of development in tune with the realities of the regional and international political and economic environment and, above all, with the aspirations of the people of Mozambique."[14]

"In tune with the realities of the regional and international political and economic environment" — a rather jejune way to describe the pattern of Mozambique's resubordination to South African and global capitalist dictate that Chissano has been forced to accept (and that we will outline further in section III of this chapter). And what about "the aspirations of the people of Mozambique"? Fry makes great play of evidence supplied by Geffray as to Frelimo's overbearing approach to local tradition — epitomized by him in the term *abaixismo* (rough translation: "down with-ism"). Yet Fry himself acknowledges that things are a bit more complicated than this when, at the end of his review, he qualifies his assertions, now invoking the need for "debate on Africa's most fundamental problem: how to reconcile the desire for modernity and the need for economic development with the equally strong attachment to very different forms of social organization from those of politically and economically dominant spheres of the world."[15] But what kind of politics follows from this kind of understanding? What kind of critique of Frelimo should it ground? We must dig deeper to find the sub-text that permits the easy swing of Fry and others to a new orthodoxy that emphasizes the negative nature of the Frelimo experience.

As noted above, the materials are available for a more careful reprise of the complex dynamics of the war's escalation, one that would demonstrate the ways in which the most assertive proponents of the "new paradigm" school have overstated their case. Here it is more important to emphasize the extent to which a "mood-swing" in the most current analytical approaches to "progressive regimes" in Africa has provided the premises that help make such overstatement possible. As noted at the outset of this chapter, what is crucial is the growing hegemony of an approach — joined at a point where left and right seem increasingly comfortable to meet — that is sceptical about the role of the state, sceptical about socialism and, at least in some of its expressions regarding Africa, sceptical about the claims of "modernity" itself.

Perhaps the strongest manifestation of this mood swing in African studies is to be found in the writings of those grouped around the influential French journal — left-leaning at its launching a decade or more ago — *Politique Africaine*.[16] Darbon, in discussing *"l'État prédateur"*, suggests that "at the beginning of the 1990s, little remains of the hopes for development that had been placed on the state structures of the African countries....The concept of the state as stimulus or promoter of development seems to have completely failed in Africa."[17] Bayart takes the point a step further:

> The state is the dominant economic agent in Africa whether the regime is single-party, pluralist or socialist. Everywhere the state's integration into the world economy has proceeded apace. Everywhere there has been primitive accumulation, that is, over-exploitation of the peasantry. State accumulation is intimately connected with individual accumulation at all levels (including the highest) and in all countries (including the most "socialist"). Power in whatever form is inevitably an instrument for the accumulation of wealth....It is, therefore, otiose to seek to establish a conceptual difference between the private and the public sector. Both are the instruments of a dominant class striving to establish its hegemony.[18]

That said, it also bears noting that the critics save their strongest fire for a state that presumes to intervene in the name of socialism. Thus Jean Médard (in his *Politique Africaine* article, *"L'État patrimonialisé"*) writes of the special temptation both liberals and socialists face of seeing the state as "the demiurge of development," based on an unlikely hope: "to realize its role, it would be necessary that the state be a pure instrument of the technocratic rationality of its leaders, who themselves would have to be animated by commitment to the 'general weal' and sufficiently detached from society to remodel it 'from outside' with a great degree of independence."[19] But it is for socialists in particular that he reserves his deepest scorn: "Within a socialist framework development is even more difficult since, if a capitalist framework at least has the merit of favouring growth, the socialist framework suffocates it. And even if we know enough not to confuse growth with economic development, we also know that there cannot be development without growth."[20]

It will be obvious that Médard's conclusion rests on a vision of the benign workings of the unfettered market-place in Africa that is difficult to square with available evidence regarding the actual experience of capitalist accumulation in Africa. Not that Médard suggests the transition to capitalist growth is, necessarily, a smooth one. But in his outlining of the impediments to such growth he highlights not contradictions that might be thought to be inherent in the logic of capitalist accumulation itself but rather those springing from the manner in which capitalism's functioning is held back in Africa by the workings of quasi-traditional patron-client relations.[21] The celebrated trajectory of Goren Hyden — in his quest for an effective means of "capturing" the peasantry — from enthusiasm for the efforts of Tanzania's "demiurgic" state to an equal and opposite enthusiasm for the free run of the market is a related case in point.[22]

But Manfred Bienefeld has, in any case, underscored the extent to which many analysts much further to the left than Hyden have come to espouse "individualistic resolutions" to development problems, manifesting extreme suspicion of any state's claim to represent "a general interest" and ready to "discount the relative dangers and inflate the expected benefits of deepening an economy's entanglement with the international market and of increasing reliance on internal markets." And this in spite of the fact that, in Bienefeld's view, "the present African crisis was most clearly foreseen by those looking at Africa from a dependency perspective in the 1960s." In the process Bienefeld neatly parries Bill Warren's much-cited assertion (remarkably close to the orthodoxy of the World Bank, Bienefeld notes) of "the historically progressive and economically efficient nature of recent capitalist development in the Third World."[23] Note, then, that it is on premises much like those Bienefeld here criticizes that Clarence-Smith grounds his own critique of the Frelimo state's original project. Any effort by Mozambique to break its links with South Africa, he suggests provocatively, would be "like asking somebody to kill the goose that lays the golden egg." And like Médard he seems to take for granted that development of "Mozambique's economy along capitalist lines" is a virtual guarantee of "growth."[24]

One further strand to today's ubiquitous critique of the state is also worth noting here — one that may appear to be rather contradictory to the point just mentioned but one that is often held in uneasy tandem with it nonetheless. Recall Geffray's influential analysis of Frelimo's practice, cited above; central to his argument is a critique of the movement's failure to take the layered complexity of Mozambique's local, "quasi-traditional" society seriously. Ultimately, he seems to go so far as to cast doubt upon the very legitimacy of Frelimo's attempt to change that society at all. As O'Laughlin summarizes his argument, "Geffray tends to assume that in Nampula there is a homogeneous peasantry, sharply differentiated from townspeople and living within a traditional world dominated by traditional cults, rules and practices. The clearest voices in this world view are those of the lineage elders." And

O'Laughlin paraphrases Geffray as suggesting that Frelimo should, among other bows to the integrity of local societies, "honour the authority of traditional leaders who were not on the side of the Portuguese."25

The implication: there is a certain "modernist" arrogance in Frelimo's decision to do otherwise.26 O'Laughlin thinks very differently. "Looking at 15 years of African independence, Frelimo saw this dualism as divisive, anti-democratic and responsible for maintaining economic backwardness in the countryside. I agree," she says.27 In short, if genuine democratic empowerment is to occur — if, as one example, the emancipation of women in rural Africa is to be facilitated — the structures of the quasi-traditional world must be challenged. To think otherwise is to be politically naive, O'Laughlin says. "Permit people to respect and honour religious figures and title-holders, to be sure, but the underlying question of how local governance and political power is to be organized cannot be conjured away." Her conclusion: "The problem is that dignity and authority were enmeshed in a system of local governance which any socialist political strategy would have to alter."28

As we will see below, O'Laughlin does not view this argument as an excuse for "well-intentioned" left authoritarianism or even for any white-washing of Frelimo's activities. Indeed, she interprets the failure of Frelimo's rural strategy as "less the 'revenge' of traditional society [as Geffray seems to suggest] than the negative fallout from weaknesses in Frelimo's own application of 'modern' socialist politics."29 It should also be clear, however, that O'Laughlin's is an increasingly unpopular way of conceiving things — at a time when most observers are so eager to distance themselves from any guilt by association with the notion of the "the state and/or party as modernizing agent" that they would dismiss her formulations more or less out of hand. Not that most such observers are actually all that "relativist" and "post-modern" in their own approach to "quasi-traditional" societies, of course. It is merely that, like Peter Fry, they are content to square this particular circle by leaving any "progressive" breaching of the supposed integrity of such societies to the workings of "impersonal market forces."

Needless to say, there are some valuable insights in the literature we have been discussing. Thus, Geffray merely overstates an otherwise important insight when he argues that the Mozambican government too often saw rural populations merely as "an arithmetical collection of desocialized individuals ... curiously just waiting for Frelimo to provide them with social organization." Médard, in his description of the "demiurgic state," also evokes something real regarding the all-too-common arrogance of ostensibly progressive elites, not least in Mozambique. And Bayart's firm emphasis upon the need to facilitate the empowerment of civil society in order to offset the African state's abusive propensities is also to the point.

But can society "reappropriate the state?" Can a "more 'equal' relation between state and society" be established? Bayart does suggest that "civil society can only transform its relation to the state through the organization of new and autonomous structures, the creation of a new cultural fabric and the elaboration of a conceptual challenge to power monopolies." Nonetheless, there remains a certain Manichean quality to Bayart's emphasis on the "epistemic gulf between state and society"[30] — a view that can picture the state forever seeking to "capture the peasantry" but cannot quite envisage the peasantry (and other popular classes) becoming capable, in any foreseeable future, of capturing the state. Indeed, for Bayart, "Africa's potential for democracy is more convincingly revealed by the creation of small collectives established and controlled by rural or urban groups (such as local associations) than by parliaments and parties, instruments of the state, of accumulation and of alienation."[31]

Yet "the state" — some state — is not about to disappear from the world in which Bayart's "small collectives" seek to find their feet; and chances are that if the state is not itself being transformed into an agent of transformation — thwarting overall societal disintegration, qualifying external dictate and widening developmental possibilities, stemming abuses of power, private and public, facilitating and defending fledgling popular initiatives — his "local associations" will themselves have only limited prospects. Bayart's is a fall-back position of very modest aspiration then, even if many might consider it a "realistic" one. And, of course, he is correct to think that the state itself is unlikely to be transformed unless — the paradox is real — the "civil society" in formation has become strong and democratically assertive enough to force the state to hold to a positive course. But this is merely to suggest the simultaneity of the need both for leadership and for mass action inherent in a process of socialist transformation — a contradiction that cannot be made to disappear, and one that demands the construction of an ongoing political process that takes both terms of this equation seriously. As we will see in the following section, Frelimo — the party, the state — at least momentarily embraced this difficult challenge, and it is this that made its project so distinctive in Africa (and, not least in the nature of its failure, so instructive).

As anticipated above and in sharp contrast to this approach, the "new paradigm" emerging in the literature on Mozambique speaks less of the dilemmas facing Frelimo (and of the errors the movement has made in confronting them) than of the fundamentally misguided nature of its entire state-ridden project.* William Finnegan, in one of the best of recent books on Mozambique,[32] goes much further than many such critics in acknowledging that "the 'Marxism-Leninism' and 'international proletarianism' of Frelimo were as rigorous as any ruling-party ideology on the continent and had clearly made sense as a framework for national liberation and development in the early days of the revolution." Yet even he can conclude that "the end of the Cold War also seemed to highlight the superficiality of Western concepts like communism and capitalism when transplanted to Africa." In fact, it is really communism/socialism he wishes to quarrel with. Capitalism may be a "Western concept" too, but Finnegan has no qualms about asserting, more or less simultaneously, that for Mozambique "some form of capitalism [has] seemed to become the only economic and political model with a future." Marxism, on the other hand, "was, *pace* Samora Machel, a European product" that really made no sense under Mozambican conditions.

---

* Note, too, one added complication here: root and branch criticism of Frelimo's "statist policy" is made both by observers who see Frelimo as having been too socialist, and by others who see it as not actually having been socialist at all! Recall the positions to this latter effect cited in the previous chapter of Heribert Adam ("the elite therefore adjusts ideological interpretations as arbitrarily as they adopt them ... because a collective ideological commitment hardly existed in the first place") and, at the opposite end of the political spectrum, Michel Cahen. Indeed, even so sensitive observer as William Finnegan is able to remark, in a somewhat parallel manner, on the "breathtaking ease" with which Frelimo now moves to "switch tracks" to "some form of capitalism." "Breathtaking ease?" Finnegan can only make this remark against the grain of the evidence of his own powerful book, the best part of which describes the terrible pounding Mozambique has endured for daring, in the first instance, to struggle against its subordination to global capitalist dictate. In so arguing, such critics choose to ignore the testimony of virtually all those who actually examined the Frelimo state closely enough in its early years to have a studied opinion on the subject. For as O'Laughlin has put the point (in her article cited earlier), "If we abstract from this history, we tend to see only the defensive measures of the 1980s and forget the optimism, sense of reconciliation and broad mass participation in activities organized by Frelimo, in both rural and urban areas, during the first years after independence." Judith Marshall also evokes the promise of this period effectively in her book *Literacy, State Formation and People's Power: Education in a Mozambican factory* (Bellville, S.A.: CACE/UWC, 1990).

One must, of course, give due weight to Finnegan's concern — so central to the current literature on Mozambique — at "the social and economic distance between the elite, whether it calls itself revolutionary or an aristocracy, and the great mass of illiterate peasants." Nor is he wrong to argue that "vanguardism has inherent weaknesses — it fosters passivity and authoritarianism — and the victories won by a vanguard in the name of the people rarely end up empowering the masses." But communism, socialism; Marxism ... all to be regarded as irrelevant notions? This would be sobering enough coming from Finnegan. Even worse is the fact that many Mozambicans have themselves now been beaten into accepting some such conclusion.[33]

Unless one shares the unreal premises of a Clarence-Smith or a Peter Fry regarding the likely fecundity of capitalism in Africa can this really be cause for celebration?[34] Surely there is a need in contemporary Mozambique for a socialist perspective that can make sense of the country's present situation vis-à-vis an ascendent regional and global capitalism, and make sense, too, of the social forces that continue to fray Mozambique's own social fabric. Equally important is the need to interrogate the demise of Frelimo's project from such a perspective if the real lessons of its failure are ever to be learned by those who must eventually seek to re-focus the energies of the poorest of the poor in order to reverse the terrible "liberation" that global capitalism has inflicted upon Mozambique. These, in any case, are the unregenerately old-fashioned premises that frame the following two sections of this chapter.

II. Evaluating the Frelimo State

We begin, then, by taking seriously the progressive opening represented in Africa by Frelimo's original socialist project, sharing Dan O'Meara's sense that "as a political movement, Frelimo had proved itself, and would prove itself again and again, capable of a domestic and international political creativity and imagination unique in Africa."[35] But there is also a need for a comprehensive critique both of Frelimo's project and its practices.[36] The movement's own failures did play some role in producing the present unhappy outcome, whatever the precise weight one might ultimately give them when measured against the impact of other factors, South African destabilization in particular. Of course, not everything now being said by the new generation of Frelimo's critics was profane knowledge to committed observers of Mozambican developments even in the heyday of Frelimo's maximum credibility. However, there is little doubt that when Frelimo came to power in 1975 it proved all too easy to overestimate both the clarity of its vision regarding the modalities of societal transformation, and the symbiotic nature of its link to the popular classes - notably the peasantry.

My own first attempts to make sense of the history-making possibilities that seemed open to the Frelimo leadership as it came to power in the mid-1970s turned around the notion (developed out of the work of Hamza Alavi) of the "overdeveloped," relatively autonomous state that was up for grabs in the fluid circumstances of Africa's initial transition to independence. Although the degree of the "post-colonial state's" autonomy remained subject to debate — and the task of transforming it much more difficult than might have been predicted — the concept seemed a helpful one. Certainly, it gave added resonance to my own conviction that the nature of the still forming group and/or class (I referred to it as a "petty-bourgeoisie-in-the-making;" Colin Leys as the "state-party apparatus;" Patrick Chabal simply as the "revolutionary leadership"[37]) that began to take shape around this state was of considerable significance in defining development outcomes. Even more concretely, this formulation anticipated that struggles within this group — such as had already occurred within Frelimo circles in exile in the late-1960s when the hegemony of a cadre of left-leaning leaders was consolidated — would be of considerable importance.[38]

It is necessary to be very precise about what is being claimed here since it seems imperative to lay to rest a canard that has served, ever since it was first articulated by Gavin Williams some years ago, to caricature this emphasis on the importance of "petit-bourgeois politics." At that time, Williams wrote: "Since the state is governed by the petit-bourgeoisie, and since their politics is indeterminate, the state may turn in any direction, depending on the ideology of those who come to control it. Like many members of the African 'petit-bourgeoisie', Saul appears to think that 'what we need is a good ruler, with a progressive ideology.'"[39] This is, quite simply, a reductio ad absurdum of my argument. Just because one grants some active role to this "group," it is not to be construed as having been removed from, and placed above, history, the production process, or the broader class structure. Moreover, nothing in the arguments surveyed by Williams suggest that it should be considered as being so isolated.

Such a line analysis did indeed suggest the importance of the fact that guerilla war had produced in Frelimo a leadership cadre, a fraction of the petty-bourgeoisie, drawn towards a progressive/socialist project. But it also made quite clear that the extent to which the potential for consolidating such a project might be realized depended crucially on three variables: the strength of the forces pressing the leadership to diverge from such a project; the nature of the links the leadership would actually forge with those popular classes in whose name it professed to speak; and the capacity of the leadership to develop clear and effective policies for realizing the kind of socio-economic transformation it envisaged. Unfortunately, on the latter two fronts the Frelimo leadership's project can be found wanting. Not flawed, *pace* the new critics, so much in the ends ("development," "socialism," "anti-imperialism") that it sought as in the means chosen to move towards those ends. This is, at any rate, the judgement underlying the argument that follows.

The constraints on their activity were real enough, of course, ranging from the drag of "historical backwardness" (the grim legacy of Portugal's primitive colonialism, an exaggerated economic dependence on South Africa, and the shortfalls in education, literacy, health standards and the like that were dramatic even by African standards) to the brutal fact of South Africa's destabilization itself. Moreover, the apparent "relative autonomy" of the newly independent state proved to be a decidedly mixed blessing. Although Samora Machel spoke eloquently at the very moment of independence of the need to transform, root and branch, the inherited Portuguese colonial state, its old-fashioned, hierarchical and highly bureaucratized structures soon began to entangle the incoming Frelimo team and, no doubt, helped encourage a certain high-handedness in its practices.[40] Did this entanglement also begin to tempt the "state/party apparatus" to develop a "class interest?" That this might have been so is one principle theme of Joe Hanlon's influential analysis of the Frelimo state's first decade, *Mozambique: The Revolution Under Fire,* for example.[41]

Yet the primary weakness of the Frelimo state was not, in the first instance, its parasitic and exploitative nature. A high level of commitment to a transformative project did move the "state/party apparatus" for many years, and both conspicuous consumption and corruption remained relatively unimportant during that time. The pull towards "high-handedness" was another matter, however. For a second danger of excessive reliance on a state apparatus that remained "relatively autonomous" was more immediately ominous than any pull towards parasitism. Perhaps if one reads, for "autonomous," such words as "ungrounded," "suspended," "free-floating" it is possible to get a sense, at least metaphorically, of the nature of the problem: *viz.,* that the Frelimo state remained suspended above the society whose liberation it sought to facilitate (Médard's demiurge!) and dangerously compromised by the great difficulty it would ultimately have in rooting its project in an active popular base.

Not that the tension, alluded to in the previous section, between "leadership" and "mass action" could merely have been willed away. Frelimo did offer a vision sufficiently coherent, in the first instance, to promise the moulding of a new, nation-wide Mozambican identity. It was also one linked closely enough to the cause of the poorest of the poor to promise policies (notably in the spheres of health and education) that could transform such people's lives in positive ways. Not relying naively on mere spontaneity to produce this result, the party used the state to help create organs of potential empowerment for women, workers and peasants. Make no mistake: this project bore the stamp, in many particulars, of "enlightened leadership," leadership that sought to help various "progressive" classes and categories to "name" themselves much more self-consciously.

Nor need this active role in helping draw to the surface of society certain self-definitions (e.g., "women," "workers," and "peasants") rather than others (e.g., "races," "tribes," and "regions") be considered to be, inherently, an arrogance. It only became so to the extent that Frelimo proved incapable of acknowledging to itself the paradox inherent in its role and risking the democratic implications of the task of empowerment it was setting itself. Here Frelimo's decision, in 1977, to pronounce itself a vanguard party became a key moment. This dictated the winding down of the messy and somewhat unpredictable — but often promisingly democratic — politics that were occurring in the *grupos dinamizadores* of the period; in addition, by further encouraging the laying of the firm hand of a fairly undemocratic centralism across the local assemblies, unions and women's organization that it had itself willed into place, Frelimo came, in time, to render many of its own progeny still-born. Perhaps we can also argue the even more formative importance of another decision, one that antedated the embracing of the "vanguard party" model *per se:* that is, the decision, inscribed in the very foundation of a one-party state, to forego pluralism in the name of revolutionary purity.[42] Of course, it is much easier to say this now, with the benefit of hindsight, than most of us found it possible to say at the time. Still, the fact remains that from the very beginning the Frelimo leadership was unwilling to put at democratic risk its own "essential" role in the transformation it wished to set in train. And the costs of the model of revolutionary leadership it adopted were to prove very high indeed.

Nor is it obvious that such costs need have been paid. Democratic leadership can, in principle, succeed in sustaining itself without the collapse into vanguardism and mere fiat that came to haunt Frelimo's practice. But to so succeed would require what O'Laughlin (as cited above) has termed "socialist methods of political work" — methods that would find the party both more sensitive to the nuance of local context and also capable of struggling, competitively, to win popular allegiance to the nobility and efficacy of its project against the pull of other poles of popular identification. This was possible, O'Laughlin insists, even in the Mozambican countryside, where peasants are alert to a diversity of possible strands of potential self-identification, including many "modernizing" ones, both economic and political, that reach far beyond Geffray's confined world of quasi-traditionalism.[43] In fact, quasi-traditionalism in its purest expression becomes most potent only as a fall-back position for peasants when other means of security and/or progress seem unavailable. But such was the hardness — externally evoked, internally generated — of Frelimo's style that the more positive possibilities of "mobilization" that O'Laughlin alludes to were all too seldom realized.[44]

Incapable of rooting itself entirely effectively in a mass politics, the Frelimo state had become instead a "developmental dictatorship" (in Eboe Hutchful's evocative formulation).[45] This fact must be central to our analysis — but so, too, must the fact that this was a developmental dictatorship of the Left. My point: we lose far too much if we permit Bayart and others to collapse the distinction between "left" and "right" in this context into one overarching abstraction, and to see all African states as belonging to one genus: the profoundly suspect, necessarily exploitative African state. We must, in short, keep open the space to assert that the weaknesses to which a "developmental dictatorship *of the Left*" is prone are rather different from those that afflict a "developmental dictatorship of the Right." For it is only by specification of the weaknesses of the former — and not from any more generalized brand of "state-bashing" — that useful lessons can be learned from the Mozambican experience.

The chief lesson? That even the most benignly left-wing but quasi-dictatorial leadership will have difficulty in sustaining its transformative project unless it allows itself (and/or is forced) to be held accountable to real rather than merely notional democratic pressures from below. Of course, it may well be argued that the costs of an undemocratic political practice in Mozambique would have been less had the Frelimo leadership not made mistakes on other policy fronts. The area of economic policy is particularly noteworthy in this regard. As I have argued elsewhere, the adoption of a model of "primitive socialist accumulation" is by no means the fated requirement of a left regime in the context of underdevelopment. In principle, Frelimo could have adopted a different approach — what I have called "the socialism of expanded reproduction" — that built on a more effective interchange between industry and agriculture, urban and rural, and better addressed the most pressing and immediate material requirements of peasants (and others). Instead of producing a "crisis of reproduction" for the peasantry, such a strategy might have provided the material foundation for the peasants actually embracing as their own Frelimo's modernizing and socializing project.[46]

Not that this failure can be delinked from the movement's own undemocratic practices. Had Frelimo been a bit less confident that it knew what was best for the peasants, it might not have so readily adopted an economic strategy that exacerbated their "reproductive crisis," nor moved quite so aggressively (at least in some areas) to "socialize" from above (via the communal village programme) their way of life. Significantly, at the one moment at which decisions about economic strategy seemed to bow to democratic input (in the run-up to the Fourth Congress, when both the need to address the reproductive crisis and to adopt a more flexible approach to the use of market mechanisms in the countryside were forced onto the agenda by popular protest), the Frelimo state came closest to striking the kind of balance between leadership and mass action that promised both economic advance and political support. By then, however, the war of destabilization had escalated to such a point that the pursuit of a more measured approach to rural development had little chance of being implemented. Soon, as capitulation to the IMF and the World Bank loomed large for the Frelimo leadership, the subtleties of pursuing a more flexible and realistic socialist strategy had given way to full-scale retreat before the logic of capitalism.

But how had Frelimo come to abandon "the peasant line" and democratic practices that had seemed so much a part of its liberation struggle against the Portuguese? In part this paradox may be more apparent than real, for the school of liberation struggle, even if it did serve to radicalize the Frelimo leadership's outlook in important and progressive ways, was probably also a much harder school than many of us realized at the time. It bred a certain ruthlessness alongside the commitment it evoked, and in Frelimo's case also a cockiness, bracing but dangerous, about the efficacy of revolutionary will in blowing aside apparently insuperable obstacles. Moreover, it is also easy to forget (as Colin Leys and I have noted elsewhere) "the climate of the times during the 'Thirty Years War' for southern African liberation (1960-1990), a climate that shaped much of the discourse both of the liberation movements themselves and of their supporters around the world. Can there be any doubt that the Left during those years of relative success (both within the region and beyond) too often took the righteousness of its cause for granted, allowing the subtle narcotic of 'correctness' to dull its democratic sensibilities?"[47]

For the Frelimo leadership there was also the Soviet factor — a factor central, militarily, to the triumph of the Mozambican struggle and one given further credibility by the Soviet regime's own apparent success in the building of "socialism." But linking its star to the Soviet Union was, for Frelimo, a fateful choice.[48] For the costs to Frelimo's project of Soviet tutelage can now be seen more clearly than ever to have outweighed the benefits. And yet it was not difficult to see, even at height of Frelimo's powers, that the movement was learning precisely the wrong lessons from what passed for Marxism in Eastern circles: lessons about the most overbearing of vanguardisms,[49] the most inflexible of primitive accumulation-driven economic strategies, the most unnuanced of class analyses, and the most unilluminating and disempowering versions of Marxist methodology.[50] Here was one kind of Marxism (one kind, one wants to insist to him!) well worthy of Finnegan's scorn. Of course, one must not overstate the case. Frelimo was not merely a prisoner of this "Marxist-Leninist" embrace. Sometimes its preachments merely meshed — all too comfortably — with the leadership's own worst instincts. And sometimes the Frelimo leadership's own sense of itself and the nature of its revolution enabled it to win more helpful insights from the revolutionary tradition. This said, however, it remains true that the impact of Soviet-style "Marxism-Leninism" was yet another reason for the difficulties Frelimo had in identifying the subtle tactics and strategies necessary to realizing its goals.

Meanwhile, the world was closing in on the Frelimo state. Might a combination of less overweening self-confidence and a sharper set of analytical tools have enabled Frelimo to neutralize some of that onslaught that Botha and Reagan had in store for it? Certainly, had the regime had greater success in fortifying itself domestically — by consolidating, democratically, its popular base and by finding the keys to greater economic advance — it would have been that much less vulnerable to attack. On the other hand, once Reagan assumed power, the odds against finessing Western hostility and advancing a radical project lengthened precipitously. Perhaps Mozambique could have found room for manoeuvre by ducking some of the fights in the region — it committed itself fully to ZANU's war in Zimbabwe, and gave what limited backing it could to the ANC — that were to prove so costly in rousing first Rhodesia's and then South Africa's merciless retaliation. But even to put the question in these terms is to underscore just how cruel was the environment of choice in which Frelimo sought to plot its course in the 1970s and 1980s. Moreover, Mozambique was a target for South Africa and its allies not merely for whatever role it played in the continuing battle for southern Africa. The symbolic and practical significance of the socialist option (warts and all) that it had chosen for itself might well have been excuse enough for its enemies. To forget this, even in the current climate of shifting paradigms and of rethinking "the state," "socialism" and so much else, would be to blame the victim indeed.

III. The State of Recolonization

Perhaps the best testimony as to how much has been lost with the virtual collapse of the erstwhile "Frelimo state" is provided by a clear description of what that collapse has left in its wake. The Frelimo state was, indeed, a "left-developmental dictatorship," one weakened (fatally or not we will never know, since it was not left to its own devices) in its purpose both by its dictatorial propensities and by other deep flaws in its strategic vision. But in potential at least, it bore the promise of providing a protective intermediary between the Mozambican people and a global/regional economy that, left uninflected, held out no positive prospect for them. It also bore the promise of ensuring a context within which the realization of a better life — a promise the mass of the population was by no means indifferent to — was at least a plausible possibility for Mozambicans. Are they offered a better promise now that the (admittedly flawed) Samoran project has been smashed and the "Frelimo state" as formerly defined is no more?

Not that getting a bead on the state of the state in contemporary Mozambique is easy to do. Its writ does not run all that broadly because of the war and the social chaos that now defines so much of Mozambican society. Still, there is a state (and still a

Frelimo party ostensibly at its helm) — even though what is left standing in Mozambique seems remarkably close to the most extreme model of the state's external determination conjured up in the "bad old days" of dependency theory. Thus Marshall writes of an "erosion of Mozambican sovereignty" and suggests that "control has shifted out of Mozambican hands in an alarming fashion."[51] This is particularly marked, most observers agree, in the free run of decision-making that the IMF and World Bank have now claimed for themselves. Certainly, these bodies make no bones about the thrust of their agenda: basic to the Structural Adjustment Programme has been, in the words of the World Bank, "the recognition that the closer integration of the Mozambique economy is essential, with domestic industrial and agricultural producers being exposed both to the incentives and disciplines of international markets."[52] And "the IMF, for its part, could see the crisis only in terms of excessive state control of the economy, excessive control of foreign exchange and too few exports, with measures of privatization and deregulation as the obvious remedies." Moreover, neither the IMF not the World Bank will brook much challenge.[53]

Is this what Peter Fry had in mind when, as quoted earlier, he hailed Mozambican President Joaquim Chissano for "his attempt to set Mozambique on a course of development in tune with the realities of the regional and international political and economic environment?" Surely we need to compare this version of events with the forlorn flavour of the remark I myself heard Chissano make in Maputo in 1990 (as quoted on p. 43, above). What could more starkly reveal just how supine Mozambique has been forced to become vis-à-vis Western dictate?

Several observers have pointed to an additional dimension to this picture. Thus Hanlon, in his most recent book,[54] provides impressive chapter and verse regarding the powerful grip of the World Bank and IMF on Mozambican decision-making. But he also emphasizes the extraordinary role that is increasingly being played by aid agencies, both foreign-governmental and private, in dictating policy outcomes. While manifesting, via food aid and other programmes, the "human face" of structural adjustment, aid agencies (World Vision and Care are two whose role he explores in particular detail) have policy agendas (the need for privatization is a common theme). Moreover, Hanlon comes close to suggesting that, in usurping its role over a broad front, such agencies actually become, to a significant degree, the state!

The costs of buying this structural adjustment package have been high for many Mozambicans. Oppenheimer, for example, writes that "price rises caused by sweeping currency devaluation and commercial speculation together with underproportional wage actualization and restraint in public sector spending contributed to the lowering of already precarious standards of living of large parts of the population."[54] And Judith Marshall's writings have further documented the "social impact" of such programmes, notably in terms of the erosion of advances in the area of health and education that were once thought to be the most notable accomplishments of the Mozambican revolution.[56] At the same time, it remains far from clear that, having been forced to swallow the pill of structural adjustment, Mozambique can now expect the kind of growth that a Clarence-Smith might foresee as flowing from the capitalist option. Experience of capitalist development strategies elsewhere in Africa is not so very promising in this respect. Nor are the early returns from Mozambique particularly favourable. Thus, one economist's recent analysis concludes, after a careful sifting of the evidence, that "prospects for growth and development are poor; unemployment is rising; inflation remains high; the balance of payment deficit is worsening; and the astronomical external debt is rising."[57] Indeed, a second analysis of recent economic trends in Mozambique (by Kenneth Hremele) suggests that a likely future for the country is "a weak and dependent form of capitalism, which basically will serve the South African economy with labour, transport routes, markets and raw materials," a situation that (in Merle Bowen's phrase) would be "all too reminiscent of the colonial era."[58]

Another dimension of the impact of opening Mozambique so dramatically to the benisons of the global capitalist economy also bears noting. For the flip side of increased deprivation for many Mozambicans is the crystallization of a distinctly novel level of socio-economic privilege for others. In Oppenheimer's words, we find "a rapid social differentiation process breaking up an economically inefficient and poverty-bearing, but relatively egalitarian, social order....Consequently, social exclusion became a wide-spread phenomenon. Abject poverty now co-existed with ostentatious consumption."[59] Moreover, this new world of "social exclusion" and differential opportunity ("opportunity" compounded of novel private sector activities and of access to jobs and other spin-offs from the large aid-giving industry now ensconced in Mozambique) creates a milieu, political and social, very different than that which existed in the past.

Thus, the fluidity that may once have marked Mozambique's petty-bourgeoisie-in-the-making and rendered it a potential seed-bed of "revolutionary leadership," seems increasingly a thing of the past. This group is now crystallizing its self-interest and "classness" around the new structure of privilege in Mozambique at a rapid rate. And as this happens so, in turn, the opportunism that characterizes petty-bourgeois politics elsewhere in Africa becomes, increasingly, the norm within Frelimo itself. The old unity of common social purpose that once bound Frelimo together seems lost forever, replaced, increasingly, by a jockeying for position that has even seen the invoking of racist appeals in the heat of battle for political advantage (the trumpeting of a narrowly-defined "African nationalism" by the prominent long-time Frelimo leader Armando Guebuza, for example [60]).

Hanlon does suggest that within ruling circles there was some attempt, at least in the early rounds of negotiation (1985-6) with the international bankers, to safeguard elements of the old progressive agenda.[61] In this he finds a remnant of the old Frelimo state that is worth defending. Indeed, he has criticized some in the international solidarity network who feel the need, increasingly, to direct their assistance to Mozambique to initiatives at the grassroots and within civil society (arguing, as they do so, that this can help revive the social base for a long-term renewal of progressive politics in Mozambique). This, Hanlon insists, is to play directly into the hands of the right-wing aid agencies with their own agenda of undermining the state and hastening the pace of market-driven privatization. In arguing his case, Hanlon seems little inclined to make requisite distinctions between initiatives designed to spawn collective forms of popular empowerment and those cast in more privatizing terms. True, Hanlon's point has some resonance: recall our earlier insistence — against the thrust of Bayart's argument — on the need to facilitate a positive role for a non-parasitic state if a meaningful process of transformation to be sustained. Yet to prove his case he would have to identify more convincingly than he does the militant attributes (in terms of both policies and personnel) of the present state that merit defending in this way.[62]

Sadly, it is no longer easy to do so in Mozambique. Nor is it any easier to paint a positive picture when one turns to examining the workings of the new, post-destabilization Mozambican state at the local level. True, the continuing chaos spawned by war makes it difficult to generalize about the reality on the ground in any case. Formally, however, the present Frelimo leadership is said to be learning a rather dubious lesson from Renamo's own manipulation of displaced chiefs to impose its order on areas it controls. For Frelimo has now begun to dismantle what were, in spite of their weaknesses, incipient structures of grass-roots participatory democracy at the level of local government in order to facilitate "a return to some form of chiefly rule ... in which rehabilitated chiefs are mandated to govern over rural populations and to collect taxes on behalf of the government ... as an expedient way of reasserting state authority and increasing state revenues in the rural areas." For Roesch, echoing Bowen's summary (above) of another aspect of contemporary Mozambican practice, this revival of a pattern of indirect rule not so very different from the Portuguese mode of governance also has to "be seen as part of the process of recolonization in Mozambique."[63] Recall, too, O'Laughlin's warning, cited earlier: "I think it would be a fundamental error to conclude that war in Mozambique shows that Mozambican peasants need colonial-style *regulos*."

More informally, the pattern of grass-roots politics as practiced by local populations faces a "retreat to tradition" about which it is equally difficult to be sanguine. For beyond the various barbarities that the collapse of civility and emergence of the rule of the gun and the *panga* have thrown up in rural Mozambique, there are other revealing developments. Take, for example, the extent to which, "in the context of the much-eroded authority of the state, an intense competition between Renamo, Frelimo and local forces has occurred for spiritually-empowered agency, and [to which] such agency has been part of 'progressive,' 'traditional,' and 'reactionary' programmes alike."[64] Recent studies, Wilson notes, highlight not only the proliferation in war-ravaged Mozambique of the truly horrendous brands of "cultic violence" and "ritualized destruction" launched by Renamo, but also "the practice of magic and ritual by Frelimo" and others (like the influential Naprama movement) in order to find an effective way "to counter Renamo ideologically." This, it must be emphasized, is a world of "spirit possession," ancestor worship and mystical chiefly powers, where, among other magical possibilities, bullets are expected by some believers to turn to water.

True, it does make some sense to understand such "religious traditionalism" as "the Mozambican peasantry's attempt to reconstitute a new system of meaning and social order out of the war shattered wreckage of Frelimo's post-independence experiment and the colonial-cum-traditional society which Frelimo sought to transform."[65] But is it merely a "Western," rationalist bias that suggests the recent analysis of Eboe Hutchful to be relevant to any attempt to make sense not only of the pattern of violence in rural Mozambique but also of this ambience of ideological response to it?

> ...in Africa, no less than in the Soviet Union and Eastern
> Europe, developmental dictatorships had degenerated in
> the process of 'orientalization,' in which strong states
> had clamped themselves on weak and subordinated civil
> societies. Beneath the political facade of orientalism,
> however, society had survived, resilient and remarkably
> unreconstructed. In the face of this nonresisting resis-
> tance, the historical project of the autonomous, bureau-
> cratized political leaderships had wilted and decayed. The
> final outcome of the peaceful capture of the enervated
> state and bureaucracy in Eastern Europe is a potent les-
> son that could be repeated in Africa, and elsewhere in the
> Third World. But to those (particularly in the West) who
> would, as a result of these revolutions and a weariness of
> 'high politics,' romanticize 'civil society' in the abstract,
> the contradictions revealed within East European society
> by the lifting of strong state power should prepare them
> to tolerate in Africa also what *Time* has aptly described as
> the 'return of the demons.'[66]

Again, we must avoid "blaming the victim;" the cruel cynicism of the South Africans in helping bring Mozambican society to this sorry pass cannot be underscored too often. But it is sad indeed that Hutchful's formulation can seem even minimally plausible as an accurate post-mortem on what is left standing in the wake of Frelimo's efforts to help effect the Mozambican people's liberation.

Social regression seems, in fact, to inform the new Mozambican polity at every turn. For the unleashing of other "demons" will almost certainly be one key ingredient of the newly competitive politics that a liberalization of the Mozambique's political system is likely to entail. Frelimo in its heyday may well be criticized for having underestimated, in the name of a new national purpose, the ethnic, regional and racial diversities/inequalities that are part and parcel of the Mozambican reality — although it is also the case that those who criticize the movement's insufficient sensitivity to possible popular resentment at the underrepresentation in its ranks of, say, "Africans" or "northerners" are generally less than clear about what a more subtle progressive politics on this front might have looked like. But the decay of Frelimo's project now finds ethnic, regional and racial parties threatening to crowd out most other political expressions on the electoral stage[67] — unless Frelimo itself can retain just enough credibility to keep alive the sense of achieved nationhood that is the one surviving feature of its original high purpose. Yet, as noted earlier, even Frelimo seems increasingly to be riven by developments that reflect the lowest common denominator of petty-bourgeois politics in Africa — with implications that may prove very bleak indeed.

In the urban areas the superimposition of structural adjustment on a situation of war-induced social breakdown (the fall-out, most notably, from the precipitous movement of vast numbers of displaced rural dwellers to Maputo and other centres) has also produced volatile conditions. Crime rates have escalated exponentially, for example. At the same time, there have been some signs of the rebirth, from the bottom up, of a more progressive politics in such settings. Judith Marshall, writing in 1991, emphasized the importance of a wave of strikes in Mozambique that seemed directly caused by reaction to the grim impact of the structural adjustment programme on the lives of ordinary Mozambicans. And she found considerable promise, too, in the fledgling activities of a trade union movement newly "autonomous" from single-party control, alongside a number of other mass-based organizational initiatives also beginning to find their feet within "civil society."[68] Perhaps it is to this kind of development, even more than to the staging of multi-party elections, that one may look for much of the long-term promise of the freeing of Mozambique's political system from Frelimo's unqualified and too often over-bearing domination.

In the short-run, however, the brand of resistance offered to the politics of structural adjustment by trade unions and other such popularly-based organizations within civil society may not immediately produce positive results. Thus, in her recent analysis of contemporary Mozambique, Merle Bowen follows Jonathan Barker in suggesting that the kind of state crystallizing out of Mozambique's present volatile set of circumstances is quickly becoming the instrument of a "triple alliance" of elements newly privileged by economic liberalization: "international financial capital (World Bank and IMF); private capital (foreign and domestic); and (progressive) small farmers." If put under pressure, those who act on behalf of this alliance may soon feel they have no alternative but to abandon any concomitant commitment to a fledgling liberal democratic system in order to control the social contradictions spawned by the economic orthodoxy they prefer.[69] At that point, Bowen suggests, "the most serious threat to ordinary Mozambicans in the approaching era of reconstruction may be the need for an increasingly repressive state to guarantee the smooth performance of the 'triple alliance.'"[70]

Trading a "left-wing developmental dictatorship" for a "right-wing developmental dictatorship?" There is some evidence that this will indeed be Mozambique's fate. Sadly, however, even this sorry denouement — a capitalist-driven rehabilitation of social order — to Mozambique's failed revolution may prove too much to hope for. How much more likely, in light of what has been argued above, is a demon-driven politics and an "unsteady state"[71] to match: if Frelimo fades away (or becomes, at best, ever more of a shell of its former self); if warlords continue to stalk the land; if the politics of race and region and religion comes to predominate .... Then, even were a Yugoslavia/Somalia situation to be avoided, any "dictatorship" that emerged from this fire-storm with a brief to restore "law and order" could prove to be very nasty indeed — and anything but "developmental."

To summarize: the costs of Frelimo's failure have been great, however future historians may ultimately judge the relative importance of the three factors — the drag of "historical backwardness;" the impact of external intervention/destabilization; the weight of Frelimo's own errors of omission and commission — that have produced the sorry denouement to Mozambique's socialist project that now confronts us. As the last section of this chapter has demonstrated, there should be very little comfort to be garnered from the decay of Frelimo's original project, however strongly one may feel inclined to decry its various weaknesses. Nor, needless to say, is the future a promising one. The question was posed earlier in this chapter whether there is good reason to expect the rebirth of a left practice that can "promise to reverse the terrible 'liberation' that global capitalism has inflicted upon Mozambique." Unfortunately — I insist that it is unfortunate, paradigm-shifters to the contrary notwithstanding — such has been the extent of the defeat of Frelimo's revolutionary undertaking that socialist advance is not on the agenda in that country for the foreseeable future. Indeed, it may be that, for some time to come, the very most that can be hoped for is that not all Mozambicans will learn the wrong lessons from what has befallen Mozambique in recent years. There are some small signs that this is the case. If so, then (to paraphrase Frelimo's antique motto) the struggle really can be expected to continue.

1   This chapter is, in effect, prolegomenon to a longer manuscript on Mozambique, now in preparation and tentatively entitled *What is to be learned? Rethinking the Mozambican revolution*. It was presented, in draft, at the Fall Workshop of the Canadian Research Consortium on Southern Africa, Queen's University, Kingston, Ontario, Canada, December 5, 1992, and first published, in something like its present form, in Ralph Miliband and Leo Panitch (eds.), The *Socialist Register 1993* (London: Merlin, 1993) under the title, "Rethinking the Frelimo State." I am especially grateful to Manfred Bienefeld for helpful comments on the earlier draft.

2   Gervase Clarence-Smith, "The Roots of the Mozambican Counter-Revolution," *South African Review of Books* (April/May, 1989), p. 10.

3   In his verbal submission to the symposium, faithfully recorded by the present writer, October 12, 1990; Slovo's position, coming from an ANC activist, might also be considered somewhat ungracious given the price extracted from Mozambique for contributing for as long as it did to the broader struggle for southern African liberation, although one also knows that the Mozambican government was itself less than gracious to Slovo and others in 1984 during the period of its all too zealous implementation of the conditions of the Nkomati Accord as they bore, negatively, on the ANC-in-residence in Mozambique.

4   Clarence-Smith, *op. cit.*, and, more recently, Alex Vines, *RENAMO: Terrorism in Mozambique* (London: James Currey, 1991), p. 74.

5   Clarence-Smith, *op. cit.*, p. 9.

6   As advanced, for example, by Jean Copans in his "Préface" to Christian Geffray, *La cause des armes aux Mozambique: Anthropologies d'une guerre civile* (Éditions Karthala, 1990) and by Clarence-Smith himself *(op. cit.)*.

7   Required reading on this subject is Robert Gersony, *Summary of Mozambican Refugee Accounts of Principally Conflict-Related Experience in Mozambique: Report Submitted to Ambassador Jonathan Moore and Dr. Chester A. Crocker* (Washington: Department of State Bureau for Refugee Programs, 1988). Equally relevant — and just as sobering — is William Minter, *The Mozambican National Resistance (Renamo) as Described by Ex-Participants* (Research report submitted to the Ford Foundation and the Swedish International Development Agency, 1989). On this subject, see also Otto Roesch's paper - prepared for the Queen's Workshop at which the present essay was itself first presented — entitled "A New Paradigm? Rethinking Renamo's War" (as well as other of Roesch's writings, as published regularly in *Southern Africa Report* (SAR) and elsewhere); my own essay, "Development and Counterdevelopment Strategies in Mozambique" in John S. Saul, *Socialist Ideology and the Struggle for Southern Africa* (Trenton, N.J.: Africa World Press, 1990); and chapters 1 and 2 in this volume.

8   William Finnegan, *A Complicated War: The Harrowing of Mozambique* (Berkeley and Los Angeles: University of California Press, 1992), p. 70.

9   The phrase is that of Margaret Hall (in the title to her article "The Mozambican National Resistance Movement (Renamo): A Study in the Destruction of an African Country," *Africa*, 6 [1], 1990). Hall sets up her own careful analysis of developments inside Mozambique — including an unsparing critique of "the structural weaknesses of the Mozambican state" — by suggesting she will focus "on the internal processes destabilization has set in train" *(emphasis added)*.
10 Gersony, *op. cit.*.
11 As defined in his "People's war, state formation and revolution in Africa: a comparative analysis of Mozambique, Guinea-Bissau and Angola," *Journal of Commonwealth and Comparative Studies*, 21, #3 (1983).
12 *Op. cit.*
13 For a further elaboration of this point see Otto Roesch, *op. cit.*. Much the best critique of Geffray's own work is Bridget O'Laughlin, "Interpretations Matter: Evaluating the War in Mozambique," *Southern Africa Report*, 7, #3 (January, 1992).
14 Peter Fry, "Between Two Terrors," *Times Literary Supplement* (November 9-15, 1990), p. 1202.
15 *Ibid.*
16 Many related themes are beginning to find their way into the English-language literature, viz., James Manor, *Rethinking Third World Politics* (Burnt Hill, U.K.: Longman, 1991) — a book to which *Politique Africaine* authors Jean-François Bayart and Jean-François Médard make important contributions in any case.
17 Dominique Darbon, "L'État prédateur," *Politique Africaine*, "Special 10e anniversaire: L'Afrique Autrement," #39, 1990 p. 37.
18 Bayart, "Civil Society in Africa" in Patrick Chabal (ed.), *Political Domination in Africa: Reflections on the Limitations of Power in Africa* (Cambridge: Cambridge University Press, 1986), pp 115-6; see also Bayart's own *L'État en Afrique* (Paris: Fayard, 1988).
19 Jean Médard, "L'État patrimonialisé," also in *Politique Africaine*, #39, pp. 25, 26.
20 *Ibid.*, p. 34. Médard refers in this context to a second paper of his, one I have not read but the title of which epitomizes, I suspect, its content: "Le socialisme en Afrii que: l'autopsie d'un mirage."
21 Médard also notes, in a rather more satisfied tone, that at least this same logic does help to hinder — or at least further distort ("l'Etat prédateur est lui-meme prédaté, l'Etat parasite est lui-même parisité") — the malign workings of the "demiurgic state"; Médard cites in this regard Bayart's notion of the "revenge of civil society" (against "l'ambition totalisante de l'Etat"!).
22 Contrast, in this regard, Hyden's *Beyond Ujamaa: underdevelopment and an uncaptured peasantry* (Berkeley: University of California Press, 1980) with his later *No Shortcuts to Progress: African development management in perspective* (Berkeley: University of California Press, 1983).
23 Manfred Bienefeld, "Dependency Theory and the Political Economy

of Africa's Crisis," *Review of African Political Economy*, #43 (1988), pp. 81, 82.
24 Clarence-Smith, *op. cit.*, p. 10.
25 O'Laughlin, *op. cit.*, pp. 27, 28.
26 For a manifestation, more generally cast, of this kind of left-leaning "bad science" regarding the claims of "modernity" see Jean Copans, *La longue marche de la modernité africaine* (Paris: Éditions Karthala, 1990).
27 *Op. cit.*, p 28. O'Laughlin sees the roots of this "dualism" in the colonial power structure as being far more important than any roots it might be thought to have in any more time-honoured "tradition." In addition, "in most of Africa after independence, this legal and administrative dualism was maintained, although the boundaries between the two systems and movement between them was made more flexible." Her conclusion: "I think it would be a fundamental error to conclude that the war in Mozambique shows that Mozambican peasants need colonial-style regulos." We will return to this point in section III, below.
28 *Ibid.*, p. 31.
29 *Ibid.*, p. 33.
30 Bayart, *op. cit.*, p. 120. The rather melodramatic formulation within which this phrase is found is also of interest: "...because they more readily lend their services to the state than to its challengers, African intellectuals (with few exceptions) have failed to provide civil society with the original conceptual instruments required for its advance. Even when they have had the courage to offer themselves to the leadership of the resistance, they have in no way been able to transcend the epistemic gulf between state and society."
31 Bayart, *op. cit.*, p. 125.
32 Finnegan, *op. cit.*, from which the several quotations in these two paragraphs are drawn.
33 Recall here my formulation from the previous chapter that found "the burden of the past (and the ideological oversimplifications of the Cold War era) resting heavily on a leader like Joaquim Chissano, who can now summarize the situation by suggesting that 'Marxism was creating problems for us' — proceeding to elide 'Marxism' with official Soviet-style 'Marxism-Leninism' in such a way as to leave himself almost no conceptual middle-ground for blunting the charge of the most unadulterated of free-market nostrums." The same might be said of Finnegan.
34 To be fair, Finnegan is himself little inclined to join in any celebration of the capitalist future he sees as unavoidable for Mozambique. As he puts the point, "Without some extraordinary natural resource, such as oil, it is not at all clear that a severely underdeveloped country, firmly on the periphery of the modern world system, has even a fighting chance of development." Moreover, he adds ominously, "in Mozambique's case its dependence is not on the developed North.

More directly and more profoundly, it is on South Africa" (*ibid*, p. 241).
35 Dan O'Meara, "The Collapse of Mozambican Socialism," *Transformation*, #14 (1991), p 82.
36 It bears noting that O'Meara's own essay *(ibid.)* is itself a powerful and measured contribution to such a critique.
37 See my paper, "The Nature of the Post-Colonial State: Further Reflections" and also Colin Leys, "State and Class in Post-Colonial Africa: Comments on John Saul's Theses on the Post-Colonial State," both presented to a panel entitled "Bureaucratic Bourgeoisie or Power Elite? - On Power in Africa", African Studies Association annual meeting, Philadelphia, 17 October, 1980. See also Patrick Chabal, *Amilcar Cabral Revolutionary leadership and people's war* (Cambridge: Cambridge University Press, 1983), especially chapter 7, "People's war in lusophone Africa: a comparative perspective."
38 See John S. Saul, "The Context: Colonialism and Revolution", being chapter 1 of Saul (ed.), *A Difficult Road: The Transition to Socialism in Mozambique* (New York: Monthly Review Press, 1985)
39 Gavin Williams, "There is no theory of petit-bourgeois politics", *Review of African Political Economy* (ROAPE), #6 (May-August, 1976).
40 See Edward Alpers, "The bureaucratic legacy of Portuguese colonial rule in Mozambique," paper presented to the 1986 Conference of the Review of African Political Economy, Liverpool, U.K., September, 1986.
41 Joseph Hanlon, *Mozambique: The Revolution Under Fire* (London: Zed Books, 1984); as it happens, Hanlon's own argument on this point is crossed in his text by several other, seemingly contradictory, emphases.
42 For further discussion of these decisions, and the general premises underlying them, see my essay, "Development and Counter-Development Strategies in Mozambique," *op. cit.*.
43 Jonathan Barker, in his book *Rural Communities Under Stress: Peasant farmers and the state in Africa* (Cambridge: Cambridge University Press, 1989) has effectively reminded us there is no single "peasant response" to their world. There is, to begin with, a considerable range of diversity within "the peasantry" — along lines of class, region, farming pattern and the like — that makes generalization risky. But even when considered in more general terms, what can be affirmed is that peasants are open to respond to a wide range of stimuli and to make them their own.
44 "Hardness", yes, but also *"falta dos quadros"* — the relative lack of trained, skilled and confident cadres below the top leadership level (this fact being itself a reflex of Mozambique's low level of overall development) — helped blunt the edge of Frelimo's positive impact vis-à-vis the populace in the countryside, and elsewhere.
45 Eboe Hutchful, "Eastern Europe: Consequences for Africa," *ROAPE*, #50 (March, 1991).

46 See my chapter, "The Content: A Transition to Socialism?" being chapter 2 in *A Difficult Road* and, for the impact of this "reproductive crisis" on the Mozambican peasantry, also Otto Roesch's doctoral dissertation, *Socialism and Rural Development in Mozambique* (University of Toronto, 1986). Not that the performance of the Mozambican economy was so terribly weak during the first five years of independence. In this sphere balancing off the impact of policy weaknesses against the impact of external shocks — flood and drought, international terms of trade (including rising oil prices) and, in the end, destabilization — is particularly difficult.

47 Colin Leys and John S. Saul, "Liberation without Democracy: The Swapo Crisis of 1976," paper presented to the Inaugural Research Seminar of the Canadian Research Consortium on Southern Africa, Montreal, November 6, 1992, p. 30.

48 Consider, however, the cruel dynamics of the Cold War context of the time; the Frelimo leadership felt it had some good reason to think that, as a regime seeking to evade the writ of global capitalist domination, it actually had little real choice in this regard.

49 There can be little doubt, for example, that Frelimo learned far too much about police methods from the East Germans and others.

50 No benefit of hindsight is necessary here. I made much the same points about the costs of Soviet influence in my chapter, "The Content" (cited above) and also in earlier writings.

51 Judith Marshall, *War, debt and structural adjustment in Mozambique: The social impact* (Ottawa: The North-South Institute, 1992).

52 This 1987 World Bank statement is quoted in Marshall, *ibid.*, p. 9

53 Marshall (*ibid.*, p. 8) is here summarizing the account of IMF negotiations with Mozambique found, in fascinating detail, in Joseph Hanlon, *Mozambique: Who Calls the Shots?* (London: James Currey Publishers, 1991); Marshall herself recounts a briefing from Jacinto Veloso, Mozambique's Minister of Cooperation, in which "we were told quite matter-of-factly that the international donor community had effectively frozen all grants, loans and credits to Mozambique until such times as Mozambique was prepared to accept an adjustment program with the IMF." (p. 8).

54 Hanlon, *ibid.*.

55 Jochen Oppenheimer, "Development Cooperation in the Context of War and Structural Adjustment: The Case of Mozambique," paper presented to the conference of the Canadian Association of African Studies, Montreal, May, 1992.

56 See, most notably, Marshall, *op. cit.*, and her numerous reports from Mozambique in the pages of *Southern Africa Report* in recent years.

57 Kim Jarvi, "Structural Adjustment in Sub-Saharan Africa and the Case of Mozambique," unpublished paper (Toronto: York University, 1992). Moreover, in Oppenheimer's view *(op. cit.)*, to the extent that economic decline was momentarily reversed in Mozambique this was "as a result of a very high and, in the long run, unsustainable influx of external assistance."

58 Here then, at the end of the day, is Clarence-Smith's "goose that lays the golden eggs!" Bowen is quoting from Hermele's *Mozambican Crossroads: Economics and Politics in the Era of Structural Adjustment* (Bergen, Norway: 1990) and adds herself that, "this trend has been reinforced by western governments who have readily accepted South Africa's self-portrayal as the stabilizing and modernizing force in the region" (in her "Beyond Reform: Adjustment and Political Power in Contemporary Mozambique," *Journal of Modern African Studies*, 30, # 2 [1992], p. 274).

59 Jochen Oppenheimer, *op, cit.*.

60 See, for example, David Ottaway, "Black Nationalist Opposition Emerges: Frelimo's Rule, Racial Equilibrium Seen Imperilled in Mozambique," *The Washington Post,* 11 December, 1990 as well as the discussion of Guebuza's politics in my article, "Mozambique: The Failure of Socialism", *SAR,* 6, #2 (November, 1990).

61 Hanlon, *Mozambique: Who Calls the Shots?* (op. cit.), pp. 117-8, where he discusses Frelimo's attempts to defend some expanded role for the state and also to make the World Bank and IMF take seriously the fact of on-going destabilization as a parameter for defining Mozambique's economic situation. But Hanlon also notes that a meeting with World Bank officials in November, 1985, "was nearly the last time anyone talked about a 'basic socialist framework.'"

62 There is a certain irony to Hanlon's emphasis here. One of his original contributions to the discussion of Mozambican politics was, as we have noted above, to emphasize — even overemphasize — the extent to which those who staffed the Frelimo state were taking on many of the attributes of a bureaucratic bourgeoisie. Now, at a point when this process is much further developed, his new book scarcely mentions the implications of this fact for thinking through the pros and cons of supporting the actually-existing state that is in place in Mozambique.

63 Otto Roesch, "Mozambique Unravels? The Retreat to Tradition," SAR, 7, #5 (May, 1992), p. 30.

64 K. B. Wilson, "Cults of Violence and Counter-Violence in Mozambique" (unpublished paper, n. d.). See also Vines, *op. cit.;* a number of case-studies by various authors currently being edited by Wilson himself at Oxford for future publication; and, *inter alia,* Margaret Hall, *op. cit.*.

65 Roesch, *ibid.*

66 Eboe Hutchful, *op. cit.,* "Eastern Europe: Consequences for Africa," pp. 57-8.

67 See Ottaway, *op. cit.,* amongst numerous other sources.

68 Judith Marshall, "Resisting Adjustment in Mozambique: The Grassroots Speak Up," SAR, 7, #1 (July, 1991).

69 For an exemplification of some of the contradictions inherent in the relationship between economic liberalization and political democratization in present-day Africa see Marcia Burdette, "Democracy vs,

Economic Liberalization: The Zambian Dilemma," *SAR*, 8, #1 (July, 1992); see also Issa Shivji, "The Democracy Debate in Africa: Tanzania," *ROAPE*, #50 (March, 1991).

70 Bowen, *op. cit.*, p. 279; the "triple alliance" model introduced here by Bowen (p. 258) is drawn from Barker's *Rural Communities Under Stress*, cited earlier.

71 On this possibility see the essay entitled "The Unsteady State: Uganda, Obote and General Amin" in my *The State and Revolution in Eastern Africa* (New York: Monthly Review Press, 1979).

Chapter 4
South Africa: Between "Barbarism" and "Structural Reform"[1]

The Mozambican case is a sobering one. Indeed it is easy to lapse into reformism now, socialism — whatever that might mean — being in retreat on so many fronts. On much of the Left, the language of "reasonableness" replaces the language of revolution, with those who hew to the nostrums of "Marxism-Leninism" and/or "Trotskyism" seeming more antiquated and naive — more "ultra-leftist" — than ever. Certainly in South Africa the present reality casts a dark shadow over these latter enthusiasms, any neat juxtaposition of "reform" and "revolution" sounding increasingly beside the point. Despite the advances epitomized in the dramatic unbanning of the opposition movements and the release of Nelson Mandela (in February, 1990), by mid-1991 — when the following chapter was first written — we were still very far from the future prophesied by Sweezy and Magdoff (noted in chapter one) when, at the height of the insurrection of the mid-1980s, they defined South Africa as "the only country with a well-developed, modern capitalist structure which is not only 'objectively' ripe for revolution but has actually entered a stage of overt and seemingly irreversible revolutionary struggle."[2] In both the short and the longer term, the way forward to a more egalitarian South Africa could be seen to present far more complicated challenges than any easy invocation of the need for a "worker's party" and the urging of some kind of maximalist confrontation with capital could hope to resolve.[3]

In the short-term? Witness the difficulties of the current political moment, one that defines itself around "negotiations" and the process of shaping a new constitutional dispensation. This is the moment that many saw, in the enthusiasms of February 1990, as bearing the promise of (minimally) a real de-racialization of capitalism and (potentially) a great deal more. Now this process itself appears flawed, grievously if not fatally, with some of those who most starkly juxtaposed the danger of "mere reform" to the drive for revolution wondering aloud whether even meaningful reform is possible in the present conjuncture.[4] Indeed, we glimpse here a concern that must haunt any approach to contemporary South Africa. For there is, currently (mid-1991), a simultaneity of two distinct moments — the negotiations moment, the post-apartheid moment — in the South African historical process, a simultaneity that both clouds analysis and compromises action. Even as South Africans press forward to shape the post-apartheid dispensation, they are dragged back, brutally, into the present, where continuing stalemate over the modalities of "democratization" has created space for the grimmest of barbarisms — all too familiar to us from endless newspaper accounts of the "killing fields" that South Africa's townships have become. Although almost worn smooth through overuse, Gramsci's epigram nonetheless rings cruelly true of contemporary South Africa: "The crisis consists precisely in the fact that the old is dying and the new cannot be born; in this interregnum a great variety of morbid symptoms appears." (No reference cited.)

And what if the new cannot, in fact, be born; if the morbidity of the interregnum merely shows South Africans the face of their own future? We must countenance this possibility in the present chapter, yet, at the same time, avoid becoming fixated with it. In the immediacy of the moment South Africans must, indeed, struggle to counter the pull towards chaos in their country — the pull towards "Lebanization" (as a number of sage South African observers would have it). But the best of South African militants are also struggling to build a future beyond the interregnum, to divine, to begin to shape, the parameters of a new, post-apartheid South Africa. True, even a democratization of South Africa that remained narrowly political would be a useful achievement in the context of the country's sad history and glowering present. Yet if this levelling impulse were not to be pressed forward to redress the socio-economic inequalities that have been inherent in South Africa's brand of racial capitalism, any new "freedom" would quickly be rendered very formal indeed for the vast mass of the black population.

In fact, as we shall see, most of the key actors in South Africa now pay at least lip service to this latter premise. But what has any such imperative come to imply for the Left *per se?* Not, for the most part, any very precipitate plunge into full blown social revolution. Rather, at its most relevant the Left seems to be groping towards something we might choose to call "structural reform." In effect, this means applying to South Africa a distinction once delineated by Andre Gorz between a "genuinely socialist policy of reforms [and] reformism of the neo-capitalist or 'social-democratic' type:" "If immediate socialism is not possible, neither is the achievement of reforms directly destructive of capitalism. [Yet] those who reject all lesser reforms on the grounds that they are merely reformist are in fact rejecting the whole possibility of a *transitional strategy* and of a process of transition to socialism."[5] But what, within such a transition, is to distinguish "structural reform" from mere "reformism?"

There are two chief attributes. One lies in the insistence that any reform, to be structural, must not be comfortably self-contained (a mere "improvement"), but must, instead, be allowed self-consciously to implicate other "necessary" reforms that flow from it as part of an emerging project of structural transformation.[6] In Gorz' phrase, any "intermediary reforms ... are to be regarded as a means and not an end, as dynamic phases in a progressive struggle, not as stopping places."[7] Secondly, a structural reform cannot come from on high; instead it must root itself in popular initiatives in such away as to leave a residue of further *empowerment* — in terms of growing enlightenment/class consciousness, in terms of organizational capacity — for the vast mass of the population, who thus strengthen themselves for further struggles, further victories. "The emancipation of the working class can become a total objective for the workers, warranting total risk, only if in the course of the struggle they have learned something about self-management, initiative and collective decision — in a word, if they have had a foretaste of what emancipation means."[8]

Why does some variant of "structural reform" have particular ideological resonance in South Africa? What are the signs that this kind of "transitional strategy" is emerging there? And what forces are most likely to sustain such a strategy? These are questions to which I will return, although one strand of the argument may be anticipated here. For there is still something to the notion articulated by Stephen Gelb and myself a decade ago — at the moment when the ANC had begun successfully to reclaim its historic primacy within the camp of popular resistance — that "just as the ANC is at the centre of things, so the centre of things is increasingly within the ANC: the continuing dialectic between this movement and the considerable revolutionary energies at play within the society has become the single most important process at work in South Africa's political economy."9 Nor was Robin Blackburn incorrect recently to find in South Africa, and precisely in "the South African UDF/ANC," one of his "new proletarian and new left movements" that "have a strong relationship to new trade unions without conforming to the old labourist model" and that hold some positive promise of "transforming the historic programmes of the Left."10

However, as I argued several years ago, this reality has never been unproblematic nor free of contradiction.11 Now this is all the more true. Indeed, the ANC has proven to be weaker, less clear-sighted, than might have been anticipated, and the dialectic between it and "the considerable revolutionary energies at play within [South African] society" less straightforward than might have been hoped even some fifteen months ago. But if the ANC is very far from being a "revolutionary vanguard" in any familiar sense of the term, this need not mean that the political process that swirls around it is without the kind of revolutionary promise Blackburn alludes to. As we will see, it is within this very swirl that one does, indeed, find the most important of the diverse centres of creativity that continue to shine out through the gathering gloom in South Africa — as well as the most likely architects of any transformed "program of the Left" there.

All this becomes possible only if a collapse into chaos is avoided in South Africa. Of course, even then there would not be clear sailing for these *potential bearers of a "structural reform" approach to socialist transition* (the rubric I would offer as best epitomizing the most promising possibilities in that country). For the alternative to chaos could still very well be cooptation ("mere reformism") rather than transformation. Such is the strength of capital and entrenched privilege in South Africa that there will be a pull on actors, both within and without the ANC, to take, in the end, the line of least resistance *vis-à-vis* established power. Indeed, even some of the least compromised of popular leaders — the most promising architects of a "transformed programme" — may have their militancy gradually eroded by having to live the half-measures inherent in a "structural reform" strategy, and may find themselves sapped, ultimately, of the kind of nervy energy it takes, day in and day out, to so balance realism against risk as to keep radical possibilities alive.

There does remain a distinctive vibrancy and radical push at the base of South African society (despite the township wars) that should prove difficult for popular leaders to ignore. But will the latter be tempted, nonetheless, to rationalize "necessary" compromises by blurring the fact it is class struggle they are engaged in? Thus Gorz, for all the circumspection of his discussion of a "socialist strategy of reforms," keeps returning, in his important essay on the subject, to the fact that "the bourgeoisie will never relinquish power without a struggle and without being compelled to do so by revolutionary action on the part of the masses,"[12] What is at stake, ultimately, is a "trial of strength" — and those popular forces in South Africa whose cumulative empowerment is seen to be so central to a project of "structural reform" will ignore this at their peril. In fact, it is precisely concern about the real measure of the UDF/ANC's revolutionary seriousness in regard to such questions that move — in their least sloganistic moments — those who critique its undertakings from the left. However sceptical one may be about the realism and likely efficacy of the programmes and prognostications such critics offer as alternatives, this kind of concern deserves the most serious consideration. In the aftermath of the ANC's own July 1991 congress, and of recent revelations ("Inkathagate") that have greatly damaged the ANC's principal political antagonists, it is a good time to take stock of a political conjuncture with both hopeful and ominous features.

I. EXPLAINING DE KLERK

As I have argued previously, the "linkage between racial domination and capitalist exploitation is as potentially contradictory as it has been mutually reinforcing" during long periods of South Africa history.[13] Moreover, since the 1970s and in a context of "organic crisis", we have seen these two structures pull apart in various crucial ways, facilitating attempts, by some in ruling circles, to reform South Africa and de-racialize its capitalist system (the better to defend this system's essential features, needless to say). In part the roots of reform have had an economic logic. In the terms of a line of analysis recently developed most fully by Stephen Gelb, the chief limitations upon South African economic development reflect a crisis in the "racial Fordist" accumulation regime — one premissed initially on "extending industrialization via the production of (previously imported) sophisticated consumer goods primarily for the white South African market" — that had spurred the country's post-war boom. Although economic crisis also reflected South Africa's vulnerability to international trends, it did produce a growing recognition of the need to break down racial restrictions on the Fordist link between mass production and mass consumption — "to overcome the limits imposed by apartheid on the labour process and labour markets," in Gelb's formulation — in order to reactivate growth.[14]

Indeed, slowly but surely business interests were working towards advocacy of an across the board "normalization," in capitalist terms, of the South African economic system. Their resolve in this respect was brought into even clearer focus by international reaction to South Africa's crisis: both politically-willed sanctions and those market "sanctions" that sprang from global business' misgivings about South Africa's investment climate. Here, of course, economic reality intersected with political realities: popular resistance that, since the Durban strikes and Soweto uprising of the 1970s, could never quite be snuffed out by the apartheid state helped trigger both the international sanctions movement and declining investor confidence. Moreover, established power in South Africa became increasingly nervous about the proto-revolutionary link being forged within the popular movement between anti-racist democratic demands and anti-capitalist resentments. Under such circumstances, a project of taming rising trade union demands and generalized political unrest by attempting to steer such pressures into bourgeois-democratic political institutions and industrial relations regimes seemed increasingly attractive.

As Dan O'Meara has shown, this shift to reform was also facilitated by a new stratification of the Afrikaner community, long-time bed-rock of support for apartheid policy and for the National Party.[15] As anticipated by some of its architects, NP rule had indeed produced Afrikaners capable of competing successfully with English business; ironically, the emergent entrepreneurial and professional strata who did succeed along such lines began to find they had as much or more in common with their class counterparts across the (intra-white) ethnic divide as with their fellow Afrikaners at lower rungs of the ladder. It was this "new Nat" leadership cadre that, as the 1980s wore on, aligned itself — very much against the statist pull of party tradition — ever more enthusiastically with the most extreme free-market nostrums of supply-side liberalism (including a drive to privatize South Africa's large state sector that sprang as much from ideological fetish as from concerns to raise revenue or, more recently, to keep assets out of the hands of any successor majority-rule government). Gradually the party began to cut itself away from its old constituency: secure in their economic privilege the new Nats inclined to leave the cause of defending fully institutionalized racism to strata more immediately vulnerable to black advance — the marginalized white farmers of the platteland and the remnants of the white working-class who have come, in turn, to provide the social base of the Far Right.

One could easily overstate this case, however. Even in the business community it was only a handful — the Premier Group's Tony Bloom and Barclay's Chris Ball (both of whom have since left South Africa), the Permanent's Bob Tucker and the Consultative Business Movement's Christo Nel — who could suggest the most far-reaching brand of deracialization of South Africa to be advisable, such advanced thinkers considering the strength of capital to be sufficient in and of itself to discipline (and/or seduce) virtually any black-majority successor regime to its purposes. However, the business consensus generally remained rather less confident than this, often content merely to bide its time on the reform question. How much more has this been true of Nationalist politicians, on even the most yuppified of whom the pull of the traditional national-cum-racial project can often still be felt.

Hence, the schizophrenic witches' brew of reform and repression that defined state policy in the 1980s. The brutal crushing of the 1984-86 insurrection that succeeded, momentarily, in derailing the resistance movement lent further weight to a growing centralization and militarization of state power in South Africa: the President's "State Security Council" continued to eclipse the Cabinet, and a new "National Security Management System" began to preempt and overdetermine conventional administrative structures. Yet accompanying dollops of reform were also felt to be essential to the coopting of black leaders and/or the winning of the "hearts and minds" of the populace.[16] Inadequate to the purpose of draining off the high level of popular resistance that boiled just beneath the surface of repression, the very inadequacy of such measures helped seal the fate of the 1980s' quintessential political figure, *die Groot Krokodil,* President P. W. Botha. Summoned to the cause of reform but a Nationalist politician of the old school, this profoundly security-oriented, long-time Minister of Defense was, in the end, torn apart by the contradictory claims history had placed upon him.

De Klerk's flawed deracialization project

Certain related contradictions find expression within De Klerk's project. Still, De Klerk did introduce something new.[17] Far more assertively than his predecessor, he has sought to take the offensive in shaping a new political terrain — albeit in ways favorable to his own purposes. More fully than Botha could do, he sensed the stalemate created by the National Party's repressive checkmating of the near insurrection of 1984-96 to be unviable — fragile politically, formidably expensive, unconvincing to potential investors and other concerned parties abroad. In particular, the hunger strikes, the widespread defiance of bannings and segregation notices, the industrial action and worker stay-aways, in short the entire spectrum of assertions that defined 1989's revival of the popular resistance movement (or "Mass Democratic Movement" as it came to be known) made it clear the government could not hope to stabilize things in the same old way. Moreover, renewed resistance could only give fresh life to the international pressures referred to above.

At this point the White House, hounded at home about sanctions, began to press Pretoria to signal new new flexibility in its policies, even as South Africa's good friend Margaret Thatcher counselled the need to "normalize" things in a more readily defensible way. A more subtly political approach also recommended itself just as those who favoured the hardest of lines in South Africa were themselves on the defensive in ruling circles — mere repression a failed policy inside South Africa, the stunning military stalemating of South Africa by joint Angolan-Cuban forces a reality in Angola, a ceding of ground to an erstwhile "terrorist" enemy (SWAPO) proceeding relatively seamlessly in Namibia. Almost simultaneously, world events further discredited the apartheid regime's old game of claiming to be a buffer against the global "red menace," while the very collapse of the Communist bloc served to raise international expectations regarding the necessity for some kind of democratic outcome in South Africa.

It was in this context that De Klerk — heretofore a denizen of the centre-right of the NP — took the bold steps of February 1990, seeking to break the political log-jam by inviting exiled political organizations in from the cold. Moreover, he has continued to promise (and in part deliver) a de-racialization of South Africa: he has formally opened the Nationalist Party to non-white members, for example, and in February of this year (1991), announced the imminent repeal of such apartheid legislative foundation-stones as the Land Act, the Group Areas Act and the Population Registration Act.[18] Such steps were dramatic, and enough to win him kudos abroad and a significant waning of the sanctions impetus in the European Community and the United States, if not yet in the Commonwealth. One could easily underestimate the novelty of the terrain upon which the popular movement now finds itself. Yet the fact remains — the old Adam in the new Nat — that

De Klerk's political intentions seem to remain dangerously limited, and this in all too familiar ways.

Thus, in one his very first utterances (to Ted Koppel on ABC-TV's *Nightline*) after Mandela's release, De Klerk still mouthed the old Nationalist line that seeks to present South Africa as a "multinational" amalgam (with all those "tribes" whose interests must be accommodated). And, phrased with greater or lesser subtlety, considerable talk about the imperative of protecting "group rights" has continued to surface in official circles, prompting O'Meara to conclude recently that "De Klerk and his colleagues quite simply will not commit themselves to the establishment of a non-racial democracy. Thus the constitutional plan they have now bruited about as their likely 'offer' when that stage of the negotiations process is reached, still provides for a strong white veto through the careful structuring of the proposed new parliament's second chamber. This reflects deep-felt concerns on the part of Afrikaners about protecting their own culture and language, as well as more prosaic concerns about defending certain important aspects of economic/racial privilege against any unchecked majority certain to be both poor and black."[19]

Still half-hearted on reform: we must return to this matter since it is from some such a starting-point that De Klerk has chosen to deal with the ANC. But the limits that may mark De Klerk's intentions bear noting here, since much current media analysis tends to explain his half-measures as reflecting merely a bow to the white Right. Not that those to the right of De Klerk — who, undeterred by nuance and smelling betrayal, resent the ground he is breaking — comprise an insignificant force. One may doubt their electoral potency (even assuming there will ever be another white election); at least for the moment, analysts tend to grant them, at best, 30 to 35 per cent. Moreover, the chief opposition party, Treurnicht's Conservative Party, seems likely, however reluctantly, to play out the political game by the rules. There are others further to the right, however — Eugene Terreblanche's quasi-fascist AWB, for example — who feel no such constraint and who seem set to inflict considerable damage on their enemies during any process of transition to a new constitutional order. Most importantly, this white Right interpenetrates with the state's security apparatus — the police, the military — in ways that may already be of considerable significance.

The white Right also has its black counterpart, the residue of previous attempts by the regime to divide and rule the subject population. One thinks of the venal layer of "Coloured" and Asian politicians, far from popular within their own communities, who staff non-white structures linked to the Tri-cameral parliament, and of various Bantustan and black-township council intermediaries of white power who have developed their own stake in the limited realms of authority allotted to them. Of course, councillors have found themselves under siege in their own communities and Bantustan leaders, too, have felt the hot breath of popular agitation at their backs. Crude autocrats like the Mantanzimas in the Transkei and Lennox Sebe in the Ciskei (with Mangope of Bophutatswana saved only by direct South African armed intervention) have been swept aside by their militaries, these militaries in turn being forced to accommodate themselves, to greater or lesser degree, to the demands of the ubiquitous, South Africa-wide popular movement.

Thus the Ciskei's Brigadier Oupa Gqozo both renounces "independence" and cedes new room for manoeuvre to trade unions whose activity was violently crushed by his predecessor; while the Transkei's Major-General Holomisa, a public advocate of the ANC's cause even before February 1990, now enthusiastically domiciles within his borders ANC military commander Chris Hani and — it appears — important residues of the armed wing of the ANC. This does not mean such "homeland" leaders — with their considerable bureaucratic and military constituencies within the homelands — will not be heard from again, and perhaps in less than progressive ways, as the jockeying for position regarding a new constitutional dispensation proceeds. Nonetheless, it is other black denizens of the apartheid structures that have come to inflict the most acute damage on the cause of democratic change. One thinks here of the vigilantes of the townships and, most problematic of all, of the Kwazulu Bantustan's Chief Gatsha Buthelezi and his Inkatha movement.

The role of Inkatha

The counter-revolutionary role of those notables who have clustered around township structures in South Africa — councillors, business types, black police personnel, alongside such *lumpen* elements as these latter can recruit to be the footsoldiers of vigilante undertakings — has been all too visible in South Africa ever since the failed insurrection of the mid-1980s.[20] But the most recent round of violence in South Africa's townships has reached particularly frightening and seemingly uncontrollable proportions. Increasingly, too, this violence seems merely overdetermined by context, a cruel but ineluctable index of the way blacks have been forced to live for decades by apartheid, and of the social distemper bred by such realities. And yet the emergence of this wasting syndrome has been anything but spontaneous; in its main thrust it has had to be politically constructed. Its principal architect? Gatsha Buthelezi, covertly prompted and subsidized by forces within the government and state.

Accepting participation in the government's Bantustan scheme in 1970 (although consistently refusing "independence" thereafter) Buthelezi revived a moribund Zulu nationalist organization, Inkatha, in 1975 in order to provide a political base for himself. Painted as a moderate because of his capitalist leanings (including a firm rejection of any form of sanctions) and his dismissal of armed struggle (and indeed of most other militant forms of confrontation with the apartheid state), he and his cronies proved, more or less from the outset, to be anything but moderate in the brutal manner of their consolidating a hold on power in Kwazulu. (Inkatha's extraordinary rape of the university campus at Ngoye in 1983 is merely one particularly graphic example of a far more general pattern in this respect.) It was from this Bantustan base that Buthelezi then made himself available for any political outcome that could further his apparently boundless personal ambition.[21]

In particular, he sought to position himself as a possible compromise candidate for the day when the contradictions of the apartheid system would finally dictate some bolder kind of reform. The discussions over a power-sharing model for Natal (orchestrated around the "Buthelezi Commission" and within the KwaNatal Indaba) represented one earnest of this intention. Yet such was the strength of pan-South African nationalism within the black community that Buthelezi could never convincingly carry his tribal-tinged and conservative politics beyond Natal. Moreover, it became increasingly apparent throughout the 1980s that the rising Mass Democratic Movement — the chief protagonist of a broader national project — was also winning increasing support amongst the Zulu people itself. Faced with the possible eclipse of its position, Inkatha slashed back brutally at ANC/UDF/COSATU supporters in Natal.

It should be noted that the violence that surfaced so dramatically in Pietermaritzburg and elsewhere in 1988 and 1989 was between political groupings *within* the Zulu community. (It was not, that is to say, "tribal violence" in any meaningful sense.) And it was largely initiated as a political tactic by Inkatha, now increasingly on the political defensive and attempting to reconsolidate its position by force of arms. 1990 brought even more bad news for

Buthelezi: the apparent recognition by world opinion of the ANC's primacy within the black community and of its claim to co-equal status with the government in negotiating the future of South Africa. With even De Klerk himself seeming to come to terms with this view, Buthelezi thus saw himself being shut out from the crucial early rounds of bargaining over a new constitution. He was no longer a preferred intermediary and, indeed, became increasingly fearful of a constitution that might ignore all his claptrap about "power-sharing" and even sidetrack the prospect of recycling the Bantustan system — so long the chief underpinning of his power — in some kind of "federal" system.

How, then, to get to the bargaining table before having to face the none-too-tender mercies of the ballot box? There was an answer: if no longer quite credible, he could at least try to make himself indispensable. If you want a peaceful transition, he seemed to say, include me in: include me in or a great many more people will die. In some such mood Inkatha, in the latter part of 1990, carried its bloody tactics beyond Natal and into the Transvaal.

As we now know, the Republic's Minister of Law and Order (sic), Adriaan Vlok, directly sponsored the resulting mayhem to the tune of several million rand. That the government should lend this degree of covert support was important to Buthelezi (although, as is now apparent, rather risky). Yet we should also understand that, however ugly, his project has had some kind of social base, especially in the remote rural areas of Kwazulu where Inkatha's machine-style politics can dispense its patronage, where its closed and aggressive methods can serve to intimidate dissenters, and where its ethnic sloganeering can have some added resonance. This kind of politics has not tended to play nearly so well in the more sophisticated urban townships of Natal. Nonetheless, in the mushrooming shanty-towns that now begin to ring the formal townships, the notorious Inkatha "warlords" have been able to establish some similar patterns of social control amongst a desperately impoverished and marginalized population. Moreover, this kind of warlord system seems to have found an echo in the tribally-exclusive and isolated migrant-labour hostels of the Transvaal cities. It is from these hostels that Zulu men have been mobilized as the cutting edge of Inkatha's terror.

The ethnic charge of this project is real, of course, and, as a kind of self-fulfilling prophesy, can encourage other ethnic-based responses. The possible result: the kind of downward spiral of internecine struggle that has already begun to affect negatively the functioning of several hitherto strong unions in the Transvaal. This kind of politics can also exploit other faultlines in local communities, inter-generational tensions for example, the seeds for which have sometimes been sewn by the the unbridled activities of militant youth within the popular movement. Yet the class question remains preeminent: the most significant development of all, perhaps, is the pull towards Inkatha of that very network of local notables we have identified as the principal instigators of earlier rounds of vigilante-style activity.

Thus, as one former Inkatha central committee member who now heads the Transvaal provincial authority's community development programme put the point, "It has taken a long time but the message is now clear. If the ANC continues with its campaign [to remove government-created local authorities] it will meet organized resistance. The spines of the councillors have been stiffened by the words of Chief Buthelezi. They know they will now be supported by Inkatha." The *Southscan* report (March 22, 1991) that carries this quote proceeds as follows: "The process has already been at work in Alexandra, where Inkatha-ANC clashes in the past fortnight left 60 dead, and tensions continue to run high. In a confidential memorandum to his four council colleagues in advance of the fighting, nominated mayor Prince Mokoena said he was 'allowing Inkatha into Alexandra....I am sick and tired of the civic and the ANC.' Just days before the first killings, Mokoena warned Moses Mayekiso, head of the ANC-aligned Alexandra Civic Organization and driving-force behind the anti-council campaign in the Transvaal: 'We are going to hit you.'"[22] Add to this pattern the various criminal elements who, amidst the resultant chaos, can find space to expand their activities (and even occasionally legitimize them under one political banner or another) and the South African picture begins to look very grim indeed.

But note: equally important to the resonance Buthelezi's brutal project has gained are forces within the white community. Haysom and others have identified a pattern, from the first appearance of the black vigilantes and throughout the country, of firm links between such vigilantes and the police and military present in the townships. Not surprisingly, in the current situation, it is Inkatha's undertakings that are particularly attractive to those right-wing whites who have a brief both to undermine the ANC and, more generally, to panic other whites, presented with the spectre of "black anarchy," away from support for democratic reform. There has been some debate about the extent to which such right-wingers are minions of the state, to what extent they represent some shadowy "third force." Given the well-documented degree of police participation in ultra-right political groups, the distinction may not be of great importance. In any case, what can be confirmed quite unequivocally — from numerous first hand accounts — is a pattern of police support for Inkatha's ravages in both Natal and the Transvaal, a pattern that ranges from blatant non-intervention to more active involvement in mobilizing and transporting death squads within the townships.

Well before the most recent dramatic revelations, it seemed clear that the involvement in the violence ran even deeper than that. Already, in 1990, a *Weekly Mail* report had documented the fact that, on at least one occasion (in 1986), an elite unit of Inkatha fighters were trained in guerilla warfare by a division of the South African Defense Force at the Hippo Base in the Caprivi Strip.[23] Further evidence pointed to the on-going training of Inkatha "hitmen" by the SADF at camps in Kwazulu itself. And there were signs of collusion, in training and in general logistics, between these Inkatha forces and Renamo (the South African-backed wrecking crew that has inflicted such damage upon neighbouring Mozambique), including suggestions that some Renamo units may actually have been actively involved with Inkatha in recent township offensives. Small wonder that the scorched earth tactics of South African vigilantes — aimed at maximum social disruption and the brute physical intimidation of local populations — have come to resemble those of Renamo so closely. As *Southscan* summarizes the point: "With some justification the ANC sees itself as the target of a sustained military campaign: those of the 3,000-plus victims of violence since the ANC's legalization who have not been ANC members or supporters, have in the main been residents of communities demonstrating significant ANC support."[24]

Government-sponsored violence

Against this background the explosion of the "Inkathagate" scandal in late July, following the publication of documentary proof that the Ministry of Law and Order had funded Inkatha campaigns, was scarcely a surprise. Nevertheless, the revelations, first published in the *Weekly Mail* in its issue of 19-25 July, should prove deeply damaging to Inkatha and to the government. Previously both parties had strenuously denied any collusion. De Klerk and Pik Botha had publicly deplored the township violence, even as their government was funding the forces behind it, while Buthelezi himself stands exposed as being, in effect, a hired tool of the security services. Moreover, beyond the proven, and now admitted payments made by the ministry to Inkatha, lies the question of the huge subversion budget as well as highly circumstantial accounts of (for example) incidents where members of the South African armed forces have been used, in disguise, to terrorize communities that supported the ANC.

Was De Klerk the architect or the prisoner of the strategy of sabotage undertaken by the security services? Something of both, perhaps. He does indeed seem hamstrung, within the white community, in dealing with the military. True, his coming to power in the wake of Botha did signal a distinct civilianization of the white polity; very quickly, he moved to up-end the State Security Council/National Security Management System structure. Yet, beyond this, De Klerk has shown little inclination to press the reigning "securocrats" hard regarding their day-to-day practices in harrassing the popular movement, much less to curb Magnus Malan, Minister of Defense, old Botha crony, and the most unyielding and outspoken of hard-liners within his Cabinet. De Klerk did not use many previous opportunities — such as his minister's implication by the Harms Commission in a whole range of "dirty tricks," or the exposure of his lies in Parliament regarding illegal disbursement of funds — to move against Malan. Under the pressure of "Inkathagate" revelations, De Klerk did at last move Malan and Vlok from the security ministries, (though retaining them in the Cabinet), and their successors do appear to be less compromised. Nonetheless, we should recall that De Klerk's critics have also emphasized "the extent to which the pattern of recent appointments — notably that of General Liebenberg to head the Defense Force, the very man who, as chief of the SADF Special Forces Command, had presided over the military destabilization of Mozambique and Angola — seems further to document De Klerk's disinclination to run too many risks in the interest of change."[25]

Moreover, there is some ground for thinking De Klerk to be even more actively complicit in security force undertakings than this suggests. De Klerk may indeed be uncertain as to just what mix of racial/ethnic privilege and capitalist socio-economic structure he can and will defend, as he seeks both to keep politically one jump ahead of the white right-wing, and simultaneously to contain and qualify the revolutionary potential implicit in an untrammeled expression of black opinion. It may also be that his decision to crack the prevailing mould of white South African politics and redefine the terrain of struggle was something of leap in the dark. Still, if the rules of the game are new and rather unclear, it remains a game De Klerk intends to win. It has not been his intention to hand over power to the ANC on the latter's own terms. Anything that weakens the ANC (and/or helps him cobble together the components of an alternative political network) might therefore be interpreted by him as pure gain.

In fact, this reading — one that finds De Klerk prepared, *in furtherance of his own purposes,* to grant both his security arm and Buthelezi's vigilantes room for manoeuvre — is also consistent with the pattern of tactics he has adopted in the post-February 1990 negotiations process. He has consistently dragged his heels on facilitating the resolution of such key pre-negotiations issues as the release of political prisoners and the indemnification of exiles. Indeed, he so finessed the ANC on such questions that the latter movement felt moved to concede a surprising amount of ground in order to keep the process alive. A case in point was its offering up, as part of last August's jointly agreed "Pretoria Minute," of a unilateral abandonment of armed struggle — much to the consternation of many of its followers. And in the jockeying for position regarding more substantive negotiations over establishment of a framework for political transition, De Klerk has shown no inclination to embrace ANC demands for election of a constituent assembly and formation of a new interim government to implement the next steps. Instead, he seeks merely to expand the ring of "consultation" amongst "concerned parties," signalling his preference for a constitution-making process that would see the existing white government in the chair throughout.

Weakening the ANC

Since its own December (1990) Consultative Conference the ANC has sought to rally in order to regain the initiative. Despite this, there can be little doubt that thus far De Klerk has managed to keep the ANC on the defensive, setting most of the terms for debate about change. Still, the question arises: will he prove, in the end, to have been too clever by half? February 1990 reflected a bold awareness on the part of the "new Nats" of the centrality of the ANC to any attempt to restabilize South African politics. In working to weaken the ANC De Klerk has been walking a tightrope, and in doing so he may both be overestimating its actual strength and underestimating the need for a coherent political center to the popular movement that can control the centrifugal pulls towards anarchy within South African society. De Klerk has bought time with respect to the ANC, to be sure, but in the meantime the situation has not stood still. The vacuum created has also provided room for a range of "morbid symptoms" to surface that beggar the imagination and begin to defy anyone's control: an internecine warfare within the black population that, whatever its origins, has taken on a grisly life and momentum of its own, and a rising level of sheer criminality that, given fresh fuel by the frustration of initial hopes for change, is reaching catastrophic proportions. "Like Gorbachev in a rapidly disintegrating Soviet Union, De Klerk too is running out of time. The one thing De Klerk requires most ... is an ANC sufficiently strong to broker with him a restabilization of South African politics. At one level De Klerk knows this. How ironic that he seems bound, simultaneously, to undermine the very ANC he needs so much."[26]

Is De Klerk overplaying his hand? How should we weight this factor alongside others in explaining the limits upon De Klerk's initiatives: his own political vulnerability within the white community (*vis-à-vis* the military, in particular), for example, and his own very divided feelings regarding the broad parameters of permissible reform? Moreover, O'Meara suggests an additional reason for a style of negotiation that seems, dangerously, to underestimate the need to legitimate the process of change in the eyes of the black population. How, after all, could De Klerk really believe it possible that the kind of white veto he seems still to contemplate be sold to this population by the ANC (even in the unlikely event that it should seek to do so), or by anyone else?

Here O'Meara sees De Klerk as victim of the old Afrikaner fixation (shades of the mad scientist Verwoerd and his Bantustan scheme!) with "social engineering." The new code word is "elite-pacting," the notion that "representative elites" can be brought together in negotiations to cut a more or less private deal above the heads of the populace — a fundamental misreading of black politics, needless to say, yet one reminiscent to O'Meara of the Afrikaners' similarly out-of-touch overestimation of the electoral chances of a deeply compromised Bishop Muzorewa *vis-à-vis* Robert Mugabe in Zimbabwe; or of the viability of the various alternatives to SWAPO that they attempted to cobble together in Namibia over the years. The result: one more ingredient of stalemate, a gap between the maximum De Klerk is prepared to grant and the minimum the popular movement can accept. Perhaps this is stalemate at a higher level than in the Botha period, but it is stalemate nonetheless, one that invites the escalation of violence, the further disintegration of the economy and even the slow melting away of majority white support for De Klerk.

Are cooler heads likely to prevail within De Klerk's own

camp? Certainly, the entrepreneurially-minded — both within and without the National Party — can hope to profit little from a slide into "barbarism" that disrupts the domestic economy and continues to discomfit overseas economic interests that might otherwise wish to engage with South Africa. Nor has the last word been heard from the popular movement. Can the ANC, in particular, hope to shift the terms of the current political equation? To this question we must turn in the second section of this chapter. But we should remember, in passing, one other underlying reality. To the "entrepreneurially-minded" in the white power structure additional questions occur; questions about change, about the ANC and the popular movement more broadly defined; questions that reach beyond the negotiations moment, however traumatic and all-absorbing that moment may sometimes appear to have become.

For there are other reasons to weaken the ANC and the popular movement than merely to force limits — whether advisedly or not — upon their constitutional demands. Even as the ultra Right seeks to side-track these latter demands, others — notably those linked most closely to capital, local and international — seek to shape the socio-economic structure of a post-negotiations, post-apartheid South Africa in line with their own interests and against too radical an outcome. This latter effort can also have a constitutional edge, of course: "hands off the economy" is one message inherent in any demand for a "white veto," and there is talk from De Klerk's team of the need for some even more explicit constitutional guarantee of "property rights"; perhaps this, too, is a good reason, from De Klerk's point of view, to "soften up" the ANC during the negotiation process. Generally, however, the tactics in this sphere are subtler, not without threat (the tacit threat of capital's withdrawal from South Africa if too socialist an undertaking were to surface, for example), but with seduction and attempted cooptation already equally pronounced ingredients of a longer-term counter-revolutionary project. Needless to say, this is also the terrain upon which attempts to define a strategy of "structural reform" must locate themselves, a subject that will provide the focus of the third section of this chapter.

II. EMPOWERING THE MOVEMENT

In an earlier essay I sketched the steps by which the ANC had re-emerged at the center of the resistance movement, broadly defined, by the mid-1980s.[27] This is a position the ANC has not relinquished to the present moment, despite the great problems that currently confront it. At one level, of course, the ANC did fail to give adequate punch and focus to the energy manifested in the nation-wide insurrection of 1984-86. The state crack-down, when it came, was a severe one, and manifestly staggered the popular movement. In the last stages of the insurrection there was much talk of moving beyond the proclaimed policy of rendering the townships "ungovernable" to an attempt to build new institutions of "people's power." But the scourging of the townships of such embryonic possibilities was amongst the clearest goals of the government's Emergency measures, as was evident in the particularly severe repression meted out to a setting like Alexandra where, under the leadership of Moses Mayekiso, this process had gone furthest. And the ANC's promise, at its 1985 Consultative Conference, that it would adapt its military tactics in such a way as to defend more effectively centres of township resistance from state repression proved impossible to deliver upon.

Not that the military dimension of the ANC's presence disappeared altogether, even if the attacks it sponsored remained much closer to the established format of "armed propaganda" than was hoped. Indeed, the symbolic value of "armed struggle" remained high. For example, a much publicized 1988 debate within the ANC about the relative merits of "hard' and "soft" targets had what, in any case, may have been its intended effect: it reminded the white populace that, without change, worse might be yet to come, even as it permitted the ANC to retain the moral high ground by ultimately rejecting, authoritatively, the soft target approach. More generally, Barrell is undoubtedly correct in concluding that "whatever the structural shortcomings of the internal underground and the post-1984 military campaign, MK [Umkhonto we Sizwe, the ANC's military wing] had played a key role in precipitating the conditions which increasingly forced a hostile power elite to contemplate alliance building with the ANC."[28] Nonetheless, the continuing strength of the apartheid state in sheer physical terms was by now perfectly manifest to the ANC/Umkhonto leadership, encouraging the latter increasingly to see armed action as merely one amongst a number of variables that could eventually undermine the apartheid regime.

Might not such variables have drawn that regime — early or late — to the negotiating table? Of course, the ANC's readiness to negotiate has been seen by some on the Left (the "Left" of both socialist and cultural nationalist provenances) to be the ANC's mark of Cain: for "negotiations" read "sell-out," in this lexicon. But surely much depends on the strength the relevant parties bring to the table in any such negotiations. It is true that some sense of its own weakness did move the ANC to step up the pace on this front. As stated, it could not hope to crush the apartheid regime militarily. Moreover, the Frontline states, battered beyond recognition by South Africa's destabilization tactics, were ever less available as rearguard bases for the ANC, while another of the movement's most important pillars of international support — the Soviet Union in particular, Eastern Europe more generally — was fading from the southern African scene.[29] Yet, simultaneously, the ANC drew confidence from the fact that the apartheid regime's repressive tactics had not worked. By 1989, such methods had manifestly failed either to solve South Africa's economic crisis or to buy it much greater credibility abroad. Moreover, the revival of mass resistance in 1988-89, in the very teeth of the Emergency, encouraged the ANC to think that, once again, "insurrection" might be brewing.

Let us recall the details. The unions were crucial, particularly COSATU, much the largest of the labour federations and the one aligned with the ANC and the UDF as part of the "Mass Democratic Movement" (as this grouping now came to be termed). The level of strike action was high, as was the level of mobilization on other fronts: the union-sponsored mass stay-away of June 6-8, 1988, against the draconian terms of the new Labour Relations Amendment Act saw some three million workers out in protest, and a related stay-away in September of the next year was also very successful. A highly visible "defiance campaign" in 1989 saw some individuals and organizations in effect "unbanning" themselves, while others carried out direct actions to desegregate beaches and hospitals or, as prisoners, mounted hunger strikes. In many of the townships consumer boycotts, rent strikes and a range of militant youth activity continued to sustain themselves, even leading to a number of dry runs for negotiations when white regional and municipal authorities found themselves compelled to treat over local issues with insistent civic associations. Perhaps these and other developments did not have quite the dimensions of the mass upsurge underway, more or less simultaneously, in Eastern Europe (a comparison much favoured by left critics of the ANC, despite the manifest difference in the regimes involved). But it had been the (unsuccessful) 1984-86 uprising that came closest, in South Africa, to that model. The 1988-89 revival of resistance seemed dramatic enough for the purposes of the moment.

If the ANC linked together this pattern of resistance, it was also experimenting with other kinds of linkages. For already, well before this most recent round of popular assertion, the ANC was being sounded out by actors traditionally closer to the other side of the political divide in South Africa. Its first meeting in Lusaka with a delegation of high-powered South African businessmen (including Gavin Relly, then Anglo-American chair) had taken place as early as 1985, and other related meetings were to follow — including the dramatic 1987 session with a range of Afrikaner intellectuals and opinion leaders in Dakar. Moreover, in 1985 the ANC also began, self-consciously, to codify for itself the tactics that should inform such talks, as well as the pre-conditions for any negotiations that might ultimately take place with the government.[30] Such pre-conditions were further formalized in 1987 and, by August 1989, actually adopted by the OAU, at ANC request, as the "Harare Declaration." The movement's demands remained militant throughout: they included the lifting of repression in South Africa and looked to negotiations that would transform South Africa into a "united, democratic and non-racial country." Perhaps, when first articulated, these (then still unlikely) demands were primarily for international consumption — to enable the ANC to keep the initiative and to suggest to backers, real and potential, just how "reasonable" it was prepared to be. But in part they were designed to keep a door open to the government for the moment when, the ANC projected, the hard reality of its situation would dawn upon it.

Even if its negotiations posture had been some time in the making, however, the ANC seemed more than a little stunned by the pace set by De Klerk once he seized upon the idea for his own purposes. True, even before Mandela's release the ANC had a sense of what was coming, predicting both that De Klerk "in all likelihood will seek to move with speed in order to catch us unprepared and off-balance ... so that the initiative remains in his hand;" and that, having done so, his "pace would logically move down several gears as it did over Namibia from 1980 — with the intention of wearing down its opposition with endless highly technical negotiations: haggling, in the expectation of a slow but steady demobilization and demoralization of the liberation movement's support base."[31] As discussed in Section I, this is precisely what has transpired in the period since that time. Yet the ANC, for all its suspicions concerning the traps that might await it on this new terrain, has so far seemed less able than De Klerk to master it effectively. The international support the ANC had concentrated so much of its energy on winning in the past has proven difficult to carry forward. The ANC's domestic failures have been even more telling; if revived popular militancy was a key to forcing De Klerk's hand in the first place, translating that militancy into bargaining power for the present round has not happened as readily as might have been anticipated.

The lure of "elite-pacting"

Has the ANC, in its own way, become trapped on the terrain of "elite-pacting?" Despite its suspicions, the ANC may have expected too much from De Klerk and concentrated too uncritically on "working things out" with him. After all, I have suggested that De Klerk, in outsmarting the ANC, might actually be outsmarting himself: the ANC had some reason to anticipate from De Klerk a much quicker and more straightforward political settlement than he has been prepared to offer. Perhaps, too, a misreading of motives has gone hand in glove with both a certain arrogance of approach and a closely related underestimation of De Klerk's guile. After all, Mandela had been engaged in some kind of negotiations with De Klerk from his prison quarters; what could stand in the way of his consummating those negotiations now that he was a free man? Add to this the frenzy of those overseas tours in the first months after Mandela's release that must have seemed to the ANC like a virtual coronation. How easy under such circumstances to overestimate international support even as, in retrospect, such support can be seen merely to have been peaking — and then receding, the Western media soon implying the apartheid problem to be solved and Western leaders inclining, increasingly, to give De Klerk the benefit of the doubt.[32]

Domestically, it may also be that the lure of "pacting" has drawn out some of the ANC's worst instincts. Although the ANC maintained its integrity and coherence in exile, there was some pull towards autocratic tendencies in its practice. These tendencies are familiar enough as part of a continent-wide pattern within African nationalism, but in the ANC they were reinforced both by Stalinist inclinations derived from close interaction over the years with the South African Communist Party, and by the seemingly inescapable fall-out from hierarchical patterns inherent in underground work and militarization of the struggle.[33] There seem also to have been some costs, alongside the considerable benefits that have accrued, to Nelson Mandela's reemergence to centrality within the movement and to the bringing to bear of his rather regal style on ANC politics. How else to explain the extreme defensiveness of much of the leadership concerning criticism of Winnie Mandela's often questionable practices, and its insensitivity in making her head, amidst much protest, of the ANC's Social Welfare department?³⁴ More importantly, such factors probably contributed to the ANC's apparent reluctance, throughout 1990, to unleash nationwide political mobilization and thus put the clout of popular protest behind its often desultory "pacting" with De Klerk.

A closely-related problem for the ANC has been its difficulties in consolidating a strong organizational presence inside South Africa. The return to South Africa of the exile leadership has been anything but smooth: a *Southscan* correspondent has identified as the ANC's "major difficulty" the "domination of its leadership and executive core by elderly former exiles still unfamiliar with the dynamics of street level politics and with its ability to provide hands-on leadership still unproven."³⁵ Moreover, the prior unity has fragmented, as returning exiles, bound to unity in Lusaka, seek their own diverse political bases at home, and as ideological differences, hitherto papered over, become more salient. There is also the question of folding into one organization both external and internal (principally UDF) structures and personnel. And how, indeed, to consolidate itself at the base. The UDF had not itself articulated the smoothest of links between central leadership and its constituent (township-based) parts. Moreover, such networks as did exist had been badly battered, at every level, by state repression. Throughout 1990 local resistances (rent-strikes, consumer boycotts, marches and the like) continued across a broad front, but so too did the ANC's "inability to harness local grievances [and] to give actions national coherence" and to ensure that "present localized campaigns, largely reactive and very concrete in their focus, ... be fused into national political action."³⁶

Finally, all such points of criticism must be qualified by awareness of context, specifically that of internal war inflicted on the ANC, as we have seen, both by the state and by actors linked to the state such as Buthelezi. Some critics have asked whether better methods of work might have enabled the ANC alliance to penetrate the Zulu hostels with an alternative politics. Others asked, even more controversially, whether something should have been done earlier to get Buthelezi on side. But his asking price, in terms of federal-cum-power-sharing constitutional gimmicks designed to safeguard his power base and that of his allies, would have been high were he finally to have bullied his way to the negotiating table in this manner. And who, in any case, could have anticipated Buthelezi's acting quite as ruthlessly as he has — or his obtaining quite so much official back-up for his misdeeds? Satisfaction that Inkathagate has now incontrovertibly exposed the latter should not blunt our awareness of the toll on the ANC of the operations mounted against it: the ruthless intimidation of its potential mass base and the diversion of the energies of its already overstretched cadres into the endless firefighting of local skirmishes engineered by Buthelezi and the security establishment. The impact of such vicious instigation and sabotage was one more critical reason why, for example, a 1990 goal of one million ANC members had not produced many more than 100,000 members at year's end (although that number was, in fact, to become far larger by mid-1991). As the *Weekly Mail's* Anton Harber headlined a September 1990 story: "The ANC begins to wobble as it nears the home straight." His lead? "Now that it has come out of the shadows, the new demythologized ANC seems to be a very troubled organization."[37]

One could as easily overstate this case as understate it, however; as Harber himself concluded in the article referred to above, "if there is cause for optimism in the ANC ... it is that there is an extremely high level of internal debate and self-criticism over these issues" — just the kind of "internal debate and self-criticism" that, only a few months later, was to surface usefully at the ANC's Consultative Conference of December 1990. Nor do all the democratic pressures felt by the ANC play themselves out within the organization itself. After all, much of the ANC's present strength has sprung from its ability to cut against some its own more autocratic temptations and risk development of a kind of creative tension between itself and a wide range of popular assertions inside South Africa. Most notable in this respect has been the interaction between the liberation movement and South Africa's vibrant and autonomous non-racial trade unions. Such "creative tension" remains in play and it is particularly interesting to note the terms in which it has come to be comprehended in South Africa, terms that seek, quite self-consciously, to illuminate the kind of political work necessary to keep this "tension" as alive and creative as possible.

In an earlier essay[38] I sought to explore this tension by drawing on Ernesto Laclau's early work and suggested the ways in which, in the South African context, "popular democratic" and "proletarian" demands might "reinforce and push each other forward." This line of argument has been taken to imply the assumption of some kind of "objective process" being at work to align nationalist/populist and working class/socialist assertions quite unproblematically ("a Second International version of Marxism - proved bankrupt since 1914," is the way Alex Callinicos charitably phrases his criticism of me in this respect[39]). But the South African activists who have come actually to *live* this problematic fully realize that only class struggle can eventually produce an alignment in these terms.

The claims of "civil society"

Class struggle — and democratic struggle. For alongside an awareness of the class provenance of diverse projects in South Africa, there is also a great deal of talk within the movement, broadly defined, about the claims of (the term is used quite specifically) "civil society." Amongst the most articulate advocates of this way of thinking has been Moses Mayekiso, General Secretary of the radical National Union of Metalworkers, South Africa (NUMSA), and President of the Alexandra Civic Association. While also a member of both the ANC and the SACP, Mayekiso has insisted that solutions to South Africa's problems are not to be found exclusively in the realm of political parties. In a typical interview[40] he argued that "civil society" — comprising a whole range of autonomous grass-roots organizations such as trade unions, township-based civic associations and rural village committees, women and youth organizations — must be built up, recruited for across party lines, and *empowered* in its own right. Mayekiso is already an articulate spokesperson for just such a role for the trade union movement. Not surprisingly, he has now become a major player in the attempt to replace the UDF, as it formally dissolves itself (in early 1991) into the ANC, with an independent organization of civic associations. As *Front File* accurately summarizes the mood: "To ensure the existence of a 'democratic culture' in a post-apartheid South Africa many grassroots activists, trade union leaders and civic leaders want a new social movement to be created particularly to place the aspirations of remote, disadvantaged communities at the center of the political debate."[41] The newly-minted CAST (Civic Associations of the Southern Transvaal) is seen, quite specifically, as a prototype for the kind of national organization that could press such township demands militantly even upon some future ANC government.

As is well-known, a discourse premissed on the claims of "civil society" is a two-edged sword, much of its original historical thrust as a concept reflecting a liberal desire to keep the hands of the state off the marketplace. This is not the manner in which someone like Mayekiso uses the term. There is a genuinely radical charge to his model, one that acknowledges the invaluable leadership-cum-coordinative role to be played by the best kind of political party, but sees autonomous popular organizations as necessary to "push any political party that may find itself in power ... for changes beneficial to the masses." "Because of the nature of the broad alliance of social forces that the ANC has come to represent," Mayekiso further argues, "there may well be limits beyond which the party cannot go" in terms of socialist policy — unless, that is, it is driven forward by the insistent voices of a well-organized civil society. Similarly, Albie Sachs, who, as a major architect of ANC constitutional thinking, has articulated eloquently the case for placing the protection of human rights front and center in the movement's project, has been equally firm about the need to extend the language of rights to encompass, centrally, the most egalitarian of demands upon the economy.[42]

We will return to these latter points. Yet one would underestimate at one's peril the value of nurturing the seeds of a democratic culture *per se* in South Africa. For those seeds, apparent, from an early date, in the practices of many of the non-racial trade unions as well as elsewhere in the progressive movement, have been counter-balanced by other, more negative trends within that very movement (as within South African society more generally). These are trends at least as dangerous as any autocratic bent the ANC may manifest from time to time. For too often the ethos of struggle and of "ungovernability" has combined with the brutal imperatives that play upon lives lived under apartheid to throw up countercultures of political intolerance. Particularly among the youth of the townships one can find the cruelest of practices against presumed enemies of progressive change. Moreover, the norms of genuinely democratic practice have too often been abused even in the in-fighting between fellow progressive organizations and political parties. In short, creation of an ethos respectful of "civil society" and "democratic rights" would be no small accomplishment in a new, post-apartheid South Africa — even in advance of their implicating a deeply democratic (read: socialist) questioning of the socio-economic inequalities that haunt the country.

Since the bearers of such democratic purposes still circle most articulately and effectively around the ANC, it remains correct to see the ANC-centered movement (in effect, the erstwhile "Mass Democratic Movement") as the core of resistance, in spite of whatever more questionable attributes may also mark it. It is self-evidently more positive than any new coalition of partners — centrist whites, black township councillors and homeland notables (including Buthelezi) — that De Klerk seems, on occasion, to have in mind; and more positive than anything on offer from that alternative claimant to liberation movement status, the Pan-Africanist Congress, still without great popular support but waiting in the wings for the ANC to stumble. Cultural-nationalist — its crypto-racism sometimes masquerading as a kind of leftism (around maximalist, but largely rhetorical, "land claims," for example) — the PAC seems intent on becoming as scarred on home ground by opportunism and internecine struggle has it has been over the long years of exile. Meanwhile other claimants to attention, such as the left-Black Consciousness position of Azapo or the militant Trotskyism of the Workers Organization for Socialist Action (Wosa), which are much more admirable than the PAC, remain far from the mainstream of movement politics. As long as that mainstream has vitality enough to promise the bringing of significant transformation to South Africa these latter must remain relatively minor players.[43]

Militancy and the Negotiating Process

We will return to an evaluation of the long-run nature of this promise. The more immediate question remains whether this "ANC mainstream" has vitality enough even to deliver on negotiations. We have seen that unleashing into the negotiations process the energy of its mass base has proved difficult for it. And some of the major constituent parts of the movement the ANC ostensibly heads have also felt themselves disenfranchised by ANC tactics. Thus a COSATU conference in November, 1990, invoked specifically the precedents of Zimbabwe and Namibia where, it was argued, workers had been "left out" of constitutional negotiations, and expressed concern about COSATU's own limited measure of influence upon the South African transition process.[44] In a similar vein, the ANC's closest ally, the SACP, felt compelled to editorialize (in its journal, *Umsebenzi*) that "if the broad popular masses become spectators in the negotiating process then our negotiating hand is drastically weakened...the revolutionary alliance has not found a formula for linking mass struggle with the main, potential cutting edge of transformation ... the negotiating process." Fortunately, the previously-mentioned ANC Consultative Conference in December did provide some antidote to this, suggesting an on-going demand for empowerment from the base of great potential significance.

In the immediate context of the conference this meant a very sharp critique from the base of the whole negotiations strategy and of the ANC's failure to facilitate popular self-defence in the townships. The refreshing irreverence of delegates clearly discomfited Mandela (who polls were soon to show to be running behind the ANC in popularity in any case), but the political vitality displayed had great resonance. It gave some promise, certainly, of a vibrant "National Conference" — scheduled to follow in July. 1991 —

when fresh elections for office-holders could be expected to alter the composition of the ANC leadership and bring to the fore a new generation of leaders, many with on-the-ground UDF and trade union backgrounds. As we will see, this would prove, at least in part, to be the case. More immediately, the December meeting itself reinforced attempts to reorganize and ventilate the movement, while also giving fresh urgency to plans both to generate volunteer "township defence forces" and to expand the range of "mass action."[45] The intention: to once more focus De Klerk's attention on the legitimate demands and real power of the popular movement.

Indeed, in the immediate aftermath of the December conference, it was felt De Klerk might have become far more flexible, *Southscan* arguing (prematurely, as things turned out) that "the past weeks have seen a major shift in government thinking. The key impetus for this was the ANC's 16 December conference. Despite a year of talks with the ANC, De Klerk and his Cabinet were entirely unprepared for both the militancy and the degree of influence exercised by rank-and-file delegates."[46] Would fear of chaos and/or fear of further radicalization of popular-movement demands and strategies[47] finally convince De Klerk to accept the full de-racializing logic of the most liberal of (pro-capitalist) positions? And would/could the ANC leadership be more assertive in pressing its demands upon him?

To some degree, in the first months of 1991, the ANC did become more militant. An ultimatum to De Klerk (no longer presented as "a man of integrity" by Mandela) that it would break off negotiations and resume armed struggle unless he ceased foot-dragging on the question of prisoners and exiles brought some movement from the state president on this issue. A related April ultimatum calling for more effective government action to curb violence — including a demand for dismissal of Defense Minister Malan and Law and Order Minister Adriaan Vlok — stirred things up some more; "ANC's Shock Therapy," *Front File* called it.[48] Predictably, a move by an (understandably sceptical) ANC to offer some kind of olive branch to Buthelezi was unsuccessful. Its attempt to strengthen its bargaining position by reaching out to other forces of more genuine opposition, notably the PAC and Azapo, in proposing a broad front around the minimum condition of insistence upon election of a constituent assembly, has been rather more promising.

Yet by May it was still not clear that any of this was working. De Klerk was continuing to drag his feet (even attempting at one point to invoke legalistic quibbles to deny the ANC the right to mobilize mass action), and the ANC was not yet able to wield its continuing majority support — so the polls say — with full effect. One suspects "negotiations" over a new constitution will come eventually, but with their form and content deeply scarred by what is now transpiring. Thus some critics began to fear that the ANC negotiating team might yet, in desperate response to continuing government intransigence, make significant concessions on questions of process (including qualifying its demands for an interim government and a constituent assembly and accepting something closer to De Klerk's preferred non-elected, multi-party format). In the event, delegates to the ANC's July conference (discussed in more detail below) were to insist militantly that no significant concessions along these lines be made. But — Catch 22 — would this, in turn, merely further widen the chasm between the ANC and the white government? Already, in May, when the ANC — well in advance of its July congress — actually did break off negotiations (however temporarily) and begin to take to the streets again, it was not clear whether the upshot would be to focus, finally, De Klerk's attention on the urgency of the moment or merely to feed further a downward spiral towards "barbarism."

For the moment, certainly, the torment of the townships continues.[49] And yet the fall-out from Inkathagate — putting the government on the defensive, gravely damaging Buthelezi and vindicating the allegations of the ANC before a wider audience — must also have an effect. In its wake, the ANC would now seem to be in a far stronger position to press its demands (especially those linked to the issues of an interim government and constituent assembly) upon a discredited government. The movement has thus been given the opportunity to regain the initiative in South Africa. Of course, this very circumstance also puts the ANC to a new test: it further calls into question any "elite-pacting" strategy towards which the ANC leadership may have been tempted, while simultaneously challenging the movement to demonstrate its popularly-based *bona fides* ever more tellingly. Revived international outrage at De Klerk's machinations may play some role in easing the transition in South Africa. Much more depends on the ability of the ANC to now so mobilize and give focus to mass political activity inside South Africa as to force De Klerk — or any successor to him — to move further.

III. REFORMISM, REVOLUTION, STRUCTURAL REFORM

At present all long-term bets are off pending the outcome of the negotiations moment. Thus, even some who have resisted most vigorously the hoary ANC argument for "a two-stage revolution" (political democracy/national liberation first, socio-economic transformation second) seem inclined, momentarily, to bracket off tough questions about democratizing the economy in order to support the ANC successfully through such negotiations.[50] Their premise: with a Lebanization of South Africa the minimally-ordered terrain on which a struggle for socialism might actually be mounted would disappear. Yet — the paradox created by such simultaneity was noted at the outset of this chapter — the fact remains that *South Africans are already living the post-apartheid moment.*

This is true, self-evidently, of such constitutional negotiations as may now emerge: any rights, vetoes, privileges, inscribed into the constitution will shape the range of policy-making possibilities in the next round in South Africa. But — to now take up a crucial issue anticipated earlier — the parameters of such possibilities will be set, in even more crucial ways, by subtler processes. Indeed, centers of established socio-economic power are already working overtime to put their own stamp on the next round. If the popular movement has such difficulties in garnering, from the existing state, a democratic outcome in the political sphere, how likely is it to face down the forces of capital, together with such remnants of that state as survive, in winning a democratic-cum-socialist outcome in the socio-economic sphere? More specifically, how likely is an *ANC-centred movement* to deliver such an outcome; how likely is it to be, in the terms developed earlier in this chapter, the key "bearer" of any "project of structural reform" that may emerge?

A neo-liberal agenda

But first: how do the holders of power seek to monopolize the agenda regarding post-apartheid South Africa? As we have seen, the diverse pressures that weigh upon him have forced from De Klerk a dangerously willful approach to constitution-making. In many ways, his approach to the *following* round has been more straightforward, and on this front he has also been much more of a "team player" alongside the representatives of the business community. Not surprisingly, private enterprise is the name of the game — accompanied by an important ideological talisman, the much repeated phrase, "growth with redistribution." As noted earlier, few in circles of political/economic power in South Africa would now speak out against some redressing of the deep-seated socio-economic inequalities (socio-economic inequalities that overlap racial inequalities, needless to say) existing in South Africa. However, the goal of capital is to define these inequalities as a welfare problem (redistribution), rather than a production problem. Growth must be left to the market-place, and to the owners of the means of production.

Not that, even then, the latter are entirely certain what a successful growth path might look like. The economic roots of South Africa's crisis run very deep indeed, with some division within government/business circles about the relative merits of an "inward-industrialization" as against an "export-oriented" growth strategy. Gelb argues that the latter emphasis is carrying the day, a ruling-class strategy emerging that "focusses on restructuring and regenerating the manufacturing sector in particular by using 'neo-liberal' (market-based) policies to alter cost structures and restore profitability, and to expand markets for manufactures, especially through exports. The emphasis is on beneficiation of minerals and other commodities currently exported in a semi-processed form, together with other intermediate manufactures."[51] We will return to a discussion of the merits of any such choice. What bears emphasizing here is that, in ruling circles, the "choice" of strategy is to be defined as being (quite literally) capital's business.

In this "neo-liberal" scenario the state will continue to bail out of the production sphere as rapidly as possible (via privatization), while further freeing the market-place of unwelcome intrusions (the repeal of the racially-defined Land Act is a case in point, giving the appearance of a progressive reform without involving any real attempt to actively redress historical injustices in that sphere). Some efforts both to free space for and to help finance African entrepreneurs are afoot, while various sectorally-defined "negotiations-frameworks" (additional to the national-political one) are also being elaborated with an eye to coopting other key actors. Thus both state and capital must hope that the link forged between the employer body, the South African Consultative Committee on Labour Affairs (SACCOLA), and the trade unions (COSATU and its fellow union NACTU) in working out a joint position on amendments to the proposed Labour Relations Act and the subsequent incorporation of COSATU into the tri-partite National Manpower Commission (NMC) signal the possible corralling of the trade unions within a controllable format of benign corporatism.

And then there is "redistribution" itself. Allocations for black health and education have indeed risen in recent budgets and much has also been made of the state-funded Independent Development Trust (the "Steyn Fund"). Yet the latter — in essence a public complement to private sector efforts (especially those of the Urban Foundation) to facilitate private home ownership — seems primarily designed to ease the upward mobility of a better-off stratum of black South Africans rather than to effect any more profound restructuring; it thus lends further credence to Gelb's conclusion that the emergent neo-liberal project will merely "reinforce and extend a dualistic structure of society," albeit with some greater measure of de-racialization of that structure. Moreover, the latest budget (of March 20, 1991) shows how limited redistributive efforts within the current structure really are. Defense expenditure remains by far the largest item, while company taxes have been lowered in favour of a new, broad-gauged VAT — thereby "shifting," in COSATU's telling phrase, "the tax burden from big business on to the shoulder of workers and ordinary people."

Such "redistribution" is pretty small beer, then. Most in the ANC are well aware of this — and of the related fact that an economy left largely to its own devices will merely reproduce, "spontaneously," a great deal of racial inequality. Yet many feel hemmed in by the power of capital, both global and local. As business now ceaselessly informs South Africans, capital is immensely mobile — Anglo-American is already active in moving some of its stake "offshore", for example — as are many of the whites whose skills help steer the system. Moreover, denizens of the World Bank and IMF are on the scene, actively reminding everyone concerned (including, quite directly, the ANC) both of the vulnerability of the South African economy in international financial circles and of the need for "sound" policies.[52] Look what happened when Mozambique tried to move towards socialism too quickly and too heedlessly: the socialist effort in Mozambique was both "premature and wrong," says Joe Slovo of the ANC/SACP. True, in Zimbabwe, where the leadership claimed to have profited from Mozambique's mistakes, things merely went too slowly to permit any very significant post-liberation alteration of the structure of colonial capitalism. "But can we really afford to rock the boat?" some nationalists ask. Shouldn't circumspection be the order of the day?

South Africa is different from Zimbabwe, of course, and even more so from Mozambique; there is a developed working-class and many other articulate bearers of grievances that spring from extreme socio-economic inequalities. Yet, as is well known, the

ANC does not speak only for such voices. It is a pan-class body, many of whose leaders pride themselves not only on being open to dialogue with big business but also on welcoming aboard its project aspirant black entrepreneurs. Nor can there be any doubt that the narrowly nationalist and petty-bourgeois instincts of many of the ANC's own long-serving cadres will now be reinforced by the rush to join the organization of others with similar instincts and aspirations. True, Mandela made a firm bow in the direction of the ANC's left-of-center vocation immediately upon his release from prison, his unrepentant insistence upon the priority of "nationalization" striking a particularly blunt note in those early days. But this was soon to be substantially qualified, not least by Mandela himself ("I must stress that the entire economy, insofar as we are concerned will remain intact [and] will continue to be based on free enterprise"[53]) — even if resistance to any further privatization has remained a prominent feature of ANC pronouncements. In part, perhaps, this can be interpreted as a short-term tactical withdrawal from more advanced positions. But it is easy to believe that there are prominent actors within the ANC prepared to buy the most modest version of the "growth with redistribution" line.

Rethinking the mixed economy

But if this is one pull upon the ANC, it must be acknowledged that there are plenty of counter-pulls and a diversity of energies within the organization; if nothing else, the Congress tradition is a protean one. For the ANC is articulating, even now, other futures than those just mentioned. True, the main emphasis found on the left of the ANC-centred movement regarding such questions — an emphasis premissed on the centrality, for the foreseeable future, of a "mixed economy" — will make many uneasy. Does this emphasis merely spring, as a vaguely "reformist" perspective, from a left practice that has opportunistically tailed "nationalist-populism" all these years and that now shows its true social-democratic colours? Some such judgement is the obvious sub-text of Alex Callinicos' sardonic dismissal of an earlier comment by Joe Slovo (a comment that heralded, it might be argued, the now predominant left perspective on socialist transition in South Africa): "It is only the indigenous representative of the disastrous Pol Pot philosophy who can project a pole-vault into socialism and communism the day after the overthrow of white rule."[54]

And there *are* grounds for suspicion of such a sentiment coming from such a source: historically the ANC/SACP's two-stage theory has, at its most crass, systematically understated the extent to which active and self-conscious working-class pressure upon capital would need to be a necessary complement to "popular-class" pressure upon the racist state in wringing significant concessions from the ruling bloc. A further smothering of militancy and class struggle — in the name of "economic common-sense" and the safeguarding of "national priorities," for example — could very well spring from such quarters in the next round. Yet this is not inevitable; as I have argued previously there has, all along, been more vitality to left initiatives within the ANC-centered movement than many ANC/SACP theoretical formulations have helped to illuminate.55 Moreover, a reading of the comparative experience of prior socialist experiments (within the region and beyond) and the hard facts of the South African situation (as defined both domestically and with reference to the international economy) suggest the warnings of Slovo and others regarding the need for extreme subtlety in seeking to democratize the South African economy to be fundamentally correct. It is fortunate, then, that somewhere between the potent pull of "reformism" and the abstract irrelevance of calls for "revolution," there are emerging in South Africa elements of a project of "structural reform" that might yet prove appropriate to the exigencies of the post-apartheid moment.

We return by this route to the "mixed economy." As the ANC-linked British economist Lawrence Harris has put the point: "A mixed economy is not necessarily socialist, but may have either a socialist or a capitalist orientation depending on the context and how it is implemented."56 And indeed, within the ANC, there are signs that the concept is beginning to be used in a promisingly expansive sense, even if this pre-planning process is still not very far advanced: "The resources which have to be generated to correct the inherited imbalances and deprivations of the majority demand, in the first place, a necessary degree of state control (involving selective forms of ownership and participation) over strategic sectors of the economy. In the second place, the necessary coexistence of a private and social sector — the balance between the 'market' and the 'plan' — must accord pride of place to the latter."57

Like Harris, other ANC economists — Max Sisulu, Tito Mboweni and Ketso Gordhan58 — have begun to draft plans stressing the extent to which more aggressive and equitable taxation policies and measures like "prescribed asset requirements" and other controls over the financial system can be used to mobilize and steer surpluses. Without abandoning it altogether as a tactic, they seek to rethink the rhetoric of "nationalization" and conceive additional possible means of controlling capital: "We could, for example, legislate that representatives of the community and workers be on the boards of all the companies, [although] this needs to be debated so that we can find other forms of ownership that lie between state and totally privately-owned enterprises." And they stress the possibility of breaking up huge (and internally self-financing) conglomerates, the better both "to realize economies of scale" and to make their decisions more subject to influence by state financial and other levers. Meanwhile, a discussion paper from the ANC Land Commission discusses a range of possible modes of intervention in the rural economy that goes far beyond anything the present government's market-limited reform of the land system could even begin to contemplate. In short, on this and other fronts, attempts to "think the unthinkable" are clearly underway.

This is especially evident when these macro-economic considerations are given the spin provided by the second conceptual point of reference (in addition to "the mixed economy") currently in extensive circulation on the South African left: "growth *through* redistribution." As Manfred Bienefeld has recently observed,[59] this catch-phrase may be misleading. For the most articulate proponents of this perspective are not merely advocating — as the phrase might suggest — a redistribution of income to the less well off in order to create a different (more "basic needs" driven) pattern of demand for capitalists to respond to. Well beyond this threshold, and against the welfarist free-marketeers of the "growth with redistribution" school, they too have begun to advocate a mode of aggressive intervention in the production process that would actually guide/force the private sector into a new pattern of investment and production. In doing so, they link a concern to redress socio-economic inequalities to the dour fact that South African capitalism does not work very well even in its own terms; that it has not found, in Gelb's formulation cited earlier, a post-Fordist growth path that would permit significant accumulation to recommence. Bienefeld suggests the phrase "growth through direction of production" to be more descriptive of the kind of activist agenda that Gelb and others advocate in order to stimulate growth on new terms.

COSATU and working-class empowerment

Such preoccupations were at their most visible at an important ANC-COSATU meeting held to discuss economic futures in Harare in mid-1990.[60] In summarizing the thrust of that meeting's formal "recommendations," Gelb (until recently co-ordinator of the COSATU-linked "Economic Trends Group") contrasted the establishment view, "trapped within a static framework offering only a choice of the appropriate point in a trade-off between growth and redistribution," with the ANC/COSATU view that "is both oriented towards dynamic development and greater equality." In spelling out this latter position, Gelb agrees that the core issue is not so much the redistribution of consumption as "the redistribution of investment. On the one hand, the level of investment in productive activity would have to be substantially increased, especially in drawing funds out of the financial markets. At the same time, the emphasis in the composition of productive investment would need to be shifted away from the current situation towards those industries and sectors targeted for accumulation as part of the overall accumulation strategy." While within this model state intervention would be selective, where undertaken it would have to be "pervasive, that is, far-reaching in shaping the activities of economic agents, as opposed to the neo-liberal reliance on autonomous responses." The projected result: an investment pattern tilted towards such new motors of growth as labour-intensive/employment-producing light industries, township housing, services and infrastructure.

There is much more to be done here, of course. Many details remain hazy; debate continues regarding the role of the "informal sector," or of an exports strategy, or of other crucial considerations within such a model; an adequate picture of the limitations likely to be imposed upon South Africa by the workings of the international economy is very far from having been elaborated. What bears affirming, however, is that some of the premisses of an approach that slowly and "realistically," *but surely and self-consciously,* tilts the balance towards an imposition of collective social purpose upon the economy are beginning to take shape within the popular movement in South Africa. Equally important is a pervasive sense that the essential guarantor must be a populace which is increasingly empowering itself to sustain the momentum of such a process. In this regard it is important to note the extent to which, at Harare and elsewhere, the "growth through direction of production" perspective has sprung from the trade-union movement, in interaction with but not in subordination to the ANC. In fact, much the strongest statements about the necessary centrality of socialist preoccupations in a post-apartheid South Africa have continued to come in recent years from these trade unions. "Socialism remains the economic order representing freedom for workers," while "nationalization remains high on the COSATU agenda," asserts that union's vice-president Chris Dlamini.[61] And NUMSA's Bernie Fanaroff warns against "economism — a preoccupation with wages rather than the economic system as a whole," while urging his union "to lay foundations for the revamping of the economy on socialist lines."[62]

This is not to suggest that, even within COSATU, there is unanimity about how working-class advance might best be achieved; some measure of the "workerist" vs. "populist" division over the terms of engagement with the broader popular movement remains.[63] At the "workerist" end of the spectrum cluster both those with narrowly corporatist and those with more broadly leftist/Trotskyist suspicions of the ANC, while at the populist end are some who might still prefer merely to tail the political movement. On this spectrum, however, it is the center position that seems both more potent and more promising. For example, this center anchors a desire, now even more widely shared than in the recent past, for a healthy degree of trade union autonomy from even the most sympathetic of political parties — with most unions also pressing the campaign to adopt a "Workers' Charter," touching on crucial working class interests, to which any post-apartheid government could be held to account. It is in some such spirit that this grouping continues to acknowledge the ANC's political centrality. "We need to be independent but we also need to be interdependent," says COSATU's Sydney Mafumedi.[64] It is also in this spirit that it continues to press its left concerns upon the ANC: in the words of NUMSA's Alec Erwin, "for all its weaknesses the ANC has the most developed economic policy of all parties."

Note, moreover, the way in which the option for sustaining such a "revolutionary alliance" in the post-apartheid period is further conceptualized. For the NUMSA radicals, for example, the struggle for a democratic economy does require a strong state able to plan and intervene decisively. At the same time, they emphasize, such a struggle can never be resolved merely by some once-for-all "seizure of power." Rather, it will have to be realized as the expression of a process of unfolding empowerment emanating from the base. As Erwin himself put the point in reflecting on the Harare Recommendations, "[These] recommendations are no blueprint for socialism. They constitute a framework for reconstruction and transition. They will be a transition to socialism if the working class can achieve this by its own organizational strength." He continued: "Do organized workers develop programmatic positions [on the role of the state, planning and mass organizations], or do they stand back waiting for state power to move them to socialism?" The choice, he asserts, depends on one's view about the nature of the struggle for socialism. "Within COSATU there has always been a majority viewpoint that believes that contesting issues in the present and doing it in a way that builds worker power and democratic processes within worker organization is to carry the struggle for socialism forward and not to abandon it."[65]

How, in short, is content to be given to a sentiment most clearly expressed in a recent COSATU document prepared for the union's first economic policy conference (May, 1991): "We can no longer sit back and watch the capitalists and the state make a mess of the economy. Nor can we simply fight for political change and hope that when it comes our economic problems will be solved."[66] One answer, currently much canvassed within COSATU, is to reach what is termed a "reconstruction accord" with the ANC. Such an accord would certainly enhance the likelihood of tying the ANC to COSATU's own "perspectives on how to achieve economic growth and redistribution in a democratic South Africa"[67] — and enhance, too, the likelihood of a future ANC government imposing such perspectives, from above, on capital. Moreover, the very process of generating the terms of such an accord would help guide COSATU members to bring pressure to bear on capital *from below* — by introducing issues crucially related to economic reconstruction into their various arenas of collective bargaining, at national, industry-wide, and company/plant levels.

Take, for example, the arena of national bargaining. It is just such a perspective that frames COSATU's own view of its controversial interface — referred to earlier — with SACCOLA and with the state, most recently through tripartite participation on the National Manpower Commission.[68] Can such sectoral "negotiations" — an instrument of potential cooptation when conceived by South African business (and by the World Bank/IMF South Africa team) in terms of their favoured outcome, a new "social contract" — be turned inside out and take the imprint, instead, of ever-expanding working class empowerment? There is an echo here of the famous "registration debate" of the late 1970s: should unions, it was then asked, refuse to "legalize" themselves within the framework of the state's new industrial relations legislation (thereby avoiding the attendant risk of cooptation and/or government control), or instead "register" and use the newly claimed legal terrain as room for manoeuvre to advance working-class interests ever more assertively?

The latter route was chosen, with benefits now seen to have outweighed any costs incurred, and much the same calculation is being made in the present situation. Already COSATU is pushing the boundaries of the NMC, insisting that "it needs to be a body that helps restructure the economy so that it serves the needs of all the people." It has been argued along similar lines that, indeed, advances might be made here on various "issues arising out of a 'reconstruction accord' such as investment priorities for public and private sector investment; investment codes for foreign investment; the role of investment funds in investment; labour market issues such as a framework for training, minimum wages, etc.; international trade controls and incentives; and worker rights."[69] Moreover, in its first major confrontation within the NMC framework, COSATU pugnaciously forced the government to back down on its attempted exclusion of farmworkers from the Basic Conditions of Employment Act — and it now seeks to do the same for domestic workers.

In this view, the NMC is to be considered as being, in effect, one more front for institutionalizing a situation of "dual power," with cooptation a risk but the on-going struggle between classes the presumptive reality, both now and in the future. There are other examples of such trends. Thus, the long-time movement-related organization, the National Education Crisis Committee (NECC), has begun to take some role alongside the government in arbitrating curriculum development, and it will no doubt play an even more active role in future in seeking to transform South Africa's grotesquely misshapen educational system. Various civic associations — increasingly reasserting their autonomous existence, as we have seen — are also locked in on-going negotiations with established (white) urban authorities in pursuit of solutions to the problems of township life that reflect a more inclusive and equitable form of urban planning. How should we assess such manifestations of popular struggle — within and without the ANC, within and without state-structured processes? And what of the possible involvement of less readily heard-from constituencies — squatters (in all those urban slums that, in South Africa, are expanding explosively outside the boundaries of the formal townships), rural dwellers, farmworkers and small-holders alike, in their vast numbers — that have been much slower to develop organizational forms of self-expression?[70] In so many impressive ways, empowerment is the language of present-day South Africa; we scarcely need reminding, simultaneously, that the fight to realize it, both within and without the constitutional negotiations process, has only just begun.

The struggle for women's rights

Much the same things could be said of the struggle for post-apartheid advance on the gender front, although here, too, some important advances are already being made. It is true, historically-speaking, that the ANC Women's League can easily be accused of having too readily subordinated the fight for women's rights *per se* to the presumed imperatives of the nationalist struggle. More recently, however, women within the ANC itself have begun to challenge such priorities and have pressed for far more advanced positions.[71] One result has been release of a far-reaching statement on the "Emancipation of Women in South Africa" by the ANC's National Executive Committee (May 1990): "The experience of other societies has shown that the emancipation of women is not a by-product of a struggle for democracy. It has to be addressed in its own right within our organization, the mass democratic movement and in society as a whole...The prevalence of patriarchal attitudes in South African society permeates our own organizations, especially at decision-making levels, and the lack of a strong mass women's organization has been to the detriment of our struggle." However, there is also awareness amongst activist women as to how much more needs to be done to ensure that this kind of sensibility determines the day-to-day practices of the movement.[72] Nor, they argue, has the ANC yet found the most effective voice in which to speak to South African women more generally (with even Inkatha appearing sometimes to have more success in this regard, albeit from a quite reactionary point of approach).

The views of ANC women are not themselves uniform, however; the recently elected president of the organization, Gertrude Shope, being considered quite conservative on many relevant issues, for example. Nonetheless, a tough fight around gender seems likely to continue to spark the organization. Thus, the Women's League's recent Kimberley national conference demanded "that at least 30 per cent of all positions in ANC structures and departments be held by women — and that women must participate in the negotiating teams and help to draw up the new constitution."[73] Sexual harrassment, gender-biased education, and the plight of domestic workers were amongst the numerous other issues surfacing at the conference. Meanwhile, there are also some who question how exclusively the struggle for women's rights should be confined to the ANC. (Not that such assertions are absent in other arenas — the trade unions being a case in point.) But — paralleling the debates of union and civics' activists in this respect — the question arises whether organizing efforts by women outside the realm of direct political party linkage is not also necessary. And some steps towards a new, more inclusive "National Alliance" of women beyond the ANC Women's League have, indeed, been taken.

That said, the struggle for women's rights does seem to find much of its strongest resonance, at least for the moment, inside the ANC. As noted, other struggles for progressive outcomes (those of the unions and civics, in particular) take place more in that grey area where the most progressive expressions of "civil society" on the one hand and the political movement-cum-party on the other overlap. It is here that a positive and progressive dialectic between the two terms of this equation could be joined: a progressive civil society to drive the party (the ANC?) forward; a responsive party to give focus and effect to the most positive urgings of that civil society — while also reminding the latter of the need to take some responsibility for working-out the difficult trade-offs between competing demands. Of course, such a dialectic cannot — must not — be frozen institutionally; the tension between its two terms must *constantly remain in the process of being struggled over and resolved politically* if progressive outcomes are to emerge. Nonetheless, positively joined around an ever-deepening programme of structural reform, it is just such a dialectical process that could, slowly but surely, deliver a popular empowerment of truly hegemonic proportions.[74]

The SACP and the question of vanguardism

Such a model will not be a welcome one to many "vanguard-party" purists: it invokes a kind of "left pluralism" that is just too fluid, too uncontrolled, *too risky*.[75] And some of the dangers such vanguardists see are real enough. For example, does the model not understate the difficulty of sustaining a political centre sufficiently strong to meet the kind of brutal challenges from class enemies and imperialist quarters that any cumulatively successful left-hegemonic project is likely to encounter?[76] Yet its very openness to uncertainty is, in other ways, the great strength of a political perspective so defined. Moreover, as one of the alternative logics of development that are actually competing against one another within the ANC-centred movement, it is both *important* (it is a logic of development that remains pregnant with positive possibilities) and *potent* (it is a logic that the undertakings of the most relevant actors in South Africa serve to advance).

There is even the distinct possibility that it is eminently *advisable*, not as some second-best route to transformation (in the absence of "revolution"), but as much the most effective way forward. Recall Lenin's statement (in "On Cooperation") about the difficulties of "implanting socialism in an insufficiently cultured country," and the consequent need for "educational work," for a "cultural revolution." Compare, in this respect, South Africa's black population, so long the victims of Bantu education and neglect. "Empowerment" is not only about developing the political will to confront centres of exploitative power (a will that is not in short supply in much of South Africa), but also about manifesting the technical capability to turn newly-won power into effective policy, and this will present a continuing challenge to South Africa's popular movement. Yet the fact that a populace is not deemed to be prepared for power "culturally" (even in the strict sense used by Lenin) can become an excuse for the kind of pseudo-benevolent authoritarianism to which the vanguard model has so often given rise in this century. Conceiving, instead, of a cumulative process of structural reform and an on-going situation of dual power as aspects of a necessary *learning experience* seems one other crucial dimension of the democratizing sensibility that marks the "post-apartheid" thinking of the best of South African socialists.

That said, the fact that the ANC is *not*, either in reality or in terms of this model, a vanguard party does give rise to concern, and not merely in Trotskyist circles. Indeed, within the Congress Alliance itself, the matter has come front and centre, debate turning around the role to be played, now and in the future, by the South African Communist Party. The SACP, so long a crucial ally of the ANC (and important to keeping some kind of socialist discourse alive in that organization, albeit of a decidedly Stalinist provenance), has been going through a rebirth, and a re-think, of its own. A widely-circulated pamphlet by party secretary-general Joe Slovo entitled "Has Socialism Failed?" has been particularly important in this regard.[77] Sharply critical of Eastern European practice, the pamphlet also sounds an unorthodox note on such key questions as the need for organizational autonomy of the popular movement: thus, the pamphlet argues, "instead of being guided by the interests and aspirations of their constituencies," the unions, as well as women's and youth organizations, became in Communist practice mere "support bases for the ongoing dictates of the state and party apparatus!" Does Slovo's pamphlet signal an actual and not merely tactical re-casting of first principles on the part of old-line SACP cadres?

There is sharp debate on this question, and Slovo's essay has been sharply criticized from the left — notably, from within the ANC itself, by senior politician Pallo Jordan — for not having come quite clean on the extent of the Stalinist rot either in the Soviet Union or in the SACP's own practices.[78] But the SACP does have a strong street-level credibility, springing from the fact that it combines both impeccable (and popular) ANC credentials and a distinctly left aura of its own. Rather surprisingly, too, it is attracting to its ranks some of the cream of the democratically-minded left leadership of COSATU. Accepting the hegemony of the ANC-centred movement but dubious as to the extent of the ANC's own left provenance, such trade union cadres argue the need for having, beyond the trade unions, the presence of some kind of workers' party within the broad popular movement. Not that such elements are naive about the weaknesses, for such purposes, of the SACP itself.[79] They realize they will have to struggle hard to overcome the dead weight of the party's past. And, of course, "if we're purged, we'll leave," as one such union activist ironically underscored the ambiguities of the exercise in recent conversation.

Meanwhile, the SACP itself is actively stretching out its hand to such cadres. As leading SACP figure Raymond Mhlaba recently put it, "The SACP and COSATU need to be as close together as possible. The ANC, on the other hand, is a mixed bag where you've got capitalists as well as workers and peasants. Now when we say we want to set up a socialist republic, the capitalists in the ANC will not agree, but the communist party and COSATU will be very good partners."[80] Needless to say, there are a host of unanswered questions here. It seems unlikely that the SACP would ever merely abandon the ANC to the Right and launch an entirely independent political-cum-electoral project of its own. Yet what can the sustaining of a close linkage between the two organizations be expected to look like on what is now much more open political terrain? Note, too, that some of those most active in the "new" SACP — especially from within the ranks of its fresh recruits — are amongst those also being looked to to revitalize the ANC itself.

Certainly, the SACP does remain a prominent player within the ANC, as elections to the National Executive Committee were to reveal at the ANC's July conference (the aforementioned Mhlaba himself being amongst the strongest finishers in polling for the NEC, for example). More generally the conference, as anticipated, did allow for some changing of the guard within the ANC, with elements from the internal movement — most notably from the erstwhile UDF — joining, and even displacing, exile politicians in positions of prominence. Particularly dramatic was the elevation of so visible an internal actor as Cyril Ramaphosa, leader of the powerful National Union of Mineworkers, to the post of ANC secretary-general. At the same time, representatives with an Umkhonto we Sizwe background also found renewed prominence — these latter, in particular, pressing the case that more be done to ground a self-defense capacity in the townships.

In fact, representatives of a very wide range of possible viewpoints were to be found on the NEC that was freshly-minted in July 1991 and the balances now struck within the "new" ANC were, if anything, even more delicate than those that had marked the old. In policy terms, a mandate for an increased politicization, from the ground up, of the negotiations process emerged as the clearest and, in light of present imperatives, the most positive outcome of the conference; here was to be found the firmest promise of the ANC's revitalization as a major shaper of the current moment. Less clear were the implications of such developments within the ANC for the probable manner of structuring a post-apartheid South Africa. The exigencies of the negotiations moment still tend to smooth over contradictions that could ultimately affect the movement's long-term socio-economic policies; under such circumstances, divining the likely vocation of the new NEC regarding such issues remains a difficult task.[81] Significantly, the conference delegates themselves postponed any sustained discussion of these matters, and of the movement's possible electoral programme, to a "special policy conference" promised for early 1992.

All of which is merely to reinforce the point that the political modalities of sustaining a process of long-term structural transformation are far from clear-cut in present-day South Africa. For the moment one may merely conclude that the dialectic between the ANC and the broader movement does hold, albeit fraying somewhat as debate continues over how the balance between the two might best be struck.[82] Beyond that echoes the closely related debate, only touched on here (as, indeed, within the movement itself), over how best to concretize the pursuit of such transformation in policy terms — including within such crucial spheres of establishment power as the army/police, the media, the health sector, and the like. Much has been accomplished in South Africa to bring the situation to the point at which it now stands. But we should not underestimate for even a moment the weaknesses of the popular movement that will now confront both capital and the remnants of the apartheid state and try to wrench a significant measure of reconstruction from them. Bracket off the fresh weaknesses being inflicted upon that movement by the harrowing realities of the negotiations moment (however much these may now be counterbalanced by the ANC's effectively seizing upon the renewed room for manoeuvre that Inkathagate has granted it) and one still confronts both the complexity of the South African socio-economic system, and the (relative) paucity of skills relevant to the most demanding tasks of the next round. We must look to an on-going process of empowerment, but we must also expect the signal advances that will be made to be harried by fresh contradictions and qualifications. And we must confront squarely the fact that either chaos or cooptation may be a more immediate prospect than the consolidation of a process of structural reform.

Launching and sustaining a process of "structural reform" is merely a chance then, even an outside chance, but the best chance for producing a socialist denouement to South Africa's travails — and not necessarily a bad chance either, by present global standards. The scenario sketched in the (admittedly speculative) final section of this chapter is less straightforward, certainly, than any maximalist left scenario for the immediate deliverance of a worker's party and a worker's state. But the identification in Section III of the components of a proto-revolutionary process of structural reform (a task that will be further pursued in the following chapter) does begin to make sense of the most interesting currents in present-day South Africa. And it is these currents that offer, in turn, the best hope to the vast mass of South Africans for a transformation of their unenviable situation. Taps for revolution? — or a revolution for the nineties? Lester Bowie, the great American jazz trumpeter and long-time member of the avant-garde Art Ensemble of Chicago, was once asked by a sceptical critic if some particular innovation marked "the end of jazz as we know it." Bowie's response: "That depends on what you know."

1. This chapter was first published, in much the present form, in *New Left Review*, # 188 (July-August, 1991).
2. Paul M. Sweezy and Harry Magdoff, "The Stakes in South Africa" in *Monthly Review* (MR), 37, 6 (April, 1986).
3. See, as examples, Alex Callinicos, *South Africa between Reform and Revolution*, (London: Inklinks, 1988), David Kitson, "Is the SACP really communist?", *Work in Progress* (WIP) (Johannesburg), #73 (March/April, 1991) and Adam Habib, "The SACP's Restructuring of Communist Theory: A Shift to the Right," *Transformation*, #14 (1991). Thus Callinicos, too abstractly but with characteristic clarity and ample documentation, urges on his readers the claims of "Trotsky's theory of permanent revolution" and, against ANC/SACP strategy, the need for a "dictatorship of the proletariat"; Habib, a member of South Africa's Workers' Organization for Socialist Action (WOSA) concludes that, contrary to present SACP practice, "the vision of the classless society can only truly be brought into realization if our theories, strategies and tactics are derived from the rich tradition of authentic Marxism-Leninism."(p. 79).
4. See, for an early example of this mood, Alex Callinicos, "Can South Africa be reformed?" *International Socialism*, #46, Spring, 1990.
5. Andre Gorz, "Reform and Revolution," *Socialism and Revolution* (New York: Anchor Books, 1973). This important essay seems even more widely relevant now than when it was first written (in France in the 1960s).
6. Gorz is alert to the paradox that such a project must both have some sense of its overall trajectory ("the workers' movement [must be] fully aware from the start of the nature of the stakes it is playing for") and yet not unduly prejudge the trajectory of the struggle that is being developed: "The error [of maximalist tendencies] consists in postulating that every engagement must now be entered upon with the clearly stated socialist intention that its ultimate aim is the overthrow of the system. This amounts to affirming that the revolutionary intention must *precede* the struggle and supply its impetus. This is a non-dialectical position which evades the problem by treating it as though it were already solved. For the fact is that the socialist resolve of the masses never springs out of nothing, nor is it created by political propaganda or scientific demonstration. Socialist resolve is built in and by the struggle for feasible objectives corresponding to the experience, needs and aspirations of the workers" (pp. 153-4). He does, of course, see a role for "leaders" (even a "vanguard of the workers' movement") who should be more alert than others to "an already existent socialist intention." But "this intention will not be asserted by speeches and revolutionary propaganda but by ability to grade the objectives, to raise the struggle to a constantly higher plane and to set 'intermediary' targets ... which must necessarily be surpassed as soon as they have been achieved" (p. 154).
7. Gorz, "Reform and Revolution," p. 148.

8   Ibid., p. 159.
9   John S. Saul and Stephen Gelb, *The Crisis in South Africa*, revised edition (New York: Monthly Review Press, 1986), p. 200.
10 Robin Blackburn, "Fin De Siècle: Socialism after the Crash," *New Left Review*, #185 (January-February, 1991), p. 65.
11 John S. Saul, "South Africa: The Question of Strategy," *New Left Review*, #160 (November-December, 1986), reproduced as chapter 5 in my *Socialist Ideology* ... (*op. cit.*).
12 Gorz, "Reform and Revolution," p. 135.
13 Saul, "South Africa: The Question of Strategy," *op. cit.*, p 5.
14 Stephen Gelb, "South Africa's Economic Crisis: An Overview," the introductory chapter to Gelb (ed.), *South Africa's Economic Crisis* (Claremont, S. A.: David Philip, 1991), a volume on the South African economy prepared by the trade union-linked "Economic Trends" group. In its early phase, the revision of "racial Fordism" sought "by linking productivity improvements to wage increases for a well-trained, fully urbanized black industrial workforce ... to both boost the size of the overall domestic consumer market (especially for durable and semi-durable goods), while simultaneously domesticating the emergent black trade unions." Gelb sees this deconstruction of "racial Fordism" as continuing apace throughout the 1980s — albeit without conspicuous success in reviving the flagging South African economy — and, quite precisely, as underlying the current moment: "The third phase ... was ushered in by the dramatic developments of late 1989 and early 1990, which opened the way to the ending of apartheid — the last important element of the old growth model." *(Ibid.).*
15 Dan O'Meara, "The Crisis of Apartheid and the Politics of the South African State," draft manuscript, 1990, among other of his recent writings.
16 The attempted greening of certain persistent township trouble-spots such as Mamelodi and Alexandra provides instructive cases in point in this regard, cases well documented in Andrew Boraine, "Security Management Upgrading in the Black Townships," *Transformation*, 8 (1989) and Karen Jochelson, "People's Power and State Reform in Alexandra," *WIP*, 56/7 (November-December, 1988).
17 The next few paragraphs draw on my article "Free at Last: The Next Round in South Africa," *MR*, 42, #3 (July-August, 1990); note that "De Klerk" is used in part as a kind of short-hand for the inchoate and rather contradiction-ridden group that centers around South African President F. W. de Klerk and currently hold the reins of formal power in South Africa.
18 Patrick Laurence, "De Klerk ready to bury last of apartheid laws," *The Guardian*, February 2, 1991.
19 See Dan O'Meara/John S. Saul, "The High Costs of Stalemate: Dan O'Meara on South Africa" in *Southern Africa Report/SAR* (Toronto), 6, #5 (May, 1991), p. 11; this article represents my own summary of

the central themes of O'Meara's various talks in the Toronto area after a recent visit to South Africa, talks that have helped shape my own understanding of developments within the white polity.

20 See Nicholas Haysom, *Mabangalala: The Rise of Right-Wing Vigilantes in South Africa*, (Johannesburg: Centre for Applied Legal Studies, University of the Witwatersrand,1986) and Josette Cole, *Crossroads: The Politics of Reform and Repression, 1976-1986* (Johannesburg: Ravan Press, 1987).

21 On Buthelezi, see Gerhard Maré and Georgina Hamilton, *An Appetite for Power: Buthelezi's Inkatha and the Politics of "Loyal Resistance"* (Johannesburg: Ravan Press, 1987), and *Gatsha Buthelezi: Chief with a Double Agenda* (London: Zed Books, 1988) by the late, and much missed, Mzala. In a particularly insightful 1987 article ("The Chief," *New York Review of Books*, February 12, 1987) Michael Massing already saw fit to present Buthelezi — the Jonas Savimbi of South Africa, as Massing characterizes him — as bent on brewing civil war; in this regard, Massing found special resonance in the statement made to him by one (unnamed) Buthelezi advisor: "Over the long run, there's only one central political process in South Africa — the conflict between the ANC and Inkatha. And there can be only one victor in that conflict."

22 *Southscan*, March 22, 1991.

23 *Weekly Mail*, September 21, 1990.

24 *Southscan*, April 12, 1991.

25 O'Meara/Saul, "The High Costs of Stalemate," p. 12. Does De Klerk fear a coup? O'Meara argues that "since the military's own alternative for dealing with the crisis — brute repression - so visibly failed in [the] years immediately preceding De Klerk's coming to power, it may not feel quite confident or clear enough about an alternative agenda to chance such a step." Nonetheless, the security establishment remains a potent player in South African politics.

26 O'Meara/Saul, "The High Costs of Stalemate," pp. 12-13; the following two paragraphs also bear the imprint of O'Meara's reflections as summarized in this same interview/article. A particularly cold-blooded, "realist" version of the"pacting" model as it is being used to guide state practice in South Africa is provided by a leading Afrikaner intellectual, Willie Breytenbach, in his unpublished paper, "South Africa: Towards 1994" (1990).

27 Saul, "South Africa: The Question of Strategy," *op. cit.*; for a somewhat fuller analysis of the immediate post-insurrection years than can be presented here see ch. 1, above.

28 As Barrell continues, "In turn, the de facto legalizing of the ANC widened the space for revolutionary activity, as a counter to the heavy toll exacted from MK, the ANC generally, and other anti-apartheid activists after the declaration of a national state of emergency in June 1986 and the security forces' suppression of most township uprisings by mid-1987" (Howard Barrell, MK: *The ANC's*

BETWEEN "BARBARISM" AND "STRUCTURAL REFORM" 137

Armed Struggle, [Johannesburg: Penguin, 1990], p. 63). One should not underestimate both MK's "key role" and the considerable heroism that went into its making its presence felt over the years — even if one accepts Barrell's overall argument that weaknesses internal to the ANC/MK were at least as important as "some of the most difficult conditions ever confronted by a revolutionary movement" in frustrating its stated goal that "revolutionary armed struggle leading to a seizure of state power was both necessary and possible" (p. 71). On this subject, see also Stephen M. Davis, *Apartheid's Rebels: Inside South Africa's Hidden War* (New Haven: Yale U. P., 1987).

29 On this subject, see chapter 2, above.
30 Howard Barrell, "The Tactics of Talks," (*WIP*), #39 (October, 1985).
31 The first quotation is from senior ANC official, Alfred Nzo (*Guardian*, January 9, 1990) and the second, from "ANC sources" in early 1989, is cited in David Niddrie, "Negotiations ... another site of struggle," *WIP*, # 60 (August-September, 1989).
32 The ANC may also have been lured, in this context, into an unrealistically "maximalist" position on sanctions, Mandela insisting in his first trips abroad on their total enforcement until some all too easily unspecifiable moment of "irreversibility" had been reached in the negotiations. In retrospect, and given that the alternative has been some slow, "spontaneous" ebbing away of sanctions, a proposal to phase their withdrawal in lockstep with an ascending series of concrete moves by De Klerk towards democratization might have enabled the ANC to make itself more of an arbitrator of the process. By the end of 1990 the ANC leadership seemed to have awakened to the wisdom of such a course, although too late to satisfy its own increasingly suspicious membership (at its December 1990, Consultative Conference) that this was not an unacceptable compromise. Too late, as well, significantly to influence international actors — although the ANC's new posture did have some positive impact on the February 1991 meeting of Commonwealth foreign ministers in London, and it remains true that sanctions have not completely disappeared as an influence on the calculations of De Klerk and his cronies.
33 At their most negative such tendencies may sometimes have turned very negative indeed. There is, for example, a disturbing ring of truth to the document prepared by a group of ANC dissidents and published in *Searchlight South Africa*, #5, July, 1990, under the title, "A Miscarriage of Democracy: The ANC Security Department in the 1984 Mutiny in Umkhonto We Sizwe;" this document specifies abuses of authority both inside the ANC's Quatro Camp in Angola and beyond.
34 The other side of the coin: when, several weeks in advance of the judgement in her trial, Winnie Mandela ran for presidency of the ANC Women's League she was roundly defeated.
35 *Southscan*, January 18, 1991.

36 *Southscan*, December 7, 1990.
37 Anton Harber in *The Weekly Mail*, Sept. 21-27, 1990, p. 7. *Southscan* came to a similar conclusion at about the same time: " the ANC is likely to end its first year of legality with neither the leadership nor the programme to extricate itself from the morass into which De Klerk has skillfully led it. In its current state the movement is virtually unrecognizable as the confident liberation movement which emerged from the shadows of illegality and exile on February 2" ("Criticism mounts as ANC bogs down in a talks strategy dictated by Pretoria," *Southscan*, October 19, 1990).
38 Cited in footnote 10, above.
39 Callinicos, *South Africa between Reform and Revolution* (op. cit.), p,192.
40 "Building Civil Society: Moses Mayekiso Interviewed," *SAR* , 6, #1 (July, 1990); interestingly, Mayekiso was already arguing in this interview that negotiations "even with the best of intentions of the ANC ... could degenerate into an intra-elite bargaining process — if mass-based organizations are not further developed to focus steady, strong pressure upon all participants."
41 *Front File*, "Mobilizing the Civics," March, 1991.
42 Albie Sachs, *Protecting Human Rights in a New South Africa* (Oxford: Oxford U. P., 1990).
43 For a detailed and instructive survey of progressive political organizations in South Africa see the special issue of *WIP*, #72, January-February, 1991, entitled "A Year in the Life of the Left: The state of play since February 2 1990 focussing on the ANC, SACP, PAC, Azapo and Wosa."
44 Significantly, the conference stated the need both for a range of provisions that would guarantee popular checks on a future state and, "since COSATU is committed to changing our capitalist economy and building socialism, we need a clause in the constitution to help us fight for these objectives;" see Drew Forrest, "A union call goes out: we want our seats" (Forrest's sub-heading: "The unions were ignored in the Zimbabwe talks ... and again in Namibia. It must not be allowed to happen here, insists COSATU"), *The Weekly Mail*, November 16-22, 1990. At about the same time a senior ANC regional organizer, Andrew Mapheto, launched an incisive and widely-cited critique (*WIP*, #68, 1990) of the ANC leadership for "falling prey to De Klerk's sweet talk" and failing to reach "people on the ground."
45 See, in this connection, the article by Ronnie Kasrils and Mandla Khuzwayo, ("two senior cadres in residual ANC underground structures," as they are described), "Voices from the underground: Mass struggle is the key," *WIP*, #72 (January-February, 1991); the same issue of WIP features instructive articles by Jenny Cargill on the state of the ANC after the December conference ("Marrying mass action and creative leadership") and by David Niddrie ("Apartheid's not dead, it just smells funny").

46 *Southscan*, January 25, 1991.
47 *Southscan* ("De Klerk, anticipating danger, prepares for a rush to reform", *ibid.*) suggests an emerging desire on de Klerk's part now to deal with the existing, reasonably pliable ANC negotiations team while this was still possible: "Crucial to all these options is rapid progress towards the point at which these details *are hammered out, and the need to pre-empt the second articulation, in June, of rank and file ANC sentiment*"(emphasis added).
48 *Front File*, April, 1991.
49 Another cruel twist: in the present uncertain moment even some of the erstwhile "progressive youth" turn "comtsotsi" (this latter an ironic amalgam, in the popular argot, of "comrade" and the word for criminal).
50 O'Meara/Saul, "The High Costs of Stalemate."
51 Stephen Gelb, "South Africa's Economic Crisis: An Overview," (*op. cit.*).
52 On the sophistication of this World Bank/IMF softening-up process, and on some of the likely terms of their long run influence, see Patrick Bond, "Closing In: The World Bank and the IMF in South Africa," *SAR*, 7, #1 (July, 1991).
53 As quoted in the *International Herald Tribune* ("Mandela Outlines Policy: Private Enterprise to be Foundation," February 27, 1990), where, however, Mandela is also said to have reaffirmed the ANC's commitment to 'nationalizing mines and banks." Elsewhere Mandela has been quoted as insisting the ANC is not "anti-capitalist" and as rejecting "the commonly-held belief that the Freedom Charter is fundamentally socialistic" (*Weekly Mail*, April 27, 1990).
54 Callinicos quotes Slovo, circa 1986, in his "Can South Africa be Reformed?" p.113, and interprets this quote as manifesting the basest kind of "Gorbachevism."
55 Saul, "South Africa: The Question of Strategy," *op. cit.*
56 Lawrence Harris, "Building the Mixed Economy," paper presented to the ANC's Department of Economics and Planning workshop, Harare, April-May, 1990, p. 10; see also Harris' earlier paper, "The Mixed Economy of a Democratic South Africa," mimeograph, June, 1989.
57 Joe Slovo, "Nudging the balance from 'free' to 'plan,'" *The Weekly Mail*, Mar.30-Apr.4, 1990
58 See the article entitled "Nationalisation," *New Nation*, March 8-14, 1991.
59 Private communication
60 Stephen Gelb, "Democratising Economic Growth: Alternative Growth models for the Future," *Transformation*, 12, 1990. See also "The Economy Beyond Apartheid: Recommendations on post-apartheid economic policy," *New Nation*, June 15-21, 1991, being the summary document produced by the ANC/COSATU consultation in Harare.

61 Even more concrete is the vigorous discussion taking place within the National Union of Mineworkers (NUM) regarding the possible wisdom of nationalization measures to shore up an increasingly vulnerable South African mining industry.
62 *Southscan,* February 16, 1990.
63 See Drew Forrest, "Rival currents at work in Cosatu," *The Weekly Mail,* April 11, 1991; with many union leaders very visible within the ANC and/or SACP one focus of recent sharp debate has been the acceptability of union leaders wearing "two-hats" (three-hats?) in this way.
64 Quoted in *Southscan,* May 10, 1991.
65 Alec Erwin, "Comment" (on the Harare "Recommendations on Post-Apartheid Economic Policy"), *Transformation,* 12, 1990. On this point see also the symptomatic review ("Rethinking Socialism," *South African Labour Bulletin* (SALB), 15, #7, April, 1991) by long-time observer of the South African labour scene, Eddie Webster, of a recent book by John Mathews, entitled *Age of Democracy: The politics of post-Fordism,* (Melbourne: Oxford U. P., 1989). Webster cites Mathews' concept of "associative democracy" ("the emphasis is on *associations* of workers and citizens as the agents of democratisation," with "trade unions [to be] involved in transforming the economy from within"), while précising approvingly Mathews' notion that "the state must be seen as the institution which supports and co-ordinates the process of change, rather than the institution which 'delivers' social transformation" (p. 82).
66 The same document (quoted in "Unions urge national reconstruction plan in face of recession," *Southscan,* May 24, 1991) calls for a policy and strategy "to change the economic situation, stop retrenchments, create jobs and begin the struggle for socialism."
67 See *SALB,* 15, # 6 (March, 1991), special issue entitled "From resistance to reconstruction: the role of trade unions in the new South Africa," and, in particular, the article by Karl von Holdt, "Towards transforming SA industry: a 'reconstruction accord' between unions and the ANC."
68 Alec Callinicos, for one, appears scandalized by such an approach; in his "Can South Africa be Reformed?" (*op. cit.*) he scorns the very first step in this process, the initial — and, when backed judiciously by the invocation of mass action, ultimately successful — negotiations with SACCOLA, as capitulation to the (to him highly suspect) overall negotiations tactic of the MDM and as virtual abandonment of class struggle.
69 Karl von Holdt, *op. cit.,* p, 23.
70 Facilitating the expression of such groups will seem all the more important if it is borne in mind that organized workers still comprise a relatively small percentage of adult South Africans. Moreover, as some trade union leaders are themselves concerned to observe, the strategic locations of many such workers within the economy,

as well as the very fact of their relatively high level of organization (and attendant bargaining muscle), could encourage their taking on some of the characteristics of a "labour aristocracy." It also bears noting, however, that much of the discussion within the unions regarding a prospective "reconstruction accord" does suggest that both civic and rural organizations must also be parties to it.

71 On these issues see Linzi Manicom, "Engendering the New South Africa: Women and the ANC," *SAR*, 6, #4 (March, 1991), which also cites the ANC's "Emancipation of Women" statement quoted below.

72 For example, a sharp and very concrete critique, written from a gender-sensitive perspective, of even the most progressive ANC advance economic planning exercises can be found in the paper "Gender and Economic Policy in a Democratic South Africa," Development and Practice Working Paper #21, Faculty of Technology, Open University, 1991 written, with Maureen Mackintosh and Doreen Massey, by leading ANC cadre Frene Ginwala.

73 *Southscan*, May 3, 1991.

74 If only momentarily: the struggle to sustain such empowerment would not end, this fact defining a state of perpetual tension - if not "perpetual opposition" - between the state and the popular forces (including workers and their trade unions). For a contrasting perspective, one more inclined to envision the ultimate disappearance of such tensions within the orbit of a workers' state, see the article by SACP activist, Jeremy Cronin, entitled, sardonically, "Preparing ourselves for permanent opposition?" *SALB* (April, 1991).

75 Recall Lenin's statement (in "'Left-Wing' Communism - An Infantile Disorder") that "History as a whole. and the history of revolutions in particular, is always richer in content, more varied, more multiform, more lively and ingenious than is imagined by even the best parties, the most class-conscious vanguards of the most advanced classes." What might have happened had Lenin himself made rather more of a virtue of this reality?

76 Then again, a progressive political centre without a suitably self-empowering base would be unlikely to sustain itself either — something already learned the hard way in the southern African region, in Mozambique for example (see chapter 3, above).

77 Joe Slovo, *Has Socialism Failed?* (London: Umsebenzi, 1990).

78 Pallo Jordan, "The Crisis of Conscience in the SACP," *Transformation*, #11, 1990. For a contrasting and depressingly orthodox riposte to Slovo by a prominent, long-time SACP activist see Harry Gwala, "Let us look at history in the round," *The African Communist*, #123, 1990.

79 See Mike Morris, "Why Are Anti-Stalinists Joining the SACP?", SAR, 6, #3 (December, 1990).

80 Quoted in *Southscan*, February 8, 1991.

81 In short, it remains extremely difficult to predict of any political revitalization the ANC itself may now experience just what will be

the relative importance to be attached to broadly populist concerns (capable, at their worst, of taking on quite demagogic proportions) on the one hand and more pointedly socialist ones on the other. Related ambiguities attach to even so prominent a figure as Cyril Ramaphosa, himself a prominent trade unionist but as often as not to be found on the "populist" wing of such "populist-workerist" divisions as have been said, from time to time, to characterize the trade union movement.

82 "Mass-based movement starts to rise on ashes of disillusionment;" so *Southscan* headlines a recent article about the trend towards increased independence vis-à-vis the ANC on the part of unions, students and civics (May 10, 1991), a trend likely to be accentuated, the paper argues, at COSATU's own July conference.

Chapter 5
Structural Reform: A Model for the Revolutionary Transformation of South Africa?[1]

▼▼▼▼▼▼▼▼▼▼▼▼▼▼▼

In 1992 I was invited to participate in the Ruth First Memorial Colloquium — a gathering intended both to repatriate, from Maputo, the annual Ruth First Memorial Lecture and to mark the tenth anniversary of her assassination in Maputo — held at the University of the Western Cape, Bellville/Cape Town, August 17-18. It seemed appropriate, on that occasion, to seek to develop further the kind of argument I advanced in the New Left Review *article that became the preceding chapter. In doing so I drew on fresh thinking I had done on the general question of appropriate socialist strategies (thinking based, notably, on a reading of Boris Kagarlitsky's* The Dialectic of Change[2]*), but also on an analysis of relevant developments in South Africa during the year since I completed the earlier text. I situated the discussion with reference to some of my own memories of Ruth First during the period, prior to her assassination, when we worked together in Mozambique.*

Words have meanings. Words are weapons. Few have given these homilies more effective weight in their own lives than Ruth First. In her voluminous writings, in her teaching, in her goading of others to more precise, more telling clarity regarding the strategies and tactics of change, she used language like a rapier to advance the cause of liberation in southern Africa. And she paid with her life for her success in doing so.

No wonder Portuguese was such a trial for her. In her Mozambican years she became competent enough in that language, but I remember from our time together in Maputo her visible frustration on various occasions when she was forced to use Portuguese to make sharp points she would much rather have been making in English. Clearly, she felt disarmed, reduced to using baby-talk (as her own Portuguese must have seemed to her) when only tough talk would do. Small wonder, as well, that one of my own last and firmest memories of her are of a debate we had, precisely, over language. At her request I had written a paper for the meeting of southern African scholars she hosted in Maputo mere days before her death. Some passing criticisms of the work of her Centre of African Studies that I made in that text where not well received by Ruth. And neither was my use, at several other points, of a particular phrase — "frozen Marxism" — to capsulize the brand of inflexible Eastern European "Marxism-Leninism" too much in evidence in Mozambique (not least in the University's Faculty of Marxism-Leninism where I taught). No great enthusiast herself for the brand of Marxism under discussion, Ruth nonetheless preferred, for purposes of facilitating interchange at the workshop, a less provocative phrase and after several prolonged conversations I agreed to alter it. (I must also confess that when the paper went forward for publication several months later — after the conference and after Ruth's death — I altered it back again!)

Since the thrust of the present discussion is also about words — about the terminology likely to be most useful in conceptualizing the on-going transformation of South Africa's socio-economic structures — I regret that she is not here to comment on it. As always when dealing with Ruth one would have hoped fervently to earn, if not her complete agreement, at least her respect for the argument made and the intention behind it. I suspect, too, she would have concurred that terminological concerns are not necessarily merely academic ones but can debouch, more or less helpfully, into the terrain of practice. In fact I myself sense that, for those of us who think of ourselves as socialists, such work is at present of especially pressing importance.

After all, many of our hopes and existing preconceptions have been badly battered by the collapse of "actually-existing socialisms" and the apparently unchecked hegemony of an ever more ambitiously globalizing capitalism. At one level this can prove liberating; for example — whatever may be the final verdict on its various strengths and weaknesses — Joe Slovo's *Has Socialism Failed?* suggests something of what can be accomplished as the incubus of "frozen Marxism" begins to be shed. But in a context in which prior revolutionary experiments (now by and large defunct in any case) offer little positive inspiration, and prevailing socialist theory only limited guidance, there is a great deal more thinking that needs to be done to develop new ways of conceiving the modalities — at once socialist and realistic — of a radical restructuring of inherited socio-economic institutions

Indeed the danger exists that the perceived setback for global revolution (taken together with the fact of global capitalism's undoubted strength) will suggest to many who are progressively-minded that only the mildest brand of reformism is "realistically" possible. As Kagarlitsky has phrased it: "If, back in 1969, revolution was the major theme of theoretical discussion on the Left, by the mid-1980s the question of reformism had moved to the forefront...[T]he current reformist myth is forcing the question of revolution out of ideological circulation."[3] The current reformist myth? Read: the time-dishonoured social-democratic notion that a mere tinkering with capitalism can humanize its rapacious logic and maximize its ability to service human needs (or — to put the terms of that "myth" more honestly — unlikely as the realization of such a hope may be, it is nonetheless the very most that can ever be expected!).

But does the simple juxtaposition of revolution vs. "mere reformism" really represent the full range of present possibilities, in South Africa or anywhere else? As we know from the preceding chapter and as will be confirmed below, in some South African circles the debate about possible futures for the country is indeed being cast in terms of just such false dichotomies. When this happens a "dialogue of the deaf" occurs that merely locks "revolutionaries" and "reformists" ever more tightly (and more self-righteously) into their own respective corners. But it is also apparent that there are other South African militants whose practice starts from different premises and whose activities give real content to the promise of a long-term socio-economic transformation of South Africa.

Such militants seek, at least implicitly, to avoid the twin dangers of, on the one hand, a romantic (and inevitably all too rhetorical) ultra-revolutionary approach and, on the other, collapse into a mild reformism that will do little to alter the balance of inherited class power and conservative/technocratic decision-making.

Indeed, in many ways South Africans — notably those within the trade union movement — are in the vanguard of global efforts to forge a theory and practice relevant to the struggle for socialist renewal in the post-Cold War era. Here I seek to further develop the argument sketched in the previous chapter: that thinking in terms of the concept of "structural reform" can help make greater analytical sense of such "socialist" struggles as are occurring in contemporary South Africa. Use of this concept, I would argue, may also contribute to developing a vocabulary, a language, in terms of which those waging such struggles can become ever more self-conscious about the logic of their activities and ever more self-assured about pressing them forward. For words have meaning. Words are weapons.

I. Structural reform: some additional considerations

As we have seen, the fact that the grim and immediate struggle against the apartheid state and the apartheid system remains front and centre in South Africa renders the discussion of "post-apartheid" socio-economic futures somewhat more abstract than it might otherwise be. At the same time, we know that important battles are also underway on a number of policy fronts that already have begun to have profound implications for the balance of power and policy in a post-apartheid South Africa. Bracketing off the current, vitally important efforts to force the pace of negotiations and counter the pull towards chaos in South Africa, we will focus instead on the simultaneous efforts of many South African militants to shape a future beyond the interregnum that begins to redress South Africa's severe socio-economic inequalities. As hinted above, most of those who have this goal are conscious of the severe constraints that will hamper, in South Africa, any attempt to develop and to implement radical social and economic change: the increased power of capital, international and domestic, in an era of accelerated globalization; the absence of any strong counterweight to capital's global writ in the post-Cold War era; and the technical, administrative and other constraints on the popular movement's capacities as it seeks to deepen its challenge to established power centres. Indeed, it is precisely because commitment to meaningful change is balanced by an acute awareness of such contextual factors that the South African Left, at its most relevant, has moved towards a project of "structural reform."

As I discussed in the previous chapter, use of this concept means applying to South Africa a distinction delineated by Andre Gorz between a "genuinely socialist policy of reforms [and] reformism of the neo-capitalist or 'social-democratic' type."[4] I then identified two essential criteria for distinguishing "structural reform" from mere "reformism". The first of these is "the insistence that any reform, to be structural, must not be comfortably self-contained (a mere 'improvement'), but must, instead, be allowed self-consciously to implicate other 'necessary' reforms that flow from it as part of an emerging project of structural transformation." In other words (and in contrast to Bernstein's "the process is everything for me, and the 'final aim of socialism' is nothing"), the popular movement-cum-party attempting a programme of structural reform must constantly articulate both to itself and to its broadest potential constituency the goal of structural transformation/socialism. It is this alone that can situate and make revolutionary sense of short-term struggles and achievements and forestall a situation in which these latter take on no more than the vulnerable half-life of free-standing, one-off ameliorations of some particularly raw attribute of otherwise ascendant capitalism.

Moreover, it is precisely such emerging self-consciousness about the long-term imperatives of transformation (and about the logic that must be seen to link the realization of any one advance to the need/possibility for a set of subsequent advances towards a transformative goal) that is also the necessary touchstone for realizing the second attribute of any "structural reform." For "a structural reform cannot come from on high; instead it must root itself in popular initiatives in such a way as to leave a residue of further empowerment — in terms of growing enlightenment/class consciousness and in terms of organizational capacity — for the vast mass of the population, who thus strengthen themselves for further struggles, further victories." (No reference cited.)

My initial proposal of this approach to transformative/ socialist endeavour elicited some favourable response[5] but also sharp criticism in a subsequent issue of *New Left Review* — from a militantly Left perspective — from Alex Callinicos.[6] The latter chose to see me advocating (a mistake on my part, of course) "structural reform" as "a detour on, rather than an abandonment of, the road to revolution." In fact, as I argued in reply, my claim was actually even bolder than that:

> All the more reason, then, to insist that a strategy of structural reforms *not* be seen as being, at best, some mere

"detour".... Under many (if not most) contemporary circumstances, including South African circumstances, it may well be the road [to revolution] itself. For it suggests a model of socialist activity that can force the most unromantic reading of the odds against any very immediate transformation of existing capitalist circumstances and yet permit a definition of sites and modes of real struggle and a concretization of tactics and strategies that opens up the possibility of moving towards just such a transformation. Moreover, it promises to underscore the saliency of substantive issues (rather than vague revolutionary nostrums) in terms of which leaderships can most effectively be held to democratic account by their constituencies and in terms of which these very constituencies can become ever more conscious of their class interests - indeed, of their very 'classness' - not as some theoretical given but as the practical content of their own lives and public activities.[7]

In his criticism of my argument Callinicos flagged the danger that attempts at anything like "structural reform" are prone themselves to collapse into "mere reformism." He also expressed a fear that they would contribute to the unhealthy bureaucratization of ostensibly progressive organizations. Fair warning and, indeed, some recent writing closer to the ground in South Africa suggests that so internally democratic a trade union as COSATU is facing just such a challenge as, at present, it becomes more active in various kinds of "negotiations" on the national stage.[8] Still, I see no reason why this should be deemed inevitable. In fact, the struggle within the movement to sustain the kind of tough bargaining stance that a transformative process implies is one of the most crucial things the politics of the transition must be about. Callinicos argues that "power necessarily shifts from the shop floor to the union head office." "Necessarily"? Surely only so long as there is not a vibrant context for debate about the terms of the "structural reform" endeavor and no effective set of democratic procedures through which movement spokespersons (of whatever organizational provenance, be it union or party or women's organization) can be held, ultimately, to account.

And what is the alternative? Of course, there are bound to be differences of opinion — and debates — within the movement about the appropriateness of some particular tactic or other (for example, the direct action at the Mercedes Benz plant which

Callinicos cites in his rebuttal to my article as having been suppressed by union bureaucrats). And there are bound to be complex struggles over the approach to be taken on issues like the National Manpower Commission and the VAT (both mentioned by Callinicos). But surely real "struggles" over such issues will take place in hotel meeting rooms and ministerial offices (even in the ministerial offices of some future "revolutionary government") as often as in the streets and in the neighborhoods. Three and a half million workers can demonstrate against the government's imposition of a VAT (Value Added Tax), as we have seen to be the case in South Africa. They cannot all crowd into a negotiating room to further pressure business and/or government on the issue. Does this automatically render the latter an illegitimate front of the class struggle?

Are there to be, in sum, no organizations, no leaders, no differences of opinion *about strategy and tactics* — in effect, no politics — within the movement that Callinicos would see facilitating a transition to socialism in South Africa? Whenever Callinicos comes up against complexities like these, complexities inherent in real rather than notional struggles for socialist advance, he backs away and invokes that magic talisman, "mass struggle," to outrank competing arguments. Moreover, he is only able to do this by simultaneously underestimating the practical significance of the fact that conservative forces with real power (power rooted both locally and internationally) are not, at any early date, going to disappear from South Africa by wholesale lot. How are they most effectively to be checked, finessed, seduced, resisted, and, one hopes, ultimately constrained to yield to transformation? Unfortunately, for all their sincerity and commitment, critics like Callinicos provide few tools which might help the South African left to answer its most pressing questions: when to confront directly? when to negotiate? with whom? over what issues? Surely, if we have learned nothing else from recent history, we know that substituting the pure flame of "revolutionism"[9] for the hard calculation and complex and subtle politics of structural reform/socialist transition is a recipe for disaster.

As noted, significant segments of the South African Left are beginning to forge a far more realistic and promising brand of militant political practice; we will return, below, to further document their attempt to wring progressive change from the difficult set of circumstances found in contemporary South Africa. First, though, some additional elaboration of the concept of "structural reform" itself may be in order, drawing on my reading of Boris Kagarlitsky's illuminating volume, *The Dialectics of Change*.[10]

Kagarlitsky, too, finds the concept of "structural reform" to be a suggestive one. He also manages to give this notion a firm and convincing pedigree within the Marxist tradition, rooting it in the first instance in Marx's own writings. He emphasizes, for example, "the patently reformist themes of Capital" (that volume's emphasis on the importance of English factory legislation, for example), noting that "Marx was convinced that they [reforms] prepare not only the revolution, but also socialism. In other words, for Marx, the value of reforms was not in that they undermined the old system — sometimes they even strengthen it — but in their creation of elements of the new system within the framework of the old society. This theme in Marx's theory has been completely ignored by revolutionaries and reformist social democracy alike."[11]

The great strength of Kagarlitsky's approach, then, is to bind revolution and reform together as being, potentially, two mutually reinforcing preoccupations and processes. "In and of itself, Marxism is neither a 'revolutionary' nor an 'evolutionary' theory. As a *theory of practice* Marxism derives from the alternation of evolutionary and revolutionary stages in history and crucially from their organic interconnection. This latter feature has been completely overlooked by both Right social-democrats and their left-wing critics."[12] Right and left? We noted earlier Kagarlitsky's suspicions, echoing Lenin's own, of ultra-leftist "revolutionism" (footnote 8). But he is also well aware that "the right wing of the workers' movement" offers no very helpful alternative. "The politics of inconsistent and indecisive reforms has led many parties to lose their socialist perspective," pushing, as he puts it, "social democrats towards technocratic ideology, which has nothing in common with socialism."[13] It is by denying the intellectual prison framed by such a polarization of positions that Kagarlitsky moves instead towards advocacy of "revolutionary/radical reformism." In doing so he also underscores the imaginative contribution of such thinkers as the (much underrated) French socialist Jaurès[14] to the identification of some fresh and promising possibilities within the Marxist tradition:

> Alone among activists in the Second International, Jaurès and his supporters genuinely understood the depth and complexity of this problem. Alone among revolutionaries, Jaurès grasped the value of reformist work, proclaiming it necessary "to take up the business of reform from the beginning and, through reform, to begin the business of revolution." Alone among reformists in the

STRUCTURAL REFORM   151

International, Jaurès attempted to elaborate an entire offensive, socialist strategy for state power in the conditions of democracy. As the supporters of Jaurès put it: "our weapon has two edges, one is the spirit of gradual reform, the other is revolution."[15]

Beyond Jaurès, Kagarlitsky sketches the importance to the development of a "structural reform" tradition of such diverse voices as Italy's Palmiro Togliatti (with his project of "reformism from below"); intellectuals linked to the Centre for Socialist Research (CERES) in France; certain elements within Poland's Solidarity; and, most significantly, militants (including Andre Gorz) grouped around France's Unified Socialist Party (PSU) in the 1960s and 70s.[16] The cumulative import of such thinking? On the one hand, "in contemporary society the road to revolution lies only through reforms." On the other, "structural reforms must lead to a gradual rupture with the existing order and not rectify the 'individual consequences of capitalism.'" In sum, "the strategy of change adopted by the French socialists was designed to replace the very logic of society and not only in individual institutions."

Not that such "revolutionary reformists" are likely to be naive about the obstacles that confront their project. Certainly, even in the short run, capital has demonstrated that it has the means ("direct sabotage, an 'investment strike,' the export of capital and so on") to make things extremely difficult for a structurally reforming movement. Moreover, "the closer the advocates of change get to the point which distinguishes revolution from reform, the more intense the social conflict becomes....Having upset the system's equilibrium, the changes destabilize the economy and jeopardize the government implementing them. The inadequacy of the reforms can be an argument in favour of new transformations, but they can also be used by supporters of the old order." The movement must remain ready to force the pace of revolutionary change if circumstances permit, but halts and even retreats under pressure may also prove necessary from time to time. In the latter case, much will depend on how "irreversible" the movement has managed to make the various reforms it has achieved up to that point — the key to an effective "defensive strategy" in this respect being, not surprisingly, the extent to which consolidation of self-management and/or popular empowerment have been central to what has been accomplished.[17]

More generally this suggests the crucial requirement that a mass movement has succeeded in building the capacity to sustain itself and its sense of long-term, overall direction.[18] For Kagarlitsky, such a movement should extend "beyond the bounds of political parties, autonomous from their day-to-day leadership and not subject to their tactical failures and party mistakes." It should have become, in effect, a movement with sufficiently deep roots in society to be able to live to fight another day! The politics of "structural reform" will be complex, then. And to sustain them "neither moderation nor revolutionary slogans can be a substitute for strategy. A serious and profound search is required which is only now beginning."[19] The next section seeks to determine just how far this necessary search actually has progressed in South Africa itself.

II. South Africa: conceptualizing change

In South Africa, as we know all too well, the road to political democratization, narrowly defined, is proving to be a distinctly rocky one. Increasingly, a wide range of commentators (including many located somewhere on the left of the political spectrum) also cast severe doubts as to how far socio-economic policy could move in a socialist direction even were constitutional issues to be resolved in a positive manner. For example, Bill Freund apparently embraces the perspective of a number of books on the economy which he is reviewing when, in a recent article, he states that "South Africa does not actually contain revolutionary possibilities at present." He sees that as in part reflecting international realities, in part the fact that "the old power in South Africa [is not] genuinely on the point of collapse or disappearance."

> A South African revolution could, therefore, only be accompanied by local devastation, with massive emigration of skilled people and capital flight, as well as in the teeth of international hostility. It would at best be a harsh, militantly policed `barracks socialism' Such a militarized socialism could organize a society with a high degree of equality but a low level of consumption and with few prospects for accumulation and development.

Freund's conclusion: "The alternative, however unwelcome to advocates of class struggle, involves conciliating much of the bourgeoisie and giving the South African middle-class of all colours a way forward."[20]

It is the generalization of such a mood that emboldens various local apostles of market liberalism (Don Caldwell, Louw and Kendall) to bombard the book-store shelves with their volumes in praise of unqualified, "de-racialized" free enterprise. Others speaking from within the leading circles of economic power in South Africa will acknowledge a little more readily the need to take positive action to redress the country's deep-seated socio-economic inequalities. Even here, however, the goal of capital is to define these inequalities as a welfare problem (redistribution), rather than a production problem. And then there are those (Peter Moll and others associated with him, for example) who present themselves as speaking a more firmly "radical" language, yet in calling for an only slightly more aggressive creaming off of surpluses from the private sector embrace a rather similar model of "growth with redistribution."[21] Some useful insights can be found in the work of such writers, yet ultimately their writings, characterized by their pugnacious "unwillingness to consider structural change," advance too narrow a view of "the art of the possible" even for Bill Freund: "the real limitation of Moll and his colleagues — through their modest and uncertain views on state intervention — is to take production and growth too much on business' terms. They are too ready ... to confine themselves to fiddling about with what slack space may remain from improving tax policies or saving on military expenditure after making business happy."[22]

However far Freund might himself want to push this point, it is an important one, potentially a crucial wedge in the reinsertion back into the South African equation — via the route of "structural reform" — of the very "revolutionary possibilities" Freund tends to downgrade. Take note, once again, of a suggestive presentation of the relevant point by Kagarlitsky: "While traditional social democratic reformism confined itself to changes in the sphere of distribution and indirect regulation of the economy, strategic revolutionary reform has to *affect the spheres of property and organization of production.*"[23] And bear in mind that this is not merely a debate amongst social analysts. Where, we might ask, would the ANC want to situate itself on the spectrum between, say, Moll and company on the one hand and Kagarlitsky on the other?

Unfortunately, it is not so very difficult to imagine what Kagarlitsky here describes as "traditional social democratic reformism" becoming the height of aspiration of the ANC itself. For the threat of a significant narrowing of the range of socio-economic options that some ANC leaders think to be open to a post-apartheid South Africa is very real. Pressures on the popular movement to indicate acceptance of a set of imperatives favoured by such worthies as Anglo-American and the IMF/World Bank (among many others) continue to intensify, for example. Is it a sign of the times that in a crucial meeting with international businessmen in Davos, Switzerland, in early 1992, the ANC delegation (led by Mandela himself) was apparently found backpedalling rapidly on various progressive economic positions and emphasizing the importance of "attracting foreign investment" to the virtual exclusion of all other questions?[24] True, such emphases have been challenged within the ANC. Nonetheless, even leading ANC/SACP theorist Joe Slavo sometimes seems content — according to a recent news report — also to cede the responsibility for "growth" to the private sector, with "redistribution" then being the task of the government. "'We don't follow the dead cow theory', he is quoted as having said recently, describing it [the dead cow theory] as an economic policy to 'kill, feast, gorge and then there's nothing left to milk.'"[25] Catchy enough, perhaps, but is this formulation ("growth with redistribution") really likely to assist the popular movement in conceiving effective ways to constrain the otherwise unencumbered dictate of capital?

In fact, Slovo's own position more often pushes past such limitations, especially when he is wearing his SACP rather than his ANC hat. While rejecting nationalization he vigorously defends the case for state intervention and certainly assigns his party the role of ensuring that, in the "inter-class line-up of forces, working-class interests are not swamped, that the working class is organized as a powerful constituency, and that the choices which are being debated for future development will be made in a way that will not prejudice the working class whom we claim to represent."[26] To be sure, the modalities of such state intervention as will ultimately prove to be necessary are not spelled out, no more than are the modalities of direct intervention by the popular classes that might actually serve to keep their interests front and centre. Those suspicious of the SACP's historical record of pseudo-vanguardist arrogance will want to hear more on these issues from the party as the post-apartheid policy struggle unfolds.

Creativity from the SACP in this respect is not impossible, of course. While some members criticize Slovo's emerging position from the quasi-Stalinist periphery, others — notably Rob Davies, writing in the *African Communist*[27] — have attempted to divine a "realistic" economic strategy that also sustains momentum in the direction of structural transformation.[28] Davies acknowledges both the "strengthened ... hand of the free market lobby in our own

STRUCTURAL REFORM 155

national economic debate," and (more controversially) predicts that "the immediate post-apartheid period will be characterized by national-democratic rather than socialist construction." Nonetheless, he underscores the fact that

> We (socialists and communists) need urgently to develop a specifically socialist perspective in particular policy options and measures. Our party has long recognized that there is no Chinese wall between the stages through which any transformation must inevitably pass. The kind of policy which emerges in the stage of national democratic construction will significantly affect the prospects of a socialist project in the future. We need therefore to become more active in identifying and struggling for policies that will be feasible under the concrete conditions likely to prevail immediately after liberation and which will both lead to immediate improvements in the lot of working people and lay a favourable base for the eventual transition to socialism. This requires a degree of clarity about the kind of socialist project we envisage.[29]

An argument is then presented that seeks to move away from the tendency to define socialization of the production process in terms that merely focus on "state ownership of the means of production." Instead Davies discusses both the need for planning that will "introduce a social direction into an economy which will continue to be characterized by commodity production," and for the introduction of a variety of collective production practices that might be encouraged in such a way as to alter, slowly but surely, "the balance of power in favour of working people in an economy characterized by a variety of ownership forms."[30]

There is promise here, and also in the work of Economic Trends (ET), a group of researchers (some of whom have themselves a great deal of direct trade union experience) closely linked to COSATU. The main concern of ET theorists focusses on the need for intervention by progressive forces in order to force upon capital an expansive growth strategy that it could not be expected to adopt "spontaneously." As noted in the previous chapter, one key to their project has been to privilege the notion of "growth *through* redistribution" (as opposed to the establishment slogan of "growth with redistribution") as one key to overcoming the visible crisis of the South African economy. This is an approach that seeks to place popular needs at the centre of the economic equation and looks for growth in the economy by reshaping production to meet those needs: "building materials, consumer durables, clothing and products produced in micro-enterprises" are prominently mentioned in this respect. Such theorists are by no means insensitive to the simultaneous requirement of an effective export strategy, and some tough economic questions do arise as to how best to conceive projected sectoral balances and the like in such terms. For present purposes, however, the crucial fact is that (as Freund writes in contrasting the ET approach with that of Moll and his colleagues) ET "insists on indicative planning that will reshape the orientation of the economy,"[31] an approach that reinforces the need to constrain substantially capital's own prerogatives.

To be sure, rather less is said in recent ET writings about the imperative of expanding the democratic prerogatives of the popular classes vis-à-vis the power of capital as an issue in its own right. Indeed, in one of his most recent articles, ET Coordinator David Lewis, writing with an ET colleague, Avril Joffe, downplays the class contradictions that some would see to be the chief motor of any attempt to narrow the writ of capital's freedom of choice and to overcome its irrationalities. They write that "a recognition of the benefits of cooperation must surely take the place of the adversarialism characteristic of the relationship between labour and capital to date....[C]ollaborative relationships — between manufacturers, companies and unions, the industry via employer federations and industrial policy makers — are an essential ingredient of any successful industrial policy."[32] But the answer to this is, surely, yes — and no. Lewis himself has written eloquently elsewhere of South African capitalism in ways that evoke class contradictions more centrally than class collaboration. Can one really hope to finesse the fact that such contradictions will also continue to cut across any new politics of industrial strategizing that may prove possible on the terrain of a more democratic South Africa? And isn't there a danger that presenting a project of growing democratic control over production merely in terms of collaboration may disarm more than it strengthens the popular classes, undermining their preparedness for the more pugnacious confrontations with capital that may well be required further down the road?

There is a paradox here, of course. Capital must feel its overall stake in the established system to be sufficiently secure to yield relatively gracefully to concessions extracted from it by the popular forces — until such forces have marshalled their power to push the envelope of structural reform a little further. Can the popular movement conciliate capital adequately without at the same time demobilizing its own forces? Certainly there are those within the trade union movement who want to test the limits of this paradox rather more assertively than the language of "collaboration" would easily allow. Thus, for such militants the democratization of the labour-capital relationship is indeed *necessary* in order to overcome the irrationalities of capital-logic in South Africa and to reactivate growth and development by impacting upon economic "restructuring."[33] Such necessary democratization is also to be valued in its own right, as part of a process to "genuinely empower the producers so that they have control over what they have produced." In this way socialism "must deliver what social democracy cannot do."[34] It is this kind of thinking that comes closest of any in South Africa to representing an agenda of "structural reform" and/or "revolutionary reformism."

For Enoch Godongwana, quoted here, makes no apologies for an approach to "restructuring which is informed by a socialist perspective and which is characterized by working class politics and democratic practice and accountability of leadership." Nor does he apologize to Alex Callinicos (whose views he specifically cites) for a struggle for socialism that is carried out across the terrain of "negotiations," "social contracts" and even "trade-offs between contending forces" and "is the product of methods of struggle that combine advances and — under certain circumstances —-tactical retreats to make way for further advances."[35] The prospect of engaging the class enemy in a measured and sustained manner does not unnerve Godongwana. For him what is critical is "how that engagement takes place."[36]

It is in much the same spirit that Geoff Schreiner discusses the way in which unions have advanced into various national forums to begin to make demands that stretch beyond the wage bargain: "There are good social contracts and bad ones, ones that work and ones that don't, ones that advance the interests of the ruling class and ones that assist in building workers' power and organization. We would be politically irresponsible to miss out on the latter."[37] And this, in turn, parallels considerations raised by one of the most astute of observers of South Africa's labour scene, Karl Von Holdt, in discussing various workers' participation schemes on the drawing boards in South Africa: "Do such projects mean abandoning socialism for a reformist, social democratic vision? Or are they steps on the long road of a democratic struggle for participatory socialism?"[38] Tough questions. Yet as long as such questions are on the agenda of the Left in South Africa, the possibility of socialist transformation, rather than a merely corporatist cooptation of the trade union movement, will remain alive.

The assertive role of the trade union movement links to another dimension of the South Africa situation that is distinctly positive from the point of view of sustaining a revolutionary struggle there by "reformist" means. For the unions are merely the most prominent amongst a number of forces in "civil society" whose projects can expand the array of pressures at play upon capital and the state that seek to ensure radical outcomes. This reality is, of course, the product of the particular process by which a broad mass democratic movement re-emerged in South Africa from the 1970s on, a movement very far from being reducible in its institutional expression to a single party/liberation movement. This process has also deposited an ideological legacy of considerable significance: the prominence of the South African Left's firm emphasis on the crucial legitimacy of the claims of "civil society" is itself testimony to this. Indeed, if an ever-emboldened sense of popular empowerment is a *sine qua non* of sustaining a project of structural reform, South Africa's recent history has given the country some real advantages in this regard.

Of course, one must be careful not to romanticize this outcome. Violence has permeated very deeply into South African society, not least amidst the decay of the social fabric — the pull towards "barbarism" — spawned by the stalemate of the past few years, and this has probably negated some of the advantages referred to above and slowed the further consolidation of democratic attitudes and practices.[39] This is just one more way in which the post-apartheid future is in hock to the uncertainties of the transitional present. Beyond this, Adrienne Bird and Geoff Schreiner have recently pointed to a quite different different kind of danger inherent in the way "civil society" is currently articulating itself within South Africa. Is it possible that some elements within the camp of the popular classes are "more equal" than others; and that, in particular, the best-off, best-organized workers might themselves be tempted to buy into a position of relative privilege within the post-apartheid dispensation? "In our view, corporatist arrangements (70/30 solutions) driven by union members together with organized (big) business and endorsed by a weak state hungry for political support, are a real danger for the future. Tripartite models will encourage these possibilities."[40] And in urging a "multi-partite model" (both now and in the future) of on-going "negotiations" over socio-economic matters, Bird and Schreiner seek the emergence of a more broadly-based approach to the representation of civil society. "In this conception, civics, women's groups, associations of the unemployed and the aged, consumer and rural organizations, and so on would be guaranteed the right to participate in appropriate bodies on key aspects of state policy, together with the Big Three."[41]

A useful warning. But the organized working-class must remain central to structural reform efforts, nonetheless. And, as we have already seen, there is a refreshing degree of self-consciousness about the role it has to play. Witness, for example, COSATU secretary-general Jay Naidoo's suggestion at the time of the dramatic anti-VAT stay-away of late-1991 that the stay-away had implications not merely for the existing white government; in his view, it should also be seen as a friendly reminder to any future ANC government of the workers' willingness to act dramatically to affect the substance of economic decision-making.[42] Perhaps this is as good a measure as any of just how far many South African revolutionaries have come from more statist definitions of socialism and development — no small achievement in light of what has happened elsewhere on the continent

But it is scarcely the last word on the prospective role of party and state if "revolutionary reform" is to be realized. Naidoo's sense of the need to keep a wary eye on the ANC does not contradict his equally bold assertion that "the [ANC-COSATU] alliance is a very important vehicle for us to achieve our ends. The forces ranged against us are very powerful — big business, imperialism, a powerful state. We ourselves will need a powerful state orientated towards the working class — the ANC has to be strong."[43] For if technocratically-inclined social democrats as well as recidivist Stalinists can easily overplay the extent to which state action is to be deemed the almost exclusive centre of "progressive" activity, protagonists of "civil society" must beware of any underplaying of the importance of the state (and of the political forces that control the state).[44] Established centres of social power are most likely to yield to demands for significant change and to compromise their own most narrowly construed vested interests only if they feel pressure both from above and from below.

Thus, for trade unionist Sipho Kubheka, there is a need for a "strong and democratic" ANC. "This will allow the ANC to balance the demands of capital and the demands of labour, but at the same time take a firm position on restructuring the economy with a bias towards labour." Not that the unions themselves can then avoid the necessity for hard battles against the employers in support of government programmes. "The government alone would not be able to force employers to do what it wants." Still, if his hopes materialize, Kubheka expects a "march to a socialist order in the long term."[45]

But how likely is the ANC, if and when it shoulders state power, to play this role in helping to squeeze capital and to realize — in creative interface with the forces of civil society — what could become, in effect, a structural reform agenda? This is too big a question to be tackled adequately here, although we have already noted some reasons for concern in this respect. Certainly the pull of big capital on the ANC will continue to be considerable, and many of the seductions of comfort and prestige that have sapped the energy of progressive political leaders elsewhere are already playing strongly upon the movement. There are also some good reasons — both economic and political (in terms of off-setting the predominance of big "white" capital on the one hand and building a successful political alliance on the other) — for the ANC to help advance the interests, within a "mixed economy" strategy, of the black bourgeoisie and petty-bourgeoisie.[46]

Yet the difficulties of so doing while also advancing the socio-economic interests of the more impoverished popular classes will not be so easily papered over in the post-apartheid phase by invocation of "national-democratic" imperatives as they once were. Certainly there already some signs of meaningful struggle within the ANC over possible post-apartheid outcomes — these cast not only in class terms but also, importantly, in gender terms.[47] As noted in the previous chapter, the efforts of some ANC economists to give a radical twist to, precisely, such concepts as "the mixed economy" do have promise of their own.[48] But can a leading political force which fails (at least to this point) to have anything like a "structural reform" perspective clearly and overtly articulated to itself or to its mass following actually be expected to become the cutting-edge of "revolutionary reformism?" Alternatively, can the pressures of the trade unions, the SACP and other elements within the mass democratic movement more broadly defined keep such a possibility alive, within and without the ANC, if the ANC (at its most narrowly defined) fails to move forward — and to the left? In short, even if the South African ambience seems one conducive, in many respects, to struggling for socialism in novel and potentially effective ways, the issue of the best political modalities for doing so is still very far from being resolved.

In this chapter we have confirmed that there are many voices in South Africa, on both the Right and the Left, that seek, for their own purposes, to suggest the choice of options open to the country to be absolute and starkly polarized: reformism vs. revolution. But we have also emphasized that neither in Marxist theory nor in practice is there any reason for adopting such a Manichean view of socio-economic possibilities. It is true, as Stephen Gelb has recently suggested, that my own presentation of the logic of "structural reform" could itself do more to analyze, for different sectors, how various concrete policy initiatives might have their full potential as structural, rather than "merely reformist", reforms drawn out. This is a challenge I hope to take up in future research and writing.

What is important to reaffirm here, however, is the fact that important actors in South Africa have themselves refused to be intimidated by the apparent elegance of over-simplified dichotomies and are instead following the logic of their own practice towards promising theorizations of the "structural reform" type. In doing so they enter into a more open and contested field of left debate than is sometimes acknowledged, and one from which they can hope to draw additional sustenance for their own activities. But the extent to which a commitment to the politics of "revolutionary reformism" ("Marxism-Jaurèsism!") already defines the more or less explicit agenda of many of those engaged in South Africa's own "great economic debate" suggests that South Africans can also expect to make their own important contribution to the renewal of socialist thinking that is necessary on both a regional and a global scale.

1 This chapter, originally prepared as a paper for the Ruth First Memorial Colloquium mentioned in the text, was first published, in much the present form, in the South African journal *Transformation*, #20 (1992).
2 Boris Kagarlitsky, *The Dialectic of Change* (London: Verso, 1990).
3 *Ibid.*, p. 3.
4 Andre Gorz, "Reform and Revolution," in his *Socialism and Revolution* (New York, Anchor Books, 1973).
5 Mala Singh, "Transformation Time!" *Transformation*, #17 (1992).
6 Alex Callinicos, "Reform and Revolution in South Africa: A Reply to John Saul," *New Left Review*, #195 (September-October, 1992).
7 John S. Saul, "John Saul replies," *New Left Review*, #195 (September-October, 1992).
8 See Bobby Marie, "COSATU faces crisis: 'Quick fix' methods and

9   organizational contradictions" and related articles in a special issue of *South Africa Labour Bulletin*, 16, #5 (May-June, 1992), entitled "COSATU: gaining influence, losing power?"

9   As Kagarlitsky writes *(op. cit.,* p. 14), "For Marxists, the word 'reformism' is no longer the term of abuse it was at the turn of the century. History has all too sternly demonstrated that one should be more wary of the empty chatter of revolutionary phrases and demagogic promises. In the last analysis, 'opportunists' have caused less damage than extremists. Lenin himself wrote in 1921 that "the greatest, perhaps the only danger to the genuine revolutionary is that of exaggerated revolutionism, ignoring the limits and conditions in which revolutionary methods are appropriate and can successfully be employed. True revolutionaries are most likely to come a cropper when they begin to write revolution with a capital R, to elevate 'revolution' to something almost divine, to lose their heads, to lose the ability to reflect, weigh and ascertain in the coolest and most dispassionate manner.' Untimely revolutionism, to use Lenin's term, is capable of inflicting (and has inflicted) major harm on the Left, particularly in periods of society's calm and peaceful development."

10 I am grateful to Stephen Gelb for pointing out to me the potential importance of Kagarlitsky's book (1990) to the development of my own analysis of the process of change in South Africa.

11 Kagarlitsky, op. cit., p. 8. Kagarlitsky does note (p. 8) that "this theme" is "also absent from Marx's and Engels' later works. It is indeed possible that after the first volume of *Capital* was published, Marx himself to some degree changed his point of view. The Paris Commune and the revolutionary struggle on the Continent compelled him to take a more decisive stance; the seemingly imminent revolution rendered reform a less immediate problem." But this fact merely reinforces Kagarlitsky's underlying premise: that, properly understood, revolution and reform are not necessarily mutually exclusive preoccupations, the shifting balance socialists must strike between them being strongly determined by context. His conclusion: "We do not have the right to pass over Marx's reformist ideas."

12 Kagarlitsky, op. cit., p. 113; as he continues, "Not only Marxist theory but the most elementary logic demands different responses in different situations."

13 *Ibid.,* p. 113. As for Kagarlitsky's own view of the costs of such a polarization: "The trouble is not that Marxists have adopted the idea of a revolutionary transformation of the world, but that they have made it an absolute by drawing the conclusion that 'genuine' changes are possible only on a revolutionary basis. There has arisen a particular moral doctrine according to which reformist politics merit disdain at best. This 'revolutionary ethic' came into being, of course, long before the appearance of Marxism. As we have seen, Marx himself never adopted such positions. But, by an irony of fate,

STRUCTURAL REFORM 163

it is precisely people who consider themselves his followers who, in the twentieth century, have become the heralds of such principles. The practice of 'opportunist reformists,' which has indeed often been inclined towards compromise, has tended to confirm these ideas by reinforcing sterile 'revolutionism' on the Left, which has degenerated into insurrectionary phrase-mongering" (p. 113).

14 Kagarlitsky adds that "the supremacy of the German social bureaucrats within the workers' movement at the turn of the century helped ensure that the Jauresists' practical and theoretical experiences remained substantially inaccessible to other parties" (*ibid.*, p. 42).

15 *Ibid.*, p. 35. Of course, as Kagarlitsky then proceeds to emphasize, "the starting point of Jaurès strategic concept, termed the 'new method,' was Engels' idea that, in conditions of freedom, the proletariat can struggle initially for a share of power, 'and then the whole of that power, in order to become enabled to change existing laws in conformity with their own interests and requirements.' The democratic state, unlike other forms of power, does not permit the bourgeoisie's complete and undivided rule. This rule is limited by certain conditions, and the class essence of democracy therefore consists in a compromise between the contending forces. In a polemic with Right social democracy, Jaurès said that, in French conditions, 'class antagonism exists and develops within democracy and is subordinate to the conditions of the democratic regime. The struggle between the two opposing classes, between the two groups of interests, cannot assume an identical form, character and means in both a democratic republic and a despotic state. This is true and indispensable'" (1990: 35). In terms of the South African situation, this gloss on Jaurès' point does help underscore the importance of current efforts to consolidate an achieved democratic dispensation — a crucial accomplishment both for helping, potentially, to pre-empt a further decline into social chaos and for opening up space for socialist agitation.

16 *Ibid.*, p. 126. As Kagarlitsky admits, "The PSU's attempts to build a mass revolutionary-reformist party fell through." And we all know what has happened to Mitterand, who was apparently much influenced by the "structural reform" ideas of CERES at a certain stage of his career. However, the PSU's failure (or indeed Mitterand's) "does not mean that it is impossible in general to create such a organization!"

17 Important not least, in Kagarlitsky's estimation (*ibid.*, p. 150), because "the efficacy of strategic defense determines the possibility of a new offensive and tasks" in some subsequent round.

18 The failure by Mitterand's government to take seriously this requirement is seen by Kagarlitsky (*ibid.*, p. 150) to be one of the two chief reasons for the evaporation of any left content from his political project once in power: "The French Socialists' second serious error

lay precisely in their underestimation of the masses' spontaneous support and their desire to carry out everything 'from above' through the channels of Party and State. Government figures themselves recognized that 'having seized the fortress of power, the Left raised the drawbridge and locked themselves in.'" (Their first/chief mistake? Not successfully neutralizing the pressure of international capital: "They made no efforts to build a united front with other left-wing governments in the West and elaborate an international policy which would have reinforced reformist tendencies in neighbouring countries." No small task, of course.) Daniel Singer's magisterial volume on the Mitterand experience, *Is Socialism Doomed? The Meaning of Mitterand* (New York: Oxford University Press, 1988), is extremely suggestive in dealing with similar themes.

19 Kagarlitsky, *op. cit.*, pp. 150-1.
20 Bill Freund,"Review; Four books on the economy," *South African Labour Bulletin* (SALB), 16, #5 (May/June, 1992), p. 85.
21 See Peter G. Moll, *The Great Economic Debate; A Radical's Guide to the South African Economy* (Braamfontein; Skotaville, 1990) and Peter Moll, Nicoli Nattrass and Lieb Loots (eds.), *Redistribution; How can It work in South Africa?* (Claremont, S.A.: David Philip, 1991).
22 Freund, *op. cit.*, p. 85.
23 Kagarlitsky, *op. cit.*, p. 146 (emphasis in the original).
24 See the articles "Mandela returns to continuing dispute on ANC economic policy" and "ANC team at Davos summit finds international business critical of policy" in *Southscan*, 7, #6 (February 14, 1992).
25 See the article "No to 'dead cow theory'"in *Southscan*, 7, 13 (April 3, 1992).
26 Joe Slovo, "Beyond the stereotype: The SACP in the past, present and future", *African Communist* (2nd Quarter, 1991)) and also his interview in Keith Coleman, *Nationalisation: Beyond the Slogans* (Johannesburg: Ravan Press, 1991).
27 Rob Davies, "Rethinking socialist economics for South Africa," *African Communist*, 2nd Quarter, 1991.
28 Of course there is also a strand of left discourse inside the country that does tend to collapse — much like the position of Callinicos (1992) — into a kind of well-intentioned but not very immediately relevant "revolutionism," with an all too easy urging of a maximalist confrontation with capital at its core. See, as examples, David Kitson, "Is the SACP really communist?" *Work in Progress (WIP)* (Johannesburg), #73 (March/April, 1991) and Adam Habib, "The SACP's Restructuring of Communist Theory: A Shift to the Right," *Transformation*, #14 (1991). As noted in the previous chapter, Habib — a member of South Africa's Workers' Organization for Socialist Action (WOSA) — concludes that, contrary to present SACP practice, "the vision of the classless society can only truly be brought into realization; if our theories, strategies and tactics are derived from the rich tradition of authentic Marxism-Leninism" (p. 79). The

case for "Marxism-Jaurèsism" is least likely to make advances in such circles.
29 Davies, *op. cit.*, p. 39.
30 *Ibid.*, p. 32.
31 Freund, *op. cit.*, p. 85; he emphasizes, in this connection, the possible need to "(break) up the stranglehold of conglomerates on investment funds."
32 Avril Joffe and David Lewis, "A strategy for South African manufacturing," *SALB*, 16, #4 (March/Aprll, 1992), p. 31.
33 Enoch Godongwana, in his "Industrial restructuring and the social contract: reforming capitalism or building blocks for socialism?", *SALB*, 16, #4 (March/April), defines "restructuring" (quoting Alec Erwin) as "significant and discernible changes in the pattern of output, input, cost structures, employment, employment practices and industrial relations, markets and production methods" (p. 23).
34 Godongwana, *ibid.*, p. 23.
35 *Ibid.*, p. 21.
36 *Ibid.*, p. 23; as Godongwana, a NUMSA Regional Secretary, concludes his article (1992: 23), "Callinicos and others who hold similar views, may argue that this approach does not have any historical precedent but the same could be said for their approach."
37 Geoff Schreiner, "Fossils from the past: resurrecting and restructuring the National Manpower Commission," *SALB*, 16, 1 (July/August, 1991), p. 35.
38 Karl Von Holdt, "'Worker control': new meanings," *SALB*, 16, #3 (January). See also the interview of related importance with NUM's Marcel Golding and entitled, significantly, "Productivity: 'participating to achieve control,'" *SALB*, 16, 2 (October/November, 1991) and, for a particularly helpful overview of debates within the trade union movement regarding alternative strategic perspectives, Von Holdt, "The Rise of Strategic Unionism" (in two parts), *Southern Africa Report (SAR)* (Toronto), 8, #s.2 and 3.
39 On some of the costs of this stalemate — itself a product of such diverse factors as De Klerk's footdragging, Buthelezi's ruthlessness and the ANC's own inability to deliver the coup de grace — see, inter alia, chapter 4, above, and also the chilling description of the present volatile state of South African youth in Colin Bundy, "At War with the Future? Black South African Youth in the 1990s," *SAR* (Toronto) 8, #l (July, 1992).
40 Adrienne Bird and Geoff Schreiner, "COSATU at the Crossroads: towards tripartite corporatism or democratic socialism?", *SALB*, 16, #6 (July/August, 1992), p. 28; as they go on to note, "In arguing this, we accept that COSATU has historically, in the absence of the major political parties, represented the interests of working people. But this tradition does not guarantee that this line of march will continue into the future."
41 *Ibid.*, p. 29; Bird and Schreiner also discuss usefully some of the

things that might be done to strengthen the hand of such sectors, "precisely the weakest, the poorest and most marginalized in society [who] experience the most difficulty in developing stable national organizations."

42 As Naidoo said in one interview ("National general strike," *SALB,* 16, [October/November. l992]), "COSATU has always been a political player and intends to remain a political player even if we have an ANC government in power."

43 As Naidoo adds (quoted in Von Holdt, "The COSATU/ANC alliance: what does COSATU think," *SALB,* 15, #8 (June), p. 26), "The working class in Europe and in the Soviet Union had a history of militancy and revolutionary struggle, and that has been lost. Our 30,000 shop stewards could become trapped in bureaucracy and inaction. Our tradition of organization and struggle could be immobilized. We are placing our hopes in the organizations of civil society — but a strong state would be an enormous help. The state defines the ways in which civil society is empowered."

44 A critique along these lines of Left preoccupations with the claims of "civil society" forms the core of a recent article by Blade Nzimande and Mpume Sikhosana, "Civil society and democracy," *African Communist* (1st Quarter, 1992) but the article makes its own case much too easy for itself by caricaturing "pluralism" and invoking the alternative model of a possible revolutionary society-in-the-making as an unlikely form of "fused group." More useful in identifying some of the strengths and weaknesses of recent invocations of civil society in South Africa — but also the limited utility, even grave dangers, of the alternative brand of vanguardist formulations à la Nzimande and Sikhosana — is Bob Fine, "Civil society, political parties and the state: an essay on South African political culture" (unpublished paper).

45 Both Naidoo and Kubheka as quoted in this paragraph are cited from an extremely helpful article — one of many such that he has penned in recent years — by *SALB* editor, Karl Yon Holdt: "The COSATU/ANC alliance: what does COSATU think," *SALB,* 15, #8 (June, 1991). Indeed, more generally, SALB has become a particularly important forum for reflecting the innovative socialist thinking that is at play in present-day South Africa.

46 This point is elaborated upon in Stephen Gelb, "The Political Economy of the Black Middle Class in a Democratic South Africa," being chapter 3 of Gelb's unpublished dissertation *The dynamics of accumulation: Essays on the theory of regulation and its application to South Africa* (Winnipeg: University of Manitoba. 1992).

47 See, for example, the paper "Gender and Economic Policy in a Democratic South Africa," Development and Practice Research Group, Working Paper No. 21, Faculty of Technology, Open University, 1991, written, with Maureen Mackintosh and Doreen Massey, by leading ANC cadre Frene Ginwala and cited in the previ-

ous chapter. More generally, see, *inter alia,* the various articles (by Pat Horn, Shireen Hassim and others) in recent issues of *Transformation* and *Agenda.*
48 See ch. 4, above, especially the sub-section entitled "Rethinking the Mixed Economy," p 32ff.

Afterword
Strategies for Resistance in the 1990s

Well over a year has passed since completion of the essay that became chapter four of this book, and the situation in South Africa has not really moved forward from that described there; indeed, with further violence, increasing factionalism and escalating crime, it has in many ways deteriorated. At the end of 1992, as this manuscript is being completed, the country remains in a situation of stalemate, without yet gaining the momentum to resolve even the crisis of "the apartheid moment," and this despite the misleading hoopla that surrounded De Klerk's smashing victory in the all-white referendum in March. The contradictions in De Klerk's own position (as described in chapter four but epitomized by his referendum slogan: "If you're afraid of majority rule, vote yes") seem still to be locked into place; this is the real meaning of the present situation. By systematically refusing to allow the meaningful institutionalization of democratic structures in South Africa, De Klerk himself is the chief architect of stalemate. At the same time, his apparent "reasonableness" has won him some measure of international credibility (with the attendant removal of many sanctions), however little deserved. Moreover, the various spurious constitutional notions he has produced from time to time — presented as being legitimate hedges against the "abuse of power" but in fact designed to block, as much as possible, the practical democratic empowerment of the vast majority of the population that is black — seem also to have won a certain credibility in some circles.[1]

Denied outright victory in the liberation struggle, the ANC also has not had the clout necessary to force the pace dramatically in the negotiations phase. Right-wing critics to the contrary notwithstanding, the movement has itself been prepared to guarantee all manner of democratic and individual rights (by means of a "bill of rights" and accession to some federalist preoccupations) while rejecting, for good reasons, claims for "group rights" and "minority vetoes." Most recently, however, it has seemed to go even further, with senior leader Joe Slovo proposing — as a way of breaking the negotiations log-jam and hedging against right-wing backlash — "sweeping concessions to the government in the form of 'sunset clauses' in a new constitution" (including a period of compulsory power-sharing and a significant guaranteeing of existing civil service and security force contracts).[2] Quite similar ideas were embraced, almost immediately, by the ANC leadership itself in its "Strategic Perspective" document of October, 1992.

Critics within the democratic movement have expressed fear that some of the concessions the ANC now seems prepared to make towards assuaging white minority concerns threaten to gut the capacity of a post-apartheid government to redress the socio-economic inequalities of South African society. For example, Pallo Jordan (himself a senior ANC cadre) suggests that the ANC has lost track of its broader goals of democratic transformation and begun to make the lowest common denominator of constitutional agreement an end in itself.[3] Perhaps, as some have charged in reply, Jordan runs the risk of substituting rhetoric for political realism here: "To be sure, there are sometimes epic, all-or-nothing moments in politics. But when one is simply not in such a moment, then all-or-nothing tactics are liable to yield ... nothing."[4] But even if this were true, it is clear that, entering 1993, the ANC is involved in a risky game. What makes it even more risky is that it remains frustratingly unclear just what goals De Klerk himself is pursuing. Thus year-end reviews published by several of the most astute analysts of South African politics echo the argument broached in chapter four: that National Party leaders are still mired in "limited and contradictory visions"[5] that preempt bold and imaginative action of their own.

There is, nonetheless, some pressure on De Klerk to move forward, a point to which we will return below. Hope springs eternal, therefore, and, as 1993 dawns, the ANC and others were to be found preparing for elections — even if the timing, form and import of such elections were issues that were still very far from being resolved. Had enough been accomplished to give promise of the eventual emergence (in 1993? in 1994?) of a political structure rather more democratic than not? Time alone will tell. And what, in any case, of the range of socio-economic policies a new ANC-centered government might feel inclined to pursue in any post-apartheid round? Here critics fear a degree of compromise with the prevailing structures of privilege and power — once again, in the name of "realism" — that is likely to be even more crippling than in the sphere of constitution-making itself.

What, they ask, are the implications of remarks like that by senior ANC negotiator Thabo Mbeki when he stated that, on economic matters, the National Party's positions "are not very different really from the position the movement has been advancing."[6] Or the implications of a smug report, as recently as January 13, 1993, from *Business Day:*

> We can look with some hope to the evolution in economic thinking in the ANC since the occasion nearly three years ago when Nelson Mandela stepped out of prison and promptly reaffirmed his belief in the nationalization of the heights of the economy. By contrast, after delivering his organization's anniversary message last week, Mandela — supported by SACP chairman Joe Slovo — went out of his way to assure a large group of foreign (and local) journalists that the ANC was now as business-friendly as any potential foreign investor could reasonably ask. He indicated further that ANC economic thinking was now being influenced as much by Finance Minister Derek Keys and by organized business as anyone else.

Of course, as the discussion in the previous two chapters has emphasized, realizing an alternative vision of societal transformation, one premissed on the goal of socialism and the practice of structural reform, is no easy task; small wonder, then, that many who are now comfortably situated in the upper echelons of the ANC have come to think it an irrelevance. As Colin Bundy has put the point: "There will be many who remain unconvinced. They believe that would-be socialists in South Africa are doomed to defeat; epochally quixotic, tilting forlornly at windmills driven for the rest of history by capitalist energies. To speak of 'prospects' for socialism, they say, requires a leap of faith." And "perhaps it does," Bundy concedes; at the very least it "requires stamina, creativity and collective resourcefulness." But there is something more:

> On the other hand: to imagine that a milder mannered capitalist order can secure a decent future for the majority of South Africans — or that de-racializing bourgeois rule will meet the aspirations of exploited and oppressed people — or that South Africa can somehow be absolved of its economic history and enter a future like that of Sweden or Taiwan: now that *really* requires a leap of faith.[7]

Fortunately, as Bundy also documents, scepticism about the promise of capitalism is indeed widespread in South Africa, whatever may be the position towards which the Mbekis and the Mandelas themselves are moving. We will return to this point. Here it bears emphasizing that, in a very real sense, the rest of the region is also forced to live the simultaneity of both the apartheid and the post-apartheid moments, and in ways that are at least as complicated as those we have seen to characterize the South African situation. In the first place, the bill for the counter-revolution sponsored for almost twenty years by apartheid South Africa (and discussed in our opening chapter) continues to be paid every day. Perhaps, as 1992 drew to a close and an accord was signed between Frelimo and Renamo, there were signs that the war in Mozambique might finally be beginning to wind down. But, "peace?" For one aid worker there, "Banditry is the shape of things to come. I don't know what you do with the soldiers on either side. The Swedes are looking at a scheme where they buy guns from them and send the soldiers to their villages to set up co-ops. But I think they've learned to live by the gun." And the situation appears to be at least as bleak in Angola, where the direct South African connection to the continuing process of socio-political decay is actually even more visible. True, for a moment, a "reconciliation" also occurred there between the government and those — Savimbi and his UNITA cronies — who have been the pawns of South Africa and the CIA.[8] But MPLA's subsequent victory in a "free and fair" election seems merely to have moved Savimbi — egged on by South African Foreign Minister Pik Botha, among others — to fight more ruthlessly than ever in an attempt to seize power.

But assume for a moment — however heroic an assumption it may be — that some kind of "peace" could eventually be established in these "Frontline states." The fact is that — as noted in chapter two — they too are already living the post-apartheid, post-destabilization moment. And this second "moment" is not a pretty sight. Indeed, if the pressures to yield to a "false decolonization" in South Africa (and to ignore the counter-claims of a continuing struggle for socialism) are powerful, one must admit that the virtual *recolonization* by global capitalism of the rest of the region suggests such pressures to be virtually overwhelming there. Mozambique may present a worst case scenario, but, as Judith Marshall wrote after a recent trip to southern Africa, the negative fall-out from "structural adjustment" and the hegemony of the World Bank and the IMF in that country is part of a more general regional pattern: "There is a dramatic increase in unemployment and a huge proliferation of the informal sector. The contrast between rich and poor becomes more stark. There is a strong degradation of the social fabric and a dog-eat-dog mentality that has come to prevail. Violence — both community and family — is on the increase."[9] In short, fragile societies now robbed of any sense of the collective social purpose they might have carried forward from the days of anti-colonial struggle have become easy pickings for the most opportunist of actors, both foreign and domestic.[10]

True, some greater measure of formal political democratization has also emerged alongside enforced economic liberalization in the region. But any positive link between the two processes could prove to be very short-lived indeed, with "economic liberalization" quickly throwing up many more contradictions than an "open" political system is likely to be able to contain. As we have seen in chapter three, the emergence of multi-party politics in Mozambique threatens an unravelling of the country into a congeries of ethnic and regional satrapies. In Zambia, the fond hopes that accompanied the peaceful overthrow of that sad old autocrat Kaunda seem very quickly to be foundering on the reefs of renewed popular resentment at the costs of structural adjustment and the crumbling of the coalition of notables grouped behind new president Frederick Chiluba.[11] And in Zimbabwe a senior trade union leader can plausibly accuse an increasingly defensive Mugabe government of being "out to destroy any sense of civic organization, be they students, trade unionists, communal farmers, the peasants themselves."[12] In sum, as the horrors of the catastrophic drought of the past few years serve further to strip the region bare, both the increased dependence on external actors and the deep internal tensions (of class, region and faction) of such countries stand even more starkly exposed.[13]

Resistance in the region

How, in the first instance, to move the South African government out of the stalemate mode and towards an embracing of genuine constitutional advance? Dan O'Meara, whose careful analyses of South African politics were cited extensively in preceding chapters, professes himself to be "dismayed" (although not entirely surprised) by the fact that "De Klerk has blown two chances to avoid stalemate" — the reference is to De Klerk's foot-dragging after both the initial release of Mandela and, again, after his overwhelming victory in the 1992 referendum. Could the ANC, he asked himself in mid-1992, actually begin to mobilize the popular pressure necessary to force De Klerk to risk a genuine political democratization of South Africa? His conclusion: "I would like to think that it could, I'm not so sure that it can."[14]

There did seem to be an earnest of hope in the outcome of the ANC's May 1992 policy conference where mass resistance — the promise of a nation-wide general strike if the government does not soon do its part to free up the transition process — was put much more firmly on the agenda.[15] Subsequent months were to see this sentiment acted upon, most notably during the week of "mass action," both national and local, that began on August 3rd. Most dramatically, Monday and Tuesday of that week saw the biggest stay-away in South African history — an estimated four million workers — while on Wednesday over 70,000 ANC supporters demonstrating outside the Union Buildings in Pretoria. Indeed, it is not fanciful to see this period of mass action as a kind of "second referendum," underscoring for those who wished to see that the vast majority of the black population were staunch in their democratic demands — and that the ANC continued to stand as the chief political vehicle of such demands.

Complemented as it was by some waning of international enthusiasm for De Klerk's fumbling approach, by the horrors of the Bisho massacre in the Ciskei, and by a fresh wave of scandal regarding his government's involvement in a range of grotesquely "dirty tricks," it was such activity that had begun, by the end of the year, to force De Klerk back into a bargaining mode. To the consternation of many, however, the political charge evoked by popular mobilization was not sustained. Thus, as we have seen, Jeremy Cronin, SACP activist and one of the clearer thinkers in the camp of the democratic movement, was quick to announce his support for the more narrow crafting of constitutional demands signalled by Slovo's "sunset" proposals and by the ANC's "Strategic

Perspective" cited above. Yet he also expressed his deep concern that "mass action" was being viewed merely as a "tap" to be turned on and off at the ANC leadership's whim as short-term calculation of advantage in the negotiation process might dictate:[16]

> It is critical that in the present we coordinate our principal weapon — mass support — so that we bring it to bear effectively upon the constitutional negotiations process. But we must not confine or inhibit mass struggle to this purpose. Instead we need to encourage, facilitate and indeed build the kind of fighting grassroots organizations that can lead and sustain a thousand and one local struggles against the numerous injustices our people suffer.... Democracy is self-empowerment of the people. Unless the broad masses are actively and continually engaged in struggle, we will achieve only the empty shell of a limited democracy.[17]

For Cronin, as for many others, it is the fact that such powerful popular energies continue to bubble up from the base in South Africa that gives politics there its peculiarly vibrant potential. But the question remains: how can these energies become focussed in such a way as to drive a process of genuine social transformation forward?

In fact, in the longer run, such energies could as easily curdle into a form of rather ugly, racially-driven populism — if growing discontent with ANC compromises were left to group behind the likes of a Winnie Mandela or the PAC (with its "one settler, one bullet" propaganda).[18] This is why the role of an organization like COSATU — with a more deeply reflective grasp of both the subtleties and the imperatives of revolutionary change — remains so important. It bears underscoring how instrumental the popular mobilization undertaken by COSATU was to the success of the "second referendum" referred to above, for example. Here was an echo of the role the union had played a year earlier when, in November 1991, it had led three and a half million people to participate in a massive stay-away against the government's imposition of a draconian new Value-Added-Tax (VAT). Is it the case that COSATU's involvement in such initiatives is more deeply felt than is that of the ANC leadership? Certainly the union seems more firmly committed than many within that leadership to carrying over the vigorous expression of such "energies" into the "post-apartheid moment."

We return by this route to my discussion of the theory and practice of "structural reform" in South Africa (presented in chapters four and five, above) as one key to understanding the actual process of and prospects for revolutionary change in South Africa. We will not reprise that discussion here,[19] but merely note that the most recent writings by activists and theorists linked to the trade union movement continue to use closely related language to keep alive a radical discourse in South Africa — at a point when many unionists fear, in sharp contrast, "that big business, the IMF and the World Bank are increasingly influential in the top ranks of the ANC leadership."[20] Thus, a year-end issue of the *South African Labour Bulletin* (November-December 1992) that crosses my desk as I conclude the writing of the present manuscript is alive with debate about the modalities of struggling for a genuine transformation of South Africa.[21]

What is it that distinguishes these contributions from the pronouncements of ANC big-wigs (Mbeki, Mandela) cited earlier? It may be, quite simply, a refusal to make a comparable "leap of faith" in the direction of capitalism. But perhaps the seemingly uncritical accommodation with capitalist power of such ANC leaders is more apparent than real, more tactical than principled. Even if this were so, however, the costs of their cautious approach could be very high. For a serious strategy of socio-economic transformation, however subtly and "realistically" it might be defined, demands some clear and public affirmation of the centrality of class struggle to the politics it proposes, and a recognition — "one essential ingredient of a coherent *via media* for South African socialists," as Bundy puts it — that, ultimately, "the transition to socialism means the replacement of rule by one class by that of another."[22] How else, one might ask, is the constituency for such a transformation to translate its scepticism regarding the appropriateness of capitalist solutions into any deeper level of understanding as to possible alternatives; how else is it to become both fully self-conscious and capable of empowering itself?

But even if, as the trade union debates suggest, the struggle to empower such a constituency does at least continue within South Africa's democratic movement, what can one say about the situation in the rest of the region? Unfortunately, identifying the forces (class actors and broad popular alliances) likely to resist recolonization there is rather more difficult — such has been the scope of the defeat inflicted on the Left in the Frontline states. As we have seen in chapter three, however, there are organizations in a country like Mozambique that are using the novel space for political manoeuvre that "democratization" has brought with it to begin to confront the strictures of structural adjustment. Throughout the region it is these organizations within civil society (unions, women's organizations, cooperatives, research and action groups) that seem, for the moment at least, to have eclipsed states and parties as the most promising agents of struggle. And it is the initiatives springing from such sources — witness the increasingly critical role being played by trade unions in Zimbabwe, for example, or the positive, if modest, initiatives of rurally-rooted cooperatives in Mozambique — that should eventually underpin more broadly-based progressive political undertakings as these again become feasible in southern Africa.

The new terms of solidarity

For activists from outside the region who seek to forge links with those in southern Africa who are continuing to marshall resistance to recolonization/neo-colonization, the challenge of support work is greater than in the past. There can be no disputing the fact that the anti-apartheid/southern African solidarity network in Western countries has begun to come unstuck. Partly this reflects "success:" apartheid is on its last legs, isn't it? Partly confusion: what are we to make of those erstwhile "progressive" Frontline states now forced into bed with the IMF and other bad actors? And what can it possibly mean to transform a South African socio-economic structure that is at once so deeply inegalitarian and so profoundly enmeshed in the circuits of global capitalism? The old solidarity network — a broad liberal/left coalition premissed on a simple, if worthy, distaste for institutionalized racism — was never likely to move intact onto this new terrain of deeper challenges and tougher questions.

Not that the "first phase" of southern African solidarity activity has exhausted itself altogether: South Africa is still very much in the "apartheid moment," as we have seen. This means, for Western activists, that whatever remnants of international sanctions we can defend — by Canada within the Commonwealth, for example — may still have some positive impact, and that whatever we can do to clarify what is really at stake in South Africa's constitutional negotiations (*not* defense of white South Africa's "distinct society," for example!) may have some immediate resonance. But, as we have seen, South Africa is, simultaneously, living the "post-apartheid moment." As a result, we are also being carried forward into defining the novel terms of solidarity activities relevant to the challenges of that new "moment." And, as regards the rest of the region, there is an even more pressing imperative, the need for us to reshape patterns of support, originally developed to link the Western solidarity network to liberation movements-cum-revolutionary governments, now that those governments have been forced, more and more, to conform to the global imperatives of capital.

Fortunately, some of the terms of a new kind of solidarity do begin to suggest themselves — and indicate a range of activities that may, in fact, link our own preoccupations as activists in Western countries even more directly than in the past with those of our counterparts in southern Africa. We have noted above the extent to which — especially in the Frontline states but even in South Africa itself — resistance to imperial dictate in the region has been *decentred*: it has become less the exclusive preserve of state and party (these latter by now often quite compromised, in any case) and more actively the vocation of what has been termed to be "organizations within civil society." Increasingly, the possibility of deepening links between such organizations in southern Africa and similar organizations in Canada has begun to be realized.

Take, as merely one example, the recent attempts by my own "home" support committee, the Toronto Committee for the Liberation of Southern Africa (TCLSAC), to give fresh resonance to our work. In doing so we have begun to reach out (through a novel "South-South-North network" which met, for the first time, in Harare in late 1991) to groups throughout the southern African region doing work similar to our own — in research, publications and popular education.[23] As we have discovered, such groups share many similar concerns to our own — around issues central to the new epoch like the impact of economic globalization (via "structural adjustment") and the promise of new forms of democratization. And they have valued the opportunity to pool information and to compare perspectives. Moreover, the South-North dimension of the exchange took on new vitality when "Northerners" found themselves encouraged to put their own struggles — around free trade, racism, violence against women, justice for native peoples — on the table in this novel context; the actual *sharing of experience,* South and North, came to seem even more important than in the days of the anti-apartheid struggle more narrowly defined.

For, as has become apparent to us, solidarity so forged is less that of the old type, based centrally on our support for the struggles of peoples and movements abroad, than it is solidarity based on a sharing of perspectives on common problems. Cast in Canadian terms, what, after all, is our own Tory government's fetishization of "free trade" if not servile prostration of Canadian interests on the altar of globalization — in effect, acceptance of a form of structural adjustment? And what are Canada's recent constitutional debates — when, at their best, they focus the demands of native people, women, disenchanted Quebecois — if not debates about how to make our own political institutions more responsive to our needs? Obviously, in making such points, we must not ignore the quite different positions within the global hierarchy occupied by southern Africa and a Western country like Canada. But, if developed with imagination, the new kinds of links to the region exemplified at the Harare meeting could prove to be important.

Such initiatives can also contribute to the consolidation of fresh constituencies in the Western countries themselves — unions, women's organizations, cooperatives and other groupings for whom the workings of the global economy and the challenges of popular empowerment are crucial concerns and who can begin to make southern African-related challenges their own issues in real and novel ways. Perhaps by this route support-work activists can begin to piece together a new southern Africa-centered network (in Canada and elsewhere), one to take up the torch from the anti-apartheid movement more traditionally defined. Of course, such activists might also be expected to integrate themselves even more actively than in the past into labour and social movements in our own countries and to shape our work — in terms of the kind of issues we take up and the kinds of linkages and information flows we promote — with more accountability to struggles for change here.[24]

Scholar activism revisited

Here, then, are some possible components of a new project for activists around southern African issues. But what of that curious, but useful, hybrid, the "scholar activist"? In the "Afterword" to *Socialist Ideology and the Struggle for Southern Africa* (my previous volume for Africa World Press) I discussed some of the ramifications of this role, and argued that, far from being an oxymoron, the notion has quite positive connotations. Certainly the scholar, in elaborating arguments, pursuing data and weighing evidence, is answerable to the most rigorous of scientific canons. But what of the kinds of questions scholars ask and the issues that preoccupy them? Quite simply, such preoccupations do not spring spontaneously from the data, but are largely brought to the data by the scholars themselves. And in my experience active engagement in political work — in this case political work around southern African issues — actually helps the "scholar activist" to pose the kind of "hard and searching questions" that a more conservative and passive approach to scholarship would tend to obscure.

In short, mere empiricism — and its attendant cohort of more theorized rationalizations for positivist approaches — provides only false answers to the need self-consciously to choose entry-points into the task of social analysis. This is a lesson I learned, first and most forcefully, from my old teacher, Hube Wilson, to whose memory this book is respectfully dedicated. But I also find myself returning to a fine old volume by Hugh Stretton for further insight into the dangers of what he, similarly concerned, terms "scientism": "Most social scientists sit comfortably high in the hierarchies of race, class, income, and power. That need not stop any one of them supplying the services which poorer classes and reforming movements have commonly received, for one reason or another, from individuals richer than themselves. But comfort is seductive, and so is scientism. Scientistic selection avoids the radical imagination or discovery of poor men's chances for social choice or change or conservation. Like other censors, it hedges science and education into the service of established winners."[25] This, then, is the case for a southern African studies that is, quite determinedly, *not* "value free."

Of course, there are also risks involved in adhering to this model of a "valuing" social science, the risk, in particular, that we will merely shape our analyses to fit our preconceptions. Hence the pressing need that scholar activists work to keep each other honest by dint of a careful reading of each other's work and, where necessary, sharp criticism. Noting this requirement in *Socialist Ideology* I also underscored the importance of such analytical rigor to the anti-apartheid movement *per se:* "For an anti-apartheid movement built on mere enthusiasm and apolitical moralizing cannot easily survive the cruel vicissitudes inevitable in so difficult a struggle as the one for southern Africa; those who stay the course, experience attests, are those who are least naive." Such a warning is as apt for any new solidarity-movement-in-the-making as ever it was for the anti-apartheid movement more traditionally defined (not least because of the very "cruelty" of the regional "vicissitudes" we have been examining in the present volume).

My own work has not itself escaped the charge of lapsing into "mere enthusiasm." Thus, not long ago, the noted Zimbabwean writer Ibbo Mandaza suggested of my work (however debatably) that "no individual writer has done so much to mobilize support throughout North America (or even throughout the world) for the liberation struggle of southern Africa." But, he added immediately, this is very far from being a good thing, such is the extent to which my writings have created a "revolutionary mythology" and "constituted a romantic rendition on the liberation struggles that are, in reality, much more complex in their historical origins and development."[26]

Rather too strong a charge, I feel - when, for example, I recall being pilloried, many years ago, by both ZAPU and ZANU for my published misgivings about their activities,[27] or recall our long struggle in Canada (especially vis-à-vis the ANC) to establish the legitimacy of a concept of "critical support" towards liberation movements.[28] In any case, readers can judge for themselves just how judicious is the balance I have struck between engagement and scholarly rigor in previous writings or, indeed, in this book. *Caveat emptor.* In more general terms, however, Mandaza's warning is a challenging one,[29] suggesting the clear and always present danger of substituting hope for cool assessment regarding southern African issues. Indeed, as will be apparent, this is much the same charge as the one I have levelled against Alex Callinicos and others, on several occasions in the final two chapters of this book, when I have advocated use of the concept of "structural reform" as a more realistic (if equally militant) way than their own of conceiving the process of radical transformation in South Africa.

At the same time, I am also uncomfortably aware of past temptations to shade my own analyses, albeit for what seemed at the time to be impeccably "good reasons": so as not to give too much aid and comfort to an implacable and unsavory enemy (the Portuguese colonialists, the apartheid regime, American imperialism, the right-wing liberals who haunt the western media) for example; or to cast my own ideas, to a degree, in the rather different language favoured by a particular popular movement, the better to contribute, unthreateningly, to drawing out the most radical potential possible from that movement's project. Again, there are no easy answers to such conundrums inherent, one way or another, in the (unavoidable) politics of scholarship. But the very real dangers of blinkering ourselves on the one hand, and the on-going need for criticism and self-criticism on the other, do serve to underscore, once again, the crucial requirement that scholar activism be both a collective undertaking and a profoundly democratic one if it is to fulfill its promise. To coin a paraphrase: "Dare to struggle. Dare to debate."

1. Consider, for example, the case of "Canada's national newspaper," the *Globe and Mail*, which has shamelessly elided claims to constitutionally guaranteed "group rights" by South Africa's white community with Quebec's (eminently reasonable) constitutional demand within Canada for "distinct society" status. Elsewhere, the Globe invokes the shade of James Madison in praise of De Klerk, suggesting the latter merely to be paralleling the eminently democratic concerns of *The Federalist Papers* in seeking, by means of various "checks and balances," to protect worthy minorities from potentially abusive majorities! (See the *Globe and Mail* editorials "Clashing rights in the new South Africa" [December 21, 1991] and "South Africa's distinct societies" [March 19, 1992.] Such calculated misrepresentation of things South African in much of the mass media indicates just how vital will be the information work of scholars and activists during the on-going negotiations process, in order to keep front and centre the legitimacy of demands for a genuine democratization of that country.
2. The phrase is from Paul Stober, "Slovo's 'sunset' debate is red-hot," *The Weekly Mail*, October 30-November 5, 1992), p. 16; the reference is to Joe Slovo, "Negotiations: what room for compromise?" *African Communist* (3rd Quarter, 1992).
3. Pallo Jordan, "Strategic Debate in the ANC" (mimeo, October, 1992); an abbreviated version of this paper appears as "Committing suicide by concession," *The Weekly Mail* (November 13 to 19, 1992).
4. Jeremy Cronin, "Nothing to gain from all-or-nothing tactics," *The Weekly Mail* (ibid.), p. 9; in Cronin's view. "Slovo reminds us we are dealing with a chastened, crisis-ridden but still powerful opponent. Both sides find themselves locked in a reciprocal siege. From our side the objective remains the total dismantling of apartheid. But we simply cannot will this objective into being. So how do we move from here to our longer term goals? Slovo suggests principled compromises...."
5. Steven Friedman, "Blind Man's Bluff?" *Work in Progress*, 86 (December, 1992); this article's sub-head reads: "If you've discovered the government's 'Grand Plan,' send a copy over to De Klerk. Judging by the evidence of the past year, he needs it." The second article referred to is by Phillip van Niekerk and entitled "This isn't a soap, FW. It's for real," *The Weekly Mail*, December 4-10, 1992.
6. From an interview with Mbeki in the ANC journal, *Mayibuye* (March, 1991), p. 2.
7. Colin Bundy, "Problems and Prospects for South African Socialists," paper presented to the Political Science Seminar, York University (Toronto), October, 1991, p. 20.
8. See the sobering article by Victoria Brittain entitled "Angola: The Final Act?" in *Southern Africa Report/SAR* (Toronto), 7, #5 (May, 1992) and, on the elections themselves and their aftermath her subsequent report in SAR, 8, #3/4 (January-February, 1993).

9   Judith Marshall, "The Struggle in Mozambique" in *SAR*, 8, #1 (July, 1992).
10   This reality can be quite dramatic; as Marshall has also noted, "We are forced to redefine our notions of what constitutes irreversible change in southern Africa as Portuguese settlers position themselves for a return [to Mozambique and Angola] from Lisbon and Johannesburg to the property and privilege of colonial times" (personal communication).
11   Marcia Burdette, "Democracy vs. Economic Liberalization: The Zambian Dilemma?" in SAR, 8, #1 (July, 1992)
12   Morgan Tsvangarai, general secretary of the Zimbabwe Congress of Trade Unions, as quoted in "Land pressure from peasant farmers is broken says union leader," *Southscan*, 7, #43 (13 November, 1992), p. 335; see also Kimberley Ludwig, "Race, Class and Land in Zimbabwe," *SAR*, 8, #1 (July 1992) and Pete Richer, "Zimbabwean unions: from state partners to outcasts," *South African Labour Bulletin*, 16, #7 (September-October, 1992).
13   See Carol Thompson, "The Politics of Drought" in *SAR* (*ibid.*).
14   "The Referendum and After: An Interview with Dan O'Meara," *Southern Africa Report (SAR)*, 7, #5 (May, 1992), p. 4. For some of the additional possible costs of an ANC failure to harness popular energies effectively in South Africa, see the chilling article on the present volatile state of South African youth by Colin Bundy entitled " At War with the Future? Black South African Youth in the 1990s" in *SAR*, 8, #1 (July, 1992).
15   Phillip Van Niekirk, "ANC threatens unrest to push for reforms: Black group gives Pretoria 30 days to accept demands for multiracial democracy," *The Globe and Mail*, June 1, 1992.
16   See Jeremy Cronin, "The boat, the tap and the Leipzig way," *African Communist* (3rd Quarter, 1992).
17   Cronin, "In Search of a Relevant Strategy," *Work in Progress*, #84 (September, 1992), p. 20.
18   Thus Ms. Mandela, so deeply compromised by the excesses of her own political practice, nonetheless strikes a potentially powerful note when, in the wake of the ANC's Strategic Perspective" document, she criticizes the "so-called power sharing deal between the elite of the oppressed and the oppressors" and speaks of the "looming disaster in this country which will result from the distortion of a noble goal in favour of a shortcut to parliament by a handful of individuals" (Winnie Mandela as quoted in "Swinging attack by Winnie indicates populist dissent," *Southscan*, 8, #2 (15 January, 1993).
19   Except to mention one other recent critique of the approach — that by Lawrence Harris in his paper "South Africa's Economic and Social Transformation: from 'No Middle Road' to 'No Alternative,'" presented to the Rethinking Marxism Conference, University of Massachusetts, Amherst, November 1992. In the course of launch-

ing salvos against the counter-revolutionary apostasy of Joe Slovo and others, Harris also manages to caricature my own "structural reform" approach to a rather startling degree (mimeo, pp. 6-7). Thus, my original notion that structural reforms must be allowed "to implicate other 'necessary' reforms [i.e. further related steps that would need to be taken if the struggle for a socialist transition were to be sustained] that flow from them" is translated by Harris as suggesting that such reform strategies are seen to "necessarily carry the movement forward to further reform" (a phrase in which, self-evidently, the notion of "necessity" has a very different connotation — one of Harris' own devising — than that in the original formulation). In addition, the idea that "structural reforms" will be ones that "leave a residue of further empowerment" is said to ground my claim that, in Harris' phrase, they "automatically strengthen further struggle" — the word "automatically" (his word) then being invoked to reinforce a charge of mindless "determinism." But does Harris really imagine that anyone would disagree with his summary counter-observation that "there is no such thing as a set of changes that necessarily flow from changes already achieved and we also know that while mass struggles can increase empowerment in the sense of heightened consciousness and the space in which to act, it is a 'residue' which is easily erased by the high powered cleaning fluid ... of reaction." No, the notion of "structural reform" is very far from being some kind of iron law of revolution. Its usefulness springs from its helping to define a sensibility that can underpin the practice, at once realistic and militant, of sustained socialist *struggle*. As for Harris, he seems content to hark back to the good old days of the "Leninist tradition" (more or less undefined but said to have once been embraced by Slovo and now abandoned by him) on the one hand, and to merely dismiss the possibility of any socialist prospect for South Africa on the other. Harris is too good a (Marxist) economist not to offer some very compelling arguments for the latter judgement, of course — and the danger he sees of a structural reform approach collapsing into mere "corporatism" is real enough. But in arguing that there is absolutely no way forward Harris spares himself the task of even discussing what a plausible revolutionary strategy for South Africa might look like.

20 Karl von Holdt, "What is the future of labour?" *Southern African Labour Bulletin*, 16, #8 (November-December, 1992), p. 34; the "special focus" of this issue is "The future of labour."
21 Ibid..
22 Bundy, "Problems and Prospects for South African Socialists", (*op. cit.*), p. 18.
23 See the feature "Time for Small Victories: Discussing Solidarity in Harare" in the special issue of *SAR*, 7, #4 (March, 1992) on "The New Terms of Solidarity"; this issue also contains a suggestive article on related question by Jonathan Barker entitled "Solidarity in a New

Key: The Reflections of a Bespectacled Solidarity Supporter."
24 The formulations in this section owe a great deal to the thinking of my friend and long-time colleague in southern African support work, Judith Marshall, who has been amongst those most active in defining possible "new terms of solidarity" for the support network in Canada.
25 Hugh Stretton, *The Political Sciences* (London: Routledge and Kegan Paul, 1969), p. 431; perhaps it is the vintage of the book that explains why Stretton did not also add "gender" to his list of relevant "hierarchies." See, in addition, Peter Novick, *That Noble Dream: The "Objectivity Question" and the American Historical Profession* (New York: Cambridge University Press, 1988).
26 Ibbo Mandaza (ed.), *Zimbabwe: The Political Economy of Transition, 1980-1986* (Dakar: CODESRIA, 1986).
27 The occasion was my article "Transforming the Struggle in Zimbabwe" in *Southern Africa* (February 1977).
28 The era when "direct links stink" was the rallying cry of the ANC and its very much less than critical supporters particularly sticks in my mind. At that time (the later 70s and early 80s) the attempt of TCLSAC and others to marry support for the ANC to a simultaneous and growing commitment to trade union struggles (FOSATU et. al.) on the ground inside South Africa caused endless problems in our relationship with the ANC and some its allies in Canada itself.
29 Less defensible, it seems to me, is the other, rather sharply-phrased, strand to Mandaza's critique, one that finds "radical paternalism" and "humiliation" in the fact that "non-nationals" like myself are engaged in debating developments in southern Africa. Without wanting to trivialize Mandaza's own obviously deeply-felt concerns in this respect, I must affirm that my own experience of over twenty-five years of direct engagement in such debates has been, almost uniformly, one of warm welcome by southern Africans of any manifestations of serious commitment (intellectual and otherwise) by "outsiders" to their cause. Virtually no southern African militants of my close acquaintance have felt either threatened or "humiliated" by strong arguments, even sharp disagreements, when they have been respectfully advanced from whatever quarter.

Index

"abaixismo," 61
Adam, Heribert, 41, 66fn
Adamishin, Anatoly, 37
Africa, 36, 60, 69, 77, 79; post-colonial, xi; crisis of, 63; the state in, 62; democracy in, 65; capitalism in, 67; African Studies, 58
African National Congress/ANC, xi, 18-20, 23, 29, 93, 97, 132-3, 181; banning of, 6-7; reemergence of, 15, 91; unbanning of, 24fn; De Klerk's approach to, 104-6; ideology of, 16-17, 49, 51, 118; political strategy and tactics of, 26, 92, 106-12, 115-7, 170, 174-5; socio-economic strategy and tactics, 120-3, 153-4, 160, 171, 176; civil society and, 113-4, 127, 129, 160; the SACP and, 8, 17, 110, 129-31; COSATU and, 8, 123-27, 159, 175; women and, 128-9, 160; Inkatha and, 99, 101-2; Transkei's links to, 98; Mozambican relationship to, 10, 74
"African Socialism," 5
Afrikaners, 94, 105
Alavi, Hamza, 68
Alexandra, 101, 107; Civic Association, 113

Anglo-American, 25, 109, 120, 154
Angola, 2-5, 8, 10-12, 19-21, 31, 35-6, 38-9, 46-8, 53, 96, 103, 172
apartheid: 21, 35; "apartheid moment," 169, 172, 175, 177; apartheid regime/state/system, 7, 146, 181; anti-apartheid movement, 177-80; neo-apartheid, 22; post-apartheid/"post-apartheid moment" 50, 90, 114, 132, 172, 146, 175, 177
"armed propaganda," 107
armed struggle, 38; in Zimbabwe, 5, 11; ANC and, 104, 107
Arrighi, Giovanni, 1, 3
Asians, 97
AWB (Afrikaner Weerstand Beweging/Afrikaner Resistance Movement), 27, 97
Azapo (Azanian People's Organization), 15, 22, 115-6

Ball, Chris, 95
Bantustans, 27, 98-100
Barker, Jonathan, 80
Bayart, Jean-François, 62, 65, 71, 77
Bernstein, Edouard, 147
Bienefeld, Manfred, 51, 63, 123
Biko, Steve, 7
Bird, Adrienne, 158
Bisho massacre, 174

Blackburn, Robin, 92
Black Consciousness, 7, 15, 115
Bloom, Tony, 95
Boputhatswana, 98
Botha, Pik, 102, 172
Botha, P. W., ix, 27, 31, 47, 73, 95, 103, 105
Botswana, 20
bourgeoisie, 93, 152,; black bourgeoisie (in South Africa), 160; "bourgeois rule," 172
Bowen, Merle, 76, 78, 80
Bowie, Lester, 133
Brezhnev, 38-9
Britain, 3, 5, 6
Bundy, Colin, 171, 176
Bush, George, 48
Buthelezi, Gatsha, 22, 98-102, 104, 111-2, 116-7; Buthelezi Commission, 99

Cabora Bassa, 9
Caetano, Marcelo, ix
Cahen, Michel, 41, 66fn.
Caldwell, Don, 153
Callinicos, Alex, 112, 121, 147-9, 157, 181
Campbell, Horace, 44,
Canada, 177-9, 181
Cape Town/the Cape, 8, 14
capital: 80; role of (SA), 95, 106, 118-9, 120, 146, 153, 159; control over (SA), 122-3, 126, 146, 156; strength of, 92, 151, 160; in Mozambique, 80
capitalism: 35, 37, 39, 62, 91, 145, 171; hegemony of, x; capitalist imperialism, 5; promise of, 172; in Africa, 67, 76; in South Africa, 30, 89, 103, 156, 177; in Zimbabwe, 11; in Mozambique, 52, 66-7, 72; "racial capitalism," 90; Africanization of, 17; deracialization of, 50, 90, 93, 116; opposition to (SA), 94; ANC accomodation with, 176

capitalism, international/global, 10, 35, 40, 52, 67, 76, 81, 106, 120, 144-5, 177-8
Caprivi Strip, 102
Care, 75
Centre for Socialist Research (CERES), 151
Central Intelligence Agency (CIA), 172
Chabal, Patrick, 60, 68
Charterists, 17
Chiluba, Frederik, 173
Chissano, Jacinto, 43, 46, 51-2, 60-1, 75
churches, 14, 23
Ciskei, 98, 174
civic associations, 45, 108, 113, 127-9, 158
Civic Associations of the Southern Transvaal/CAST, 113
civil society: 79; empowerment of, 65; claims of (SA), 113-4; in South Africa, 129, 158, 160, 177-8; in Mozambique, 53, 77
Clarence-Smith, Gervase, x, 57, 59, 63, 67, 76
classes (social): 6, 173, 176; structure, 17, 59, 68; struggle of, xii, 36, 113, 152; power of, 145; alliance of, 16; consciousness of, 147-8; collaboration of, 156; "progressive classes," 70; popular classes, 156, 158; Inkatha and, 101
Cold War, x, 35-6, 40, 48-9, 51-2, 66, 146
"Coloureds," 97
COMECON, 39
Commonwealth, 96, 177
communal villages, 72
Congress Alliance, 7
COSATU (Congress of South African Trade Unions), 22, 29, 108, 120, 175; formation of, 13; and the ANC, 15-16,

123-4, 159; and the SACP, 131; and Inkatha, 99; "populists"/"workerists" within, 17, 125; in negotiations, 115, 148; and economic strategies, 123-7, 155
Conservative Party, 27, 97
cooperatives/cooperativization, 11, 53, 177, 179
constitution: negotiations over (SA), xi, 117-8; 170-1; Buthelezi and, 100
"Consultative Conference" (ANC): at Kabwe, Zambia (1985), 19, 107;in South Africa (1990), 104, 111, 115
counter-revolution: in southern Africa, x, 3, 19-21, 31; in South Africa, 8, 30
Crocker, Chester, 46, 48
Cronin, Jeremy, 174-5
Crossroads, 22, 27
Cuba, 12, 19, 38, 46-7, 96
Cuito Cuanavale, 46

Darbon, Dominique, 61
Davies, Rob, 154
De Beer, Zac, 21
de Klerk, F. W., 27, 31, 93, 100; influence of Eastern European developments on, 49; his project, 95-7, 103, 118, 135fn, 170; and the ANC, 104-6, 109-11, 174; and "dirty tricks," 102-4; 116-7
decolonization, 6, 16
democracy, 148, 151; in Africa, 58, 65; in South Africa, xi, 21, 29, 94, 101, 109, 131, 156-159, 169-71, 175-6; "democratic culture" (SA), 113-4; in Namibia, 13; in Mozambique, 53, 80; Frelimo and, 70-4, 78; in Angola, 53
democratization, 178; in South Africa, 89, 174, in Mozambique, 51; the economy (SA), 29, 49, 118, 157
dependency, 63, 75, 173
deracialization, 16, 20, 95-6
destabilization, x, 8, 10, 20, 39, 44, 57, 59-60, 68, 72, 77, 81, 108, 173
development, 57, 69
"developmental dictatorship," 71, 74, 81
Dlamini, Chris, 125
Durban, 7, 94 (strikes)

Eastern Europe, 36-7, 45, 49, 79, 108, 130
Economic Trends Group, 124, 155-6
elections, 80
elite-pacting, 110, 117
Emergency (SA), 6, 18, 21-23, 24fn, 26, 28, 29, 108
End Conscription Campaign, 23
Erwin, Alec, 125
European Community, 96
Fanaroff, Bernie, 125

"false decolonization," 4
federalism, 170
feminism, xii
Finnigan, William, 60, 66-7, 73
First, Ruth, 143-4
Fituni, Leonid, 38
Fordism, 93, 93 (racial fordism)
FOSATU (Federation of South African Trade Unions), 7, 14
France, 3
Freedom Charter, 15
Frelimo (Frente da Libertacao de Mocambique), 41, 57-81 (various topics), 172; armed struggle, 4-6; its project, x, 9-10, 53; its retreat, 42-4, 51-3; the Frelimo state, ix, 57-81
Freund, Bill, 152-3, 156
Friedman, Steven, 24
Frontline states, xi, 8, 13, 20, 31, 38, 51, 108, 172, 176-7
Fry, Peter, 60-1, 67

GAWU (General and Allied Workers' Union), 15
Geffray, Christian, 60-1, 63-4, 71
Gelb, Stephen, 91, 93-4, 119-20, 123-4, 161
gender, 128, 160
GDR (German Democratic Republic), 36, 43
Godongwana, Enoch, 157
Gorbachev, Mikhail, 48, 105
Gordhan, Ketso, 122
Gorz, Andre, 24fn, 91-3, 147, 151
Gqozo, Oupa, 98
guerilla warfare, 3-4
Guebuza, Armando, 42, 52, 77
Gramsci, Antonio, 90
Guevara, Che, 4
Guinea-Bissau, 3

Halliday, Fred, 37-8
Hani, Chris, 98
Hanlon, Joe, 69, 75, 77
Harare: "Harare Declaration," 109, "Harare Recommendations," 125, Harare meeting of South-South-North network, 178-9
Harber, Anton, 112
Harris, Lawrence, 122, 183-4fn
Haysom, Nicholas, 101
Hermele, Kenneth, 76
Holomisa, Major-General Bantu, 98
Hussein, Saddam, 47
Hutchful, Eboe, 71, 78-9
Hyden, Goran, 63

ideology: 39, 42, 68; of the liberation movements, 5; of Frelimo, 66; of the Soviet Union, 36, 40
Inkatha, 22, 98-102
"Inkathagate," 93, 103, 133
insurrection (in South Africa, 1984-86), 14, 18-19, 21, 24fn, 95-6, 107-8

International Monetary Fund/IMF, x, 10, 12, 19-20, 41, 44, 50, 72, 75, 80, 120, 126, 154, 173, 176-7

Jaurès, Jean, 150-1, 161
Joffe, Avril, 156
Jordan, Pallo, 131, 170

Kaunda, Kenneth, 173
Keys, Derek, 171
Kubheka, Sipho, 159
Kagarlitsky, Boris, 143, 145, 149-51, 153
Keynesianism (global), 41
Kissinger, Henry, 2, 30
Kokorev, Vladimir, 37-8
Kolko, Gabriel, 40
KwaNatal, 99
Kwazulu, 98-100

Labour Relations Amendment Act, 108, 119
Laclau, Ernesto, 112
Lancaster House, 6
land: reform in Zimbabwe, 11; reform in South Africa, 123; Land Act (SA), 96, 119
Lebanization, 90, 118
Lenin, V. I., 130
Lesotho, 20
Lewis, David, 156
Leys, Colin, 68, 73
liberalization, 173
liberation, ix, 11, 13, 17, 29, 39, 66, 72, 79, 81, 120, 144; liberated areas, 5, 9; liberation movements, 2, 5, 112, 114, 178, 181; liberation struggle, 3, 45, 72, 181
Liebenberg, General, 103
Louw, Leon and Kendall, Frances, 153
Loxley, John, 42
Luanda, 47
Lusaka, 19, 109, 111

Machel, Samora: leadership of, 45, 69; regional tactics of, 44; left populism of, 52; Marxism of, 66; his project smashed, 74
Magdoff, Harry, 29-30, 89
Mafumedi, Sydney, 125
magic, 78
Malan, Magnus, 103, 116
Mandaza, Ibbo, 11, 180-1, 185fn
Mandela, Nelson: 15, 28, 154, 172, 176; release from prison of, xi, 13, 24fn, 31, 89, 97, 109, 174; reemergence as leader, 110; and nationalization, 121, 171
Mandela, Winnie, 27, 110, 175
Mangope, Chief Lucas, 98
Mantanzime, Chief Kaiser, 98
Maputo, 41, 46, 143-4
Marshall, Judith, 42, 66fn, 75-6, 80, 173
Marx, Karl, 150
Marxism, xi-xii, 37, 51, 59; in Mozambique, 4, 40-1, 43, 51, 66-7, 73; in Zimbabwe, 6; "frozen Marxism," 144-5; and "structural reform," 150, 160-1
"Marxism-Jaurèsism," 161,
Marxism-Leninism, 39, 89; in Mozambique, 10, 37, 51, 66, 73, 144
"Mass Democratic Movement" (SA), 96, 108, 114, 158
Mayekiso, Moses, 101, 107, 113-4
Mbeki, Thabo, 171-2, 176
Mboweni, Tito, 122
McFaul, Michael, 46-8
Médard, Jean, 62-4, 70
Mhlaba, Raymond, 131
military: South African, 97, 101, 102-3, 105; militarization of state power (SA), 95; Bantustan, 98 (SA), 105; underground (SA), 26; ANC activities, 26, 107, destabilization of southern Africa by, 103
Mocumbi, Pascal, 42
modernism: arrogance of, 57, 64; modernity, 61; modernizing project, 72; post-modern, 64
Moll, Peter, 153, 156
MNR (see Renamo)
MPLA (Movimento Popular de Libertaçao de Angola), 4, 19, 51, 172
Mondlane, Eduardo, 45; University of, 41
Mozambique: on all themes, see chapter 3, 57-81; xi, 8-9, 21, 35, 52-3, 143, 177; recolonization of, x, 31, 54; destabilization of, x-xi, 9-10, 19-20, 47, 103; war in, 172 liberation of, 2-5, 8; socialism in, 4-5, 39; reversal of socialist project, 41-5, 51-2, 120, 173; democratization of, 176; Zimbabwe and, 6, 9, 11-12; Soviet Union and, 36-9; Crocker and, 46-8; Marxism and, 51
Mugabe, Robert, 11, 105, 173
Murphy, Craig, 40
Muzorewa, Bishop Abel, 105

Naidoo, Jay, 159
Namibia, 12-3, 46, 96, 105, 109, 115
Naprama movement, 78
Natal, 27, 99-100, 102
NACTU (National Council of Trade Unions), 15-6, 119
National Forum, 15
National Manpower Commission (NMC), 119, 126-7, 149
National Security Management System (SA), 22, 95, 103
National Security Study Memorandum (NSSM) 39, 2, 30

National Union of Mineworkers (NUM), 13, 132
National Union of Metalworkers (NUMSA), 113, 125
nationhood: in Mozambique, 80
nationalism: "African [cultural] nationalism," 77, 114; radicaliza-tion of, 3-4, 6, 8; in southern Africa, 3, 20; in Zimbabwe, 6; in South Africa, 17, 110, 120, the ANC and, 16, 121
National Education Crisis Committee (NECC), 18, 24, 127
National Party (NP/Nats), 27, 94-7, 104, 106, 170
native people, 178-9
Ndebele, 5, 11
"negotiations" (in South Africa), x, 13, 29, 31, 89, 104-6, 108-9, 115, 117-8, 132, 148, 157, 177
Nel, Christo, 95
neo-colonialism, ix, 1, 3, 177
New World Order, 58
Nickel, Herman, 43
Nkomati Accord(s), 10, 44, 46
North America, 7, 180

O'Laughlin, Bridget, 63-4, 66fn, 71, 78
O'Meara, Dan, 67, 94, 97, 105, 174
Operation Production, 52
Organization of African Unity (OAU), 109
Oppenheimer, Jochen, 76

Pan-Africanist Congress/PAC, 6, 15, 114-6, 175,
"paradigm shift," 57, 59, 61
peasantry, 1, 63; Bayart and, 65; Frelimo and, 4, 10, 63, 68, 70-2; in Mozambique, 78; in Zimbabwe, 11, 173,
Pentagon, 41

people's power, 107,
people's war, 4
"petty-bourgeois politics," 68; in Mozambique, 77, 80
petty-bourgeoisie: in Mozambique, 69; in Zimbabwe, 11; in South Africa, 16-17, 121, 160
Pietermaritzburg, 22,
Pol Pot, 121,
police: in South Africa, 22, 27-28, 97-8, 101
Politique Africaine, 51, 61, 62
Portugal, 1-2, 4-5, 8-9, 64, 68, 78, 181
Pretoria, 3, 21, 46, 59, 96;
"Pretoria Minute," 104
Quebecois, 179

race, 79; racial pride, 7; racial privilege, 177; non-racial, 35
racism: institutionalized, 94, 177; oppression by, 6; opposition to, xii, 94, 178; in Mozambique, 53
Ramaphosa. Cyril, 132
Reagan, Ronald, 20, 40, 43-4, 46, 73-4
recolonization, x-xii, 58, 74, 78, 173, 176-7
redistribution: growth with, 119-121 120, 123, 154-5; growth through, 123, 155; of investment, 124
referendum (SA), 169
reform: socialist strategy of, 91, 93, 151; Marx and, 150; by SA government, 21, 50, 97, 105, 119, 123; business and (SA), 95
reformism: "mere reformism," 24, 50, 91-2, 161; vs. revolution, 89, 122, 145, 147-8, 160; in Marx, 150; revolutionary reformism, 151, 153; 153, 158-61; social-democratic reformism, 153, 157 (see also

"structural reform/ism")
religion, 78
Relly, Gavin, 109
Renamo (National Resistance Movement/MNR), 9, 20, 22, 45, 59, 60
revolution, 89, 180; vs. "reform," 90, 145; and "structural reform," 122, 133, 147-8, 150-4; "revolutionary reform', 159-60; in southern Africa, *ix*-xi, 3, 178; in Mozambique, 4, 57ff. 70-1; in Zimbabwe, 11; in South Africa, 13, 18, 30-1, 51, 115, 118ff; revolutionary potential (SA),103; "revolutionary leadership," 68, 77; revolutionary alliance, 125; "two-stage revolution," 118
Rhodesia, *ix*, 2, 3, 9
Roesch, Otto, 42, 78

Sachs, Albie, 114
sanctions, 94, 177
Saul, John S., 68
Savimbi, Jonas, 19, 48, 172
SAAWU (South African Allied Workers' Union), 15
SACTU (South African Congress of Trade Unions), 7
scholar activism, 179-81
Schreiner, Geoff, 157-8
September, Dulcie, 23
Sharpeville, 6
Shona, 5, 11
Sisulu, Max, 122
Slovo, Joe, on socialism, 130, 145; and destalinization, 49-50; on South Africa, 121, 154, 170-1, 174; on Mozambique, 39, 58-9, 120
Smith, Ian, *ix*, 3, 9
"social contract," 126, 157
social-democracy, 150, 157
socialism, xi, 57-9, 74, 89, 143, 171, 176; as a global option,
49, 144; Soviet bloc and, 35-9, 43; scepticism towards, 61-2, 66-7, 74; and "structural reform," 146ff; and democracy, 51; politics of, 64, 71; in southern Africa, 3, 8, 20, 35, 40 54; in Mozambique, 5, 9, 19, 42-6, 52-3, 58-9, 69, 81, 120; in Angola, 5, 19, 48; in South Africa, 6, 118, 160; the ANC and, 16, 49, 114; trade unions and (SA), 124-6, 159; SACP and, 155; Joe Slovo on, 121; and the "mixed economy" (SA), 122; "primitive socialist accumulation," 72; "socialism of expanded reproduction," 72
solidarity/support work, 77, 177-9
Solidarity (Poland), 151
Somalia, 80
South Africa, on all themes see ch. 4, pp. 89-133; 2, 30-1, 43; resistance within, *ix*, xi-xii, 6-8, 13-19, 174-5; destabilization by, x, 9-10, 19-20, 26, 38, 44, 59-60, 67, 74; in Angola, 44, 46-48; and Namibia, 12-13; stalemate in, 26-7, 169-70; negotiations in, 35; and the Soviet Union, 48-50; and structural reform, 50-1, 143-9, 153-61, 181; and socialism, 171-3, 176; sanctions against, 177
South African Consultative Committee on Labour Affairs (SACCOLA), 119, 126
South-South-North network, 178
Southern Africa, *ix*-xii, 8, 35, 48, 73-4, 144; liberation struggle in, 1-2, 180; revolution in, xi, 1, 12, 30; socialism in, 51; Marxism and, xii; counter-revolution in, x, 31; "peace" in, 35, 48; recolonization of, *ix*; Cold War and, 35ff; the

Soviet Union/Eastern Europe and, 36, 40, 108; Western involvement, 38; solidarity work, 177, 179; studies of, 180-1
South African Defence Force (SADF), 102-3,
Southern African Development Coordination Conference (SADCC), 20
South African Communist Party/SACP, 8, 17, 39, 49, 51, 58, 110, 113, 115, 120-2, 129-31, 154-5, 160, 171, 174,
South-West Africa, 12
Soviet Union/USSR, 12, 36, 38-39, 43, 47-9, 50-51, 73, 105, 108
Soweto, 2, 7, 8, 27
Stalinism, 159; and the SACP, 49-51, 110, 131, 154; destalinization of SACP, 49-51
state: in Africa, 61-2, 65, 79; "the overdeveloped state," 68; "the unsteady state," 81; "demiurgic state," 62-3, 65; statism, 159; "the Frelimo state," ix-x, 57, 67-71, 74, 77; in Mozambique, 10, 58, 66, 75, 77-8; in South Africa (also, "the apartheid state"), 15, 99, 101, 107, 118, 132, 146; positive role for (SA), 159
State Security Council, 103
State Security System, 95
stay-away, 108
Steyn Fund, 120
Stretton, Hugh, 180
structural adjustment, x, 53, 75, 76, 80, 173, 176, 178-9
"structural reform," 146, 149, 153, 181; Gorz on, 24, 91, 93, 147; Callinicos on, 147-8; Kagarlitsky on, 149-52; in South Africa, xii, 24, 50, 92-3, 106, 122, 130, 133, 143, 146, 156-61, 175; the ANC and,

118
students, 7, 14, 28, 173
Sweezy, Paul, 29-31, 89
SWAPO, 12, 13, 96, 105

Terreblanche, Eugene, 97
Thatcher, Margaret, 96
Togliatti, Palmiro, 151
Third World, 63
Toronto Committee for the Liberation of Southern Africa/TCLSAC, 178
townships, 98, 108, 111, 113, 116, 127
trade unions, 92, 130, 148; in South Africa, 7, 13-6, 24-5, 100, 112, 155-7; within civil society (SA), 113-4, 129; and the ANC, 49, 159-60; and SACP, 50, 130-1; and corporatism (SA), 119, 157; and women (SA), 128; and stratification of the working-class (SA), 28fn; in Mozambique, 45, 53, 70; resistance to structural adjustment (Mozambique), 80; 155-7, 159-60, 176- in Zimbabwe, 177; in Western countries, 179
Transkei, 98
Transvaal, 100-2
Treuernicht, A. P., 97
tri-cameral parliament, 14, 98
"triple alliance," 80-1
Trotskyism, 89, 115, 125, 130
Tucker, Bob, 95
Tutu, Desmond, 25

Umkhonto we Sizwe/MK, 107, 132
Unified Socialist Party/PSU (France), 151
Unilateral Declaration of Independence (UDI), ix, 3, 5
UNITA, 19-20, 172; US & SA assistance to, 46

INDEX 195

United Democratic Front (UDF), 14-16, 18, 22-23, 92-93, 99, 108, 111, 113, 116, 131
United Nations, 12, 41
United States, 10, 12, 20, 38, 40-1, 43-44, 47-8, 60, 96
Urban Foundation, 120

Vaal triangle, 15
Vilas, Carlos, 39
vanguard party/"vanguardism": Frelimo and, 4, 10, 39, 45, 70-71, 73; the ANC and, 8, 49; the SACP and, 8, 129ff, 154
Veloso, Jacinto, 42
Verwoerd, Hendrik, 105
Vines, Alex, 59
Vlok, Adriaan, 100, 103, 116
Von Holdt, Karl, 157

Warren, Bill ("Warrenite"), 51, 63
Williams, Gavin, 68
Wilson, H. H., v, 180
Wilson, Ken, 78
women: emancipation (Mozambique), 4, 9; in South Africa, 14, 129; rights of, 128-9; within the ANC, 128; in Canada, 178-9
women's organizations: in southern Africa, 177; in Mozambique, 45, 53, 70; in South Africa, 113, 158; ANC Women's League, 128-9; Slovo on, 130; structural reform and, 148, in Western countries, 179
Workers' Charter," 125

Workers Organization for Socialist Action (WOSA), 115
working-class/workers, 89, 133; and structural reform, 91; in South Africa, 2, 7-8, 13, 15-16, 25, 120, 122, 125-6, 157; and empowerment, 123ff; and corporatism (SA), 158; and socialism (SA), 159-60; workers' participation(SA), 157; in stayaways (SA), 96; and SACP, 49-50; in Zimbabwe, 6, 11; in Mozambique, 70
"workerist"; vs. "populist," 15; within COSATU, 125; vs. "Charterists," 17
World Bank, x, 41-3, 47, 50-1, 63, 72, 75, 80, 120, 126, 154, 173, 176
World Vision, 75

youth, 2, 7, 14, 101, 108, 113-4, 130,
Yugoslavia, 81

Zambia, 53, 173
Zedong, Mao, 30
Zimbabwe, 3-12, 20, 45, 53, 74, 115, 120, 173, 177, 180
Zimbabwe African National Union/ZANU, 4-6, 8-9, 11, 74, 181
Zimbabwe African People's Union/ZAPU, 5-6, 181; "super-ZAPU," 20
Zimbabwe People's Army/ZIPA, 6
Zulu, 99

AFRICA WORLD PRESS, INC.

BACK TO AFRICA

George Ross and the Maroons: From Nova Scotia to Sierra Leone

MAVIS C. CAMPBELL

Back to Africa chronicles the odyssey of a group from the diaspora who made their sojourn from Jamaica to Nova Scotia and finally to Sierra Leone in West Africa at the beginning of the 19th Century. In this newly formed West African Society, they encountered two other groups from the diaspora who had previously made their return home to Africa, the chief of these being the African-Americans who won their freedom by fighting on the side of the British during the American War of Independence, who were also sent first to Nova Scotia before going to Sierra Leone.

Back to Africa, gives insight into the lineages among African, Caribbean and Afro-American history on African soil, and should therefore make for a better understanding of why these and other African people from the diaspora such as Paul Cuffee's group and the "Liberated Africans" were to form the very nucleus of the important creole society of Sierra Leone.

0-86543-383-6	Cloth	$39.95
0-86543-384-4	Paper	$12.95

Write or call for our complete catalogue

Africa World Press, Inc.
P.O. Box 1892 • Trenton NJ 08607 • (609) 771-1666 • FAX (609) 771-1616

Title	Cloth	Paper	Quantity	Amount
BACK TO AFRICA: George Ross & the Maroons	$39.95	$12.95		
			SUB TOTAL	
			* SHIPPING & HANDLING	
			TOTAL	

Please make payment by Check or Money Order.
We also accept VISA, MASTERCARD, or AMERICAN EXPRESS. Thank You.

0993-23

Name
Address
City
Telephone
Card Number   Expiration Date
Signature

*TO ORDER:
United States: send $3.00 For the first book, and 0.50 for each additional title.
Foreign (Includes Canada):
Surface: $4.00 For the first book, and 1.00 for each additional title.
Air $15.00 For the first book, and 7.00 for each additional title.
New Jersey Residents add 6% sales tax.

AFRICA WORLD PRESS, INC.

THE SWAHILI
Idiom and Identity of an African People

Alamin M. Mazrui and
Ibrahim Noor Shariff

Are the Swahili a community of Africanized Arabs? Arabized Africans? or are they a peculiar combination of both? Are they genetically a "hybrid" people or merely socio-cultural "mutants?" Are they no more than a social-linguistic unit of a sort, or do they constitute an ethnic entity in some genetic sense of the word? Do they personify the domestication of Islam in Africa, or the dislocation of African spirituality?

To the modern research-oriented scholar, the scenario is so bewildering that the verdict on Swahili identity is said to await further empirical investigation into the community and its psychological predisposition.

What we have attempted to do is to give a sketch of the historical forces that lie behind the relativity of some of the paradigms of identity.

- from the Introduction

| Write or call for our complete catalogue | 0-86543-310-0 | Cloth | $39.95 |
| | 0-86543-311-9 | Paper | $14.95 |

Africa World Press, Inc.
P.O. Box 1892 • Trenton NJ 08607 • (609) 771-1666 • FAX (609) 771-1616

Title	Cloth	Paper	Quantity	Amount
THE SWAHILI: Idiom and Identity of an African People	$39.95	$14.95		
			SUB TOTAL	
			*SHIPPING & HANDLING	
			TOTAL	

Please make payment by Check or Money Order.
We also accept VISA, MASTERCARD, or AMERICAN EXPRESS. Thank You.

0993-23

Name
Address
City
Telephone
Card Number   Expiration Date
Signature

*TO ORDER:
United States: send $3.00 For the first book, and 0.50 for each additional title.
Foreign (Includes Canada):
Surface: $4.00 For the first book, and 1.00 for each additional title.
Air: $15.00 For the first book, and 7.00 for each additional title.
New Jersey Residents add 6% sales tax.

AFRICA WORLD PRESS, INC.

THE LIFE AND WORK OF KWAME NKRUMAH

Kwame Arhin, editor

This unique book about the late Dr. Kwame Nkrumah, president of Ghana from 1960 to 1966, grew out of a symposium organized by the institute of African Studies, at the University of Ghana, which he founded. All of the contributors are Ghanian scholars of various academic disciplines. The book is divided into three major sections and covers the following:

- Nkrumah's cultural policy and leadership style
- Foreign Policy and Performance
- Economic Policy and Development
- Origin and Performance of the State-owned Enterprises
- Agricultural Policy: Industrialization, Foreign Trade and Neocolonialism

Write or call for our complete catalogue			
	0-86543-395-X	Cloth	$49.95
	0-86543-396-8	Paper	$16.95

Africa World Press, Inc.
P.O. Box 1892 • Trenton NJ 08607 • (609) 771-1666 • FAX (609) 771-1616

Title	Cloth	Paper	Quantity	Amount
THE LIFE AND WORK OF KWAME NKRUMAH	$49.95	$16.95		
Please make payment by Check or Money Order. We also accept VISA, MASTERCARD, or AMERICAN EXPRESS. Thank You.			SUB TOTAL	
0993-23			*SHIPPING & HANDLING	
			TOTAL	

Name
Address
City
Telephone
Card Number   Expiration Date
Signature

*TO ORDER:
United States: send $3.00 For the first book, and 0.50 for each additional title.
Foreign (Includes Canada):
Surface: $4.00 For the first book, and 1.00 for each additional title.
Air: $15.00 For the first book, and 7.00 for each additional title.
New Jersey Residents add 6% sales tax.

AFRICA WORLD PRESS, INC.
Our Books Define Your World

AFRICANS IN BRAZIL:
A Pan-African Perspective

Abdias Do & Elisa Larkin Nascimento

0-86543-239-2 **Paper** $12.95
0-86543-238-4 **Cloth** $39.95

THE RASTA COOKBOOK

Laura Osborne

0-86543-133-7
Paper $12.95

EDUCATION IN A FUTURE SOUTH AFRICA:
Policy Issues for Transformation

Unterhalter / Wolpe/Botha, editors

0-86543-334-8 **Paper** $16.95
0-86543-333-X **Cloth** $45.00

SPIRIT OF AFRICA:
The Healing Ministry of Archbishop Milingo of Zambia

Gerrie Ter Haar

0-86543-269-4 **Paper** $12.95
0-86543-268-6 **Cloth** $45.00

Frontline Nationalism in Angola & Mozambique

David Birmingham

0-86543-368-2 **Paper** $12.95
0-86543-367-4 **Cloth** $39.95

Orature in African Literature Today No. 18

Jones / Palmer / Jones, editors

0-86543-351-8 **Paper** $14.95
0-86543-350-X **Cloth** $45.00

Education and the Struggle for National Liberation in South Africa

Neville Alexander

0-86543-346-1 **Paper** $14.95
0-86543-345-3 **Cloth** $45.95

Research on WOLE SOYINKA

Lindfors / Gibbs, editors

0-86543-219-8 **Paper** $14.95
0-86543-218-X **Cloth** $45.00

Write or call for our complete catalogue

STOLEN LEGACY
Greek Philosophy Is Stolen Egyptian Philosophy

George G. M. James

0-86543-362-3 **Paper** $ 9.95
0-86543-361-5 **Cloth** $24.95

JACOBUS ELIZA JOHANNES CAPITEIN:
The Critical Study of an 18th Century African

Kwesi Kwaa Prah

0-86543-332-1 **Paper** $ 8.95
0-86543-331-3 **Cloth** $29.95

SEME:
Founder of the ANC

Rive / Couzens

0-86543-313-5 **Paper** $ 9.95
0-86543-312-7 **Cloth** $29.95

Transforming Southern African Agriculture

Seidman / Mwanza / Simelane / Weiner

0-86543-132-9 **Paper** $16.95
0-86543-131-0 **Cloth** $45.95

Africa World Press, Inc.
P.O. Box 1892 • Trenton NJ 08607 • (609) 771-1666 • FAX (609) 771-1616

Title	Cloth	Paper	Quantity	Amount
			SUB TOTAL	
			*SHIPPING & HANDLING	
			TOTAL	

0993-23

Please make payment by Check or Money Order.
We also accept VISA, MASTERCARD, or AMERICAN EXPRESS. Thank You.

Name
Address
City
Telephone
Card Number   Expiration Date
Signature

*TO ORDER:
United States: send $3.00 For the first book, and 0.50 for each additional title.
Foreign (Includes Canada):
Surface: $4.00 For the first book, and 1.00 for each additional title.
Air: $15.00 For the first book, and 7.00 for each additional title.
New Jersey Residents add 6% sales tax.